Caging the Lion

NEW STUDIES IN AESTHETICS

Robert Ginsberg
General Editor

Vol. 13

PETER LANG
New York • San Francisco • Bern • Baltimore
Frankfurt am Main • Berlin • Wien • Paris

Bruce E. Fleming

Caging the Lion

Cross-Cultural Fictions

PETER LANG
New York • San Francisco • Bern • Baltimore
Frankfurt am Main • Berlin • Wien • Paris

Library of Congress Cataloging-in-Publication Data

Fleming, Bruce E. (Bruce Edward)
    Caging the lion : cross-cultural fictions / Bruce E. Fleming.
      p. cm. — (New studies in aesthetics ; vol. 13)
    Includes bibliographical references.
    1. Aesthetics.   2. Criticism.   I. Title.
II. Series.
BH39.F617   1993   306—dc20   92-5799
ISBN 0-8204-1912-5   CIP
ISSN 0893-6005

Die Deutsche Bibliothek-CIP-Einheitsaufnahme

Fleming, Bruce E.:
Caging the lion : cross-cultural fictions / Bruce E. Fleming.—
New York; Berlin; Bern; Frankfurt/M.; Paris; Wien: Lang, 1993
  (New studies in aesthetics ; Vol. 13)
    ISBN 0-8204-1912-5
NE: GT

Cover Design by James Brisson.

The paper in this book meets the guidelines for permanence and durability of the Committee on Production Guidelines for Book Longevity of the Council on Library Resources.

© Bruce E. Fleming, 1993

Printed in the United States of America.

There is no Frigate like a Book,
To take us Lands away

—*Emily Dickinson*

To the memory of my brother, Keith A. Fleming, Ph.D.

Acknowledgements

An earlier version of my consideration of *For Whom the Bell Tolls* appeared in *The Dutch Quarterly Review of Anglo-American Letters*; a version of Chapter Five appeared in *College Literature*, a version of Chapter Seven in *The Nation*, Chapter Eleven in the *New Orleans Review*, and a version of Chapter Eight in the *New Dance Review*. Parts of Chapter One appeared in another form in *Dance Magazine*. My consideration of Brontë in Chapter Four is included with the kind permission of Northern Illinois University; an earlier version of it appeared in their journal *Essays in Literature*.

Research which made possible sections of this book was conducted with the help of funds provided by the U. S. Naval Academy Research Council, for which I would like to express my gratitude. In addition I am heavily indebted to the efficiency and professional help of the librarians at the Naval Academy's Nimitz Library, whom I would like to thank here, and to the scrupulous editing of Robert Ginsberg.

Three people, palm trees, and Atlantic Ocean: Saint-Louis du Sénégal, 1987.
Photograph by author.

Contents

I

The Current State of Affairs

Chapter One

Interest in the Other

The interest by American intellectuals in cultures other than American, and especially other than Occidental, has never been higher. At university after university, courses are being required in non-Western cultures, to the point where a best-seller of the late 1980s to which I turn at the conclusion of this study, Allan Bloom's *Closing of the American Mind*, took this trend to task, and was fiercely opposed in return. The cover story by Dinesh D'Souza in the *Atlantic Monthly* current as I write this makes a point of listing some of the universities where courses in non-Western cultures, but none in Western, are required. Literature conferences as well as dance and theater festivals, such as the 1990 Los Angeles Festival, which I consider here, are increasingly devoted to non-Western art forms. And a sizeable scholarly literature exists on what is called "Otherness": the essentialization, or reification, of differences into absolutes. It is to this literature that the present study is a contribution; at the same time it is a contribution to contemporary aesthetics, being a study of the relation of artworks, and our reactions to them, to the societies which produce them.

The scope of my consideration is broader than usual in scholarly studies, including, in addition to literary works, reflections on my experiences teaching Western literature in Rwanda, a consideration of the divergent ways Acquired Immune Deficiency Syndrome (AIDS) is viewed in Africa and in the West, an analysis of watching a Kabuki performance as paradigm for viewer difficulties in coming to terms with the art forms of foreign cultures, a consideration of the popular film *Dances With Wolves*, and an overview of the landscape of contemporary domestic debate in literary theory—of which the specialized interest in the world outside is a lush but thoroughly logical offshoot.

Such interest in the exotic is not limited to the groves of academe or to the audiences that attend major arts festivals. The popularity of recent Hollywood films like *A Passage to India*, *Out of Africa*, and *Gorillas in the Mist* suggests that a deep-seated common chord is waiting to be touched in the general movie-going public by stories of Europeans in exotic climes. Many scholars, such as Renato Rosaldo, in *Culture and Truth*, go this level of popular interest in the Other one better, pointing out the Eurocentric stance such films invariably adopt; Rosaldo calls this "imperialist nostalgia." For, aimed at an American and Western European audience as they are, the films always put the whites in the center of things while the local people of color are condemned to remain at all times subsidiary.

To remain for a moment with cinema, there is "good" subsidiary, as in Sydney Pollack's *Out of Africa* or the BBC television series of Elspeth Huxley's childhood memoir, *The Flame Trees of Thika*, and there is "bad" subsidiary, as in numerous adventure films, from the three versions of H. Rider Haggard's *King Solomon's Mines* to the Indiana Jones sagas of our day. There is also bad-yet-fascinating subsidiary, as in David Lean's *A Passage to India*, which made explicit the sexual fascination of the white person with the dark-skinned native that was not so nakedly portrayed in the E. M. Forster original, or the BBC production of *The Jewel in the Crown*, based on Paul Scott's works and opening, as did the novel of this title, with the predictable rape of a white woman by non-white native men. In the most popular of all of these, Pollack's *Out of Africa*, the first five minutes of the film establish the European point of view through a tone of nostalgia so strong—produced by the framing shots of the aged Karen Blixen remembering her youth, Meryl's Streep's world-weary "I hed a faahm in Aafrica . . .," as well as the elegaic music—that the viewer knows from the outset that these Other are going to be subsidiaries of the good sort. After all, we do not feel nostalgia for what threatens us or what puts our fundamental values in question; we feel it only for the comforting and valorizing.

Finally, we may consider such well-attended and widely discussed art exhibits as New York's celebrated 1984 Museum of Modern Art show on "'Primitivism' and Modern Art," with the first word written between quotation marks—one of the favored typographical nuances of the 1980s and now 1990s—that have emphasized the indebtedness of Western art to non-Western sources. Scholars such as James Clifford, in his important *Predicament of Culture*, and Marianna Torgovnick, whose *Gone Primitive* has justifiably garnered much scholarly attention, have gone further, criticizing the show's organizers for having been Western-centered in their approach. Clifford, after challenging the show's juxtapositions of Modernist works with the "primitive" pieces—with which they display what the curators William Rubin and Kurt Varnedoe called "affinities"—comes to the following conclusion:

> the catalogue succeeds in demonstrating not any essential affinity between tribal and modern or even a coherent modernist attitude towards the primitive but rather the restless desire and power of the modern West to collect the world. (p. 196)

This touches on a principal theme of the present book, namely that our interest in the world outside is an expression more of our Westernness than of anything else, and that this Westernness consists precisely in the desire, and capability, to respond positively to worlds outside ours.

Most of such interest, whether academic or general, is exhibited at one end of the contemporary intellectual spectrum, on what I call—in the interests of schematic comprehensibility—the intellectual left. I use the terms of left and right in the course of this study as non-pejorative short-hand, and neither bears much resemblance to the corresponding political position from which I borrow the term. At its most extreme, the intellectual right is dismissive of other cultures; at its most measured it tends to be skeptical of the usefulness of involvement by Westerners in such cultures. On the side of the intellectual left, which has assumed by default the burden for talk about other cultures, we discover a situation that is equally questionable. What at first glance seems a vector relation of interest toward the outside turns out to bend back towards the perceiver; Otherness is only conception for our own purposes and in terms of ourselves. Indeed, much of our current interest in the world outside reveals itself as a form of Western self-involvement, being the expression of our own needs; it will be my attempt here to justify this claim, and show why it is the case. At neither end of the current intellectual spectrum do we find the real contact with the outside that remains a viable option.

Yet we should almost be able to say beforehand that this would be so, given that for the majority of scholars and generally interested viewers, curiosity about other cultures is sparked by, and usually remains limited to, those few quite unrepresentative products of other cultures which can be easily integrated into our own culture. Almost always this means the artistic products of these cultures, or at least the things we are able to regard as such. At the same time, such a specific interest is confounded with an objective appreciation of the culture as a whole; the result is the largely unjustified feeling of having left the confines of the West.

An example of this confusion was provided by the 1990 Los Angeles Festival, directed by Peter Sellars and devoted in its entirety to arts of Pacific Rim countries — or at least to the "traditional" or "indigenous" cultures of those countries. The terms "traditional" and "indigenous" were used interchangeably at the opening ceremonies, presumably to underscore the difference between what we were about to see and the arts of our non-traditional and non-indigenous society. These opening ceremonies, set at the spectacular site of Angel's Gate in San Pedro, high on a bluff with a view of the sky-blue expanse of the Pacific, placed side by side Maoris with what they referred to as their "younger cousins" from the islands of Wallis and Futuna, wearing beautifully painted bark cloth; these in turn rubbed shoulders with Australian aborigines decorated largely with body art, with Korean Shamans in immaculate white robes and high black hats, and with Ikooc dancers from Mexico in scarlet headbands and loincloths. Native Americans brought welcome and blessings; indeed, each group brought welcome, prayers, and in most cases, dances.

Yet as soon as the dances were over, many of the most interestingly "native"-looking of the performers pulled on jeans and jogging shoes that had been left aside for the ceremony; I concluded that these were their normal everyday clothes. Disappointed despite myself, I realized that part of our interest in the dances was the feeling that what the dancers wore to perform sprang "naturally" from their culture as it now is. I wanted to say: either they should be dancing in their T-shirts and quartz watches—in which case we would have thought their native culture polluted, and have been radically less interested in watching them—or we should accept this state of (un)dress as a costume in the same sense as our own Western tutus and tights. In this case, however, the result would have been no more "traditional" and "indigenous" than a *Giselle* in New York or Paris. At any rate, I felt condescended to, for one of the pre-conditions of respectful attention to the Other is that the Other stay Other—and not look too much like us.

Such moments revealed the Festival as a show for the haves where the have-nots were meant to stay in their places, remain colorful, photogenic, and (if possible) naked. At the same time the tabloid-sized program was touting the whole enterprise as a step forward in comprehension of the world, assuring us that "finding out about our ancient and completely contemporary neighbors on the Pacific turns out to be . . . extremely interesting, occasionally shocking, moving, mysterious, and profound, and again and again a huge amount of fun." Though intermittantly moving and mysterious, the Other is, according to this booklet, at bottom essentially "fun." It is composed of entire cultures whose purpose for us is to add yet another taste to the variety of our urban smorgasbord.

One morning during the Festival the strange status of those invited to parade their Otherness seemed particularly paradoxical. The aboriginal dancers taught a class outside on the campus of California State University, Los Angeles, where the Dance Critics Association was meeting for its annual conference. As a television crew dangled state-of-the-art microphones over their heads and circled them with cameras, the critics tried out trilling like birds and throwing imaginary spears while the eerily beautiful sound of the didgeridoo breathed in the background. Since the dancers were all citizens of a Western, Anglophone country, namely Australia, they acted in ways and spoke a language comfortingly comprehensible to the media representatives, as well as to the critic-dancers hanging on their words and gestures. One of the Australians wore a T-shirt that said "Florida" in flamingo pink. We would, I thought, have been less eager to pay respectful attention if the guests had rejected chairs or been afraid of the microphones, and we would have been unable to understand them at all if they—or someone with them—had not spoken our language. On one hand, they were emissaries from another world; on the other hand, they were just dancers, like dancers everywhere. How mysterious yet how reassuring; in short, how very much fun.

Watching the airplanes circle out over the ocean and descend toward the Los Angeles airport that day at the opening ceremonies, I reflected that in spite of our delicious feeling as audience members of having left behind the bustle of our alienating industrial society by retreating to this gorgeous spot on the Pacific, none of these ceremonies would have been audible without the bank of microphones that were continually going on the blink and bringing everything to a grinding halt, and they could not have happened at all without the airplanes that had brought the participants to Los Angeles to begin with. The paradox was that this very festival was impossible without the technological achievements of the society to which the groups invited to participate were supposed to present an alternative. The informative program had assured us that the Festival was "sparked by . . . an impulse to return to our spiritual essence through image, song, and dance." If we Westerners have lost our "spiritual essence," as the program clearly assumed, how ironic that we could only get it back through the very things that—according to most versions of the story of an Eden lost to us by our having moved away from our agrarian roots—are the sign of our loss.

The hottest items in the sales area at the booth marked "Tahiti" — set next to other booths bearing the signs of places primarily interesting to Westerners as getaway islands — were T-shirts with a silk-screened print by Gauguin, a European artist whose paintings memorialized Tahiti as an Eden already lost, his sighs of longing now turned into "indigenous" export. This was a classic example of how easily Schiller's distinction between "naive" and "sentimental" can be subverted: the sentimental attitude, Schiller thought, seeks the natural; the naive lives naturally. Here the confusion was complete: sentimental offered as naive — our own point of view reflected back at us and sold as the world beyond our borders.

The contact with a world outside offered by the Los Angeles Festival of 1990 was limited from the beginning by the nature of the medium of contact, namely works of art. Usually artworks provide the primary point of intersection between stay-at-home Westerners and non-Western cultures. Yet artworks are highly suspect as sources of information about societies. They are over-determined, somehow denser bits of the world, criss-crossing nodes that are solid enough to be lifted entire from their background — wherever we may draw the boundary between work and background. This is not to say that we are unable to draw conclusions about a society from looking at its art objects. Yet it is likely that such conclusions will only be on the meta-level, as the most interesting Marxist criticism, such as that of Georg Lukács, or Fredric Jameson, suggests that what characterizes Western art past a certain date is precisely a lack of overt link between it and the world outside of it.

The understanding of art which underlies the preceding paragraph, of course, implies a Western value system, one codified by Kant and made dogma by the Romantics. This notion of non-functionality, of art as the object of disinterested contemplation, as Terry Eagleton points out in his *Ideology of the Aesthetic*, forms the core of our understanding of the "aesthetic." Paradoxically, much of the interest by viewers in programs like these presented at the Los Angeles Festival is the result of their feeling that these *do not* correspond to this definition of art — at least, not for our societies, so that we are looking at works which are more integrated into their societies than comparable works are integrated into ours.

Whatever these works were in their own worlds, they only enter ours under our Western rubric, as separated artworks to be looked at. The process is like translation: whether the words are *Brot*, *pain*, or *pane*, they all become "bread" in English, because that's the word they are closest to in our system—even if German bread is different from French bread which is different from American bread.

For Westerners, art objects are those objects to which we devote our most undivided attention. The twentieth century has realized that symptom can become cause: having us devote our attention to something in this manner suffices to make it art. This is the nature of the "found object." Yet aesthetic attention is attention of a specific sort: attention for no other purpose than pure perception. Whatever the particular content of the things may be that are presented to us as art, we will treat them, most fundamentally, as art objects. In whatever way the people receive them in the world from which these art entities come—and we suspect that they participate more and look less—we can do nothing else but give works the same attention of the non-involved that is the hallmark of our relation with the objects we designate art. It was only necessary to look at the silent respectful audience of the Westerners that day at Angel's Gate to see this.

Another example of this permutation is provided by the way most Western museums nowadays display the African cult objects that we have come to call art, after decades of denying them this honorific label—namely, the same way that the Modernist works they influenced are displayed. In both cases, discrete units of wood, metal, or stone are spot-lit in plexiglas boxes set against white walls. Such presentation gives rise to the useful fiction that tribal ritual objects really are the same as our self-consciously artistic products of individual expression, a phenomenon Clifford and Torgovnick consider in detail. And so they are—for us—as long as we display them in this manner. Like many postmodernist art works, their exposition as objects of our undivided, passive attention makes them art. The museum creates its objects: for us, art is what is now displayed in a museum.

We can, to be sure, imagine things that are not amenable to such passive display; we can even pay them the same attention in order to broaden our understanding of "art." Many of the creations of John Cage have as their purpose just this broadening of attention. But such broadening merely subsumes more material under the same framework, as if to democratize access to its honorific status; it does not fundamentally change the framework itself. The postmodernist work that challenges the frame, the proscenium arch, or the constraints of plot resolution still ends up in a museum, a performance space, or between covers. This challenge only makes sense if we pay it the same attention we paid works which stayed within the boundaries that it is flouting.

The current trend in the appreciation of non-Western art works, which involves an emphasis on precisely those aspects which do not separate so easily from their society—such as the dances of which African masks are an integral part, as in the work of Robert Farris Thompson—and so opposes our now so-easy equation of Picasso with the Fang, or Klee with Pacific Island art, is not a rejection of this Western notion of art as object-to-be-contemplated. Instead, it is an extension on the inter-cultural front, as we have experienced an extension on the domestic one, of the kind of material that can be subject to it. The process of re-dissolving such bits of other cultures into their societal backgrounds that Clifford envisions in part three of *The Predicament of Culture*—insofar as this is possible—and an emphasis on the slippages of the boundaries between art and ethnography, "classic" tribal works and contemporary works, are only thinkable as a second step whose first is that of the separated object. Such re-contextualizing can, moreover, never be effected totally. We can put only a small group of people on an airplane, and if what they wish to do for us does not have a beginning, middle, and end—even if these divisions are not easily distinguishable by the Western viewer—we cannot show them off, and do not know how to designate what we are seeing.

Even if we had the wherewithal to import an entire society and have it live among us with all of its functions on view, it would still be "on display," like an ant farm: the whole society as art object. We can understand an alternative to ourselves only in terms of ourselves: any alternative to us must fit into our conceptual structure as alternative in order to be comprehensible. This is what the Other is: something that serves as an alternative at the level of the specific but not at the level of the general. Yet frequently we conflate a variation of the species level—a variation minor with respect to ourselves— with one of the genus, with what for our point of view would be a real alternative.

Interest in other cultures is not a new phenomenon in the West; we may see it as a resurgence of a main stream of post-Romantic Western thought. In his magisterial work on *Victorian Anthropology*, George W. Stocking, Jr. documents this stream in detail. He charts the divergent positions that preceded that codification of British anthropology's view toward less-"developed" cultures into the evolutionist equation of non-Western cultures with prior stages of our own development which had become the norm in thought by 1851, the time of the exposition in the Crystal Palace. However Stocking makes clear that, though this "Victorian" view was dominant in Britain, if not so much in Germany, there had always existed simultaneous with it the notion of something positive about the state of more "primitive" peoples, resurfacing at various times and more strongly in specific places.

The proto-Romantic form of this notion with which we are most familiar is Rousseau's conception, in his *Discourse on the Origin of Inequality*, of the "noble savage"—the idea that less "civilized" people were somehow kinder, freer, or more in touch with their feelings than the decadent Europeans. And this was also at the base of all of the wanderings into a world Out There of the later Romantics which produced the "Orientalism" that Edward Said has so exhaustively considered, as well as, subsequently, the interest analyzed by Torgovnick of the Modernists in what they perceived as the more direct sensuality of African carvings.

In *Haunted Journeys*, Dennis Porter's fascinating and mercifully non-polemical consideration of travel writings by European men from the eighteenth century to the present, the specifically French expression of this Romantic interest is summarized as follows, through a contrast of Flaubert with Stendhal, who in this sense was more akin to Stocking's British Victorians:

> The purpose of travel for Stendhal . . . was to move up the scale of civilization, not down. . . . To travel in the opposite direction would certainly have struck him as perverse.
> Yet by the late 1820s Stendhal appears to have been something of an exception in his homeland. . . . It was non-Europe that interested [travelers with literary and artistic ambitions] . . . ; they were drawn to otherness for its own sake, the otherness of "the uncivilized" or of lands at least uncontaminated by the Christian religion, Enlightenment humanism, democratic politics, or industrial progress. (p. 165)

Porter lists a few such travelers, especially those drawn to the "so-called Orient": Hugo, Delacroix, and Flaubert himself— and a few paragraphs later he produces a longer list, including Chateaubriand, Lamartine, Théophile Gautier, Gérard de Nerval, Pierre Loti, and Maurice Barrès. Porter's subsequent analysis of Freud's *Civilization and Its Discontents* links Freud's work to works by D. H. Lawrence, T. E. Lawrence, and André Gide, and concludes that all of them

> are expressions of the impulse to overcome the perceived decadence of European culture through the embracing of different forms of "primitivism." It was a problem that was also addressed, in a different way, by anthropologists from Bronislaw Malinowski to Claude Lévi-Strauss. (p. 199)

This list, as well as any close perusal of the works by the writers Porter considers, shows that at the base of this Western fascination with the non-Western was a mixture of admiration and scorn, a masochistic love of degradation. Speaking of travel in the Romantic period, Porter suggests:

> travel becomes self-consciously an end in itself, in a way that is often difficult to explain fully in terms of pleasure. The phenomenon begins with Byron but is most apparent in the Oriental journey of a Flaubert, where it appears in the lurid colors of the "romantic agony" as an orientation to death. (p. 11)

Stocking provides support for Porter's inclusion of two contemporary ethnographers in this list by making clear that the search for an alternative to Western civilization (or "civilization") is still at the basis of much ethnography. Speaking of the shift away from Victorian evolutionism after World War I, Stocking notes:

> although anthropologists did their fieldwork under an umbrella of colonial power, they tended to identify with the tribal cultures they studied . . . . In sharp contrast to the evolutionary period . . . a romantic preservationsism with strong undertones of "Noble Savagery" became the attitudinal norm of sociocultural anthropology.   Despite a questioning of relativism in the aftermath of World War II . . . this romantic tendency to view the societies they study as outside the historical processes of modern civilization has continued strong until the present. (p. 289)

Yet if, as I suggest, we cannot totally enter into Otherness, this is because the Other in a real sense is already part of ourselves. To this extent my consideration here echoes a theme common in contemporary thought: the insistence, as Wendy Steiner puts it in a review of Patrick Brantlinger's recent *Crusoe's Footprints*, that "the trauma of the humanities is the confrontation of the Other and the discovery following fast upon it that that Other is ourself." Barbara Johnson, representing an entire generation of Derrideans, makes the point on a yet more theoretical level: "the differences *between* entities . . . are . . . based on a repression of differences *within* entities, ways in which an entity differs from itself" (quoted by Porter, p. 7). Indeed, the Freudian notion of "the uncanny" central to so many of Porter's analyses suggests at the psychological level as well that in seeking the Other we are seeking a part of ourselves. As Porter puts it:

> Decisions concerning flight or exile from the "homeland" along with the embracing or rejection of the countries through which one travels, often derive from identifications dependent less on objective factors than on the projection of early prototypes onto geographic space. . . .
>   In . . . "The Uncanny," Freud both connects the question with the search for origins and reverses our usual understanding of it by implying that love of "place" is prior to love for a human object, that it is, in fact, homesickness for the lost world of prenatality. . . . There is a sense

in which our desire to leave a given home is at the same time the desire
to recover an original lost home. (pp. 11-12)

The level of my consideration is more concrete than Johnson's, less psychological than Freud's. With Porter and Stocking—as well as most anthropologically-oriented thinkers—I
insist that we can seriously consider the possibility of
differences between our culture and others, and I insist that
this distinction should not be allowed to dissolve into an easy
theoretical blurring of boundaries, given that it is based on
real, perceived differences. The question for me is not
whether differences exist, but what their nature is.

Another commentator who expresses this quite clearly is
Christopher L. Miller, in his beautifully balanced *Theories of
Africans*. Speaking of what might at first glance seem a
laudable reticence of Westerners to say anything at all about
non-Westerners, Miller asks the following question: "What
becomes of difference in a methodology that trusts only self-
reflexivity?" His answer points out the disadvantages of such
false modesty: "The impulse to leave the other alone rejoins
the impulse to obliterate the other" (p. 10). If we do not
acknowledge the possibility of difference (even if not of Difference), we end up assuming that the whole world is like us,
leaving undefined our own nature.

Like Miller, I am concerned that we preserve distinctions at
least long enough to scrutinize them. Yet the kind of Otherness Steiner and Brantlinger are referring to is different from
what which primarily concerns me. What they mean by the
Other is what I call the intra-cultural Other, to distinguish it
from the inter-cultural Other that is my primary consideration. In Chapter Two I develop the claim that the source of
much of our muddled thinking regarding inter-cultural
Otherness is caused by our confounding it with the intra-
cultural sort; an Other conceived of as outside our world is not
the same as an Other within it. I do not deny that one of these
may become the opposite—usually, in the direction of intra-
cultural to inter-cultural. But this does not mean that the two
categories themselves merge and become indistinguishable.

The same program book for the Los Angeles Festival—as near-perfect a barometer of contemporary taste as I have found—gives an example of this confusion, offering a different (and illegitimate) reason for bringing the outside in, namely the assertion that it's there already. In this booklet, penned by an anonymous author, we read the following:

> We've arrived at the last decade of our century and it's a new world out there. With 85 languages spoken in the Los Angeles school system, it turns out that most of that new world is alive and living right here in this city.

Yet this cannot justify bringing in works from "out there"; because the only possible conclusion from this is that, in Gertrude Stein's famous phrase, there is no "there" there. If this is the situation, we are past the stage of the Trojan horse: the gates of the city must already have been torn down. Precisely to the extent that we can still make the distinction between in here and out there, these works from out there must differ from those of the world within because of some quality, or degree of visibility. The suggestion is that if the soup already has some salt, we ought to add the whole box. While this may be a good idea, the reason stated cannot serve as justification for doing so.

Such an argument is based on the perception that groups whose characteristics we had previously held to be signs of Otherness are now within the cluster of qualities we define as our own. It does not eliminate Otherness *per se*; it merely decouples a specific perception of it from certain qualities, the way hair color is now largely non-essentializing in American culture. (By contrast, we read in British novels of the turn of the century of women being divided into the two categories of "fair" or "dark," based on hair color.) For this argument, Otherness is not found to be ourselves; instead, we have merely transferred specific groups from the column of Them to the column of Us.

Nor does what we might call a global perspective on things—seeing us all as one big world—deconstruct the distinction between intra- and inter-cultural Otherness, or eliminate Otherness *per se*. Steiner continues, in the review

quoted above, summarizing Brantlinger by quoting H. Bruce
Franklin:

> If we who study and teach literature wish that our profession survive,
> we must adjust our vision to a world in which most people are
> nonwhite, over half are female, the overwhelming majority are work-
> ers, and all live in a time of transformation so intense that it may consti-
> tute a metamorphosis.

Such a view rules out the relation of what I call inter-cultural
Otherness: groups in the world outside being perceived as
foreign—for it is literally the world that is meant here. Yet
this passage reinstates the criterion that must serve to re-
establish differences, even if they are different than those
being occluded: those who "study and teach literature" do so
within the context of, and to an audience drawn only from,
one kind of society—one defined by its acceptance of rationalistic debate, which is characteristic of the West.

Steiner quotes Brantlinger, who is himself drawing on
Raymond Williams: "To note the historical origins of literature is already a challenge to its status as an absolute category
having a timeless, transcendent role in human affairs." True
enough, but this also challenges the status of literature as an
absolute geographical category or undertaking. What redraws
the lines of Otherness in this argument are the limitations of
the mechanism of looking, irrespective of the catholicity of
object that is urged on us. The medium of contact with the
world is composed of works of art, however these are defined.

My point is more theoretical than the position of many
contemporary scholars, including Torgovnick. She writes, à
propos of Rubin and Varnedoe's MOMA show: "there is . . . no
guarantee that ethnographic knowledge can ever reproduce
an Other's viewpoint or that even the fullest ethnographic
knowledge will fully overcome cultural conditioning" (p. 130).
Yet this difficulty is a theoretical impossibility, not just a
practical unliklihood, as Torgovnick suggests. The relation of
Otherness means that we can never reproduce the viewpoint
of the Other—which is to say, adopt it for our own primary
viewpoint. Unlike Torgovnick, I see alternatives to Otherness
as a relation with the world outside.

The same distinction so central here between inter- and intra-cultural Otherness helps indicate the limits of the undeniable kinship between my arguments and those of another group of current thinkers. My claims at first glance may appear similar to those of thinkers like Stanley Fish who have become celebrated for insisting that we cannot escape the perception-patterns—or better, the expression-patterns—of our own group. A version of such thought relevant to the discussion at hand that emphasizes the impossibility of ever expressing the point of view of a true Other is offered in Fish's recent *Doing What Comes Naturally*. Christopher Norris gives a useful and accurate summary of the argument in his *What's Wrong with Postmodernism*:

> On the one hand, any truly radical theory . . . would *ipso facto* be wholly unintelligible to people within the relevant community . . . . On the other, any theory that *claimed* to be 'radical' but in fact enjoyed widespread acceptance—or even a modest degree of success . . . would for this very reason have to be seen as part of an existing consensus . . . . In short, critical theorists . . . are caught . . . in a classic double-bind predicament, since their claims to speak genuinely on behalf of an alternative, dispossessed or minority culture must become less plausible with each new step toward gaining a wider currency for their views. (p. 79)

This last-mentioned process defines the current discourse of the intra-cultural Other. Yet Fish's claim is more temporal than geographic; the assertion that we cannot stand outside of ourselves in the first sense differs from my claim that we can really do so in a geographical sense: we have airplanes but not time machines.

Yet a more direct response is available to Fish's claims— more direct than that produced by Norris after considerable intellectual labor, though I sympathize with Norris's attempt to produce this. In his critique of Fish and several related thinkers, Norris attempts to make theory *per se* both cerebral and muscular—both justified in its own terms and applicable to domestic political action. He does this by attempting to rescue Kant from those who, in his view, have gone too far in centralizing the notion of the aesthetic, such as Baudrillard, Lyotard, and Fish. Norris admires Habermas for trying to work in a properly Kantian fashion, though he thinks Habermas got Derrida wrong: even Derrida turns out to be on the side of the angels.

Such a tortuously acquired intellectual solution only makes sense if no easier one is available. But one is. In a thinker who makes a distinction between action and thought (as Norris does, in trying to wed them), action becomes the equivalent of Kant's noumenal realm. Norris's entire enterprise becomes one of thinking his way back to action. Yet it isn't necessary to justify action with thought (Fish would say: it isn't possible); instead, thought explains action — and each of us is capable of ceasing thought and entering this "noumenal" realm. In the same way, all Western talk, even about the Other, simply defines our Westernness. Yet we can leave this Western world without riding on the boomerang of conception in terms of the Other.

The limits of similarity are quickly reached as well between my position and what hovers behind the spate of what Renato Rosaldo, in an article for the *Village Voice*, calls "the-invention-of" books. The article in question considers three such works, *Machines as the Measure of Men* by Michael Adas, *The Invention of Africa* by V. Y. Mudimbe, and *The Invention of Ethnicity* by Werner Sollors. Rosaldo summarizes the world-view of such works as these as follows:

> The whole world, it seems, is constructed — socially, culturally, historically . . . . [The result is that] humanity has lost its origins. People grow out of the endless accretion of cultural practices, rather than resting, as it once seemed, on solid biological foundations. (p. 27)

Such works have in common that they are a logical extension, via the works of Michel Foucault, of Ferdinand de Saussure's suggestion that signs have meaning only in the context of a system of other signs. This became the cornerstone of structuralism — in anthropology, that of Lévi-Strauss — and, in its turn, of the deconstructionist or hermeneutic perception that words beget words and can only be understood in other words. The initial conclusion to this is that the world is only a construction of words; its extension to the debate on Otherness is effected by saying that cultural structures are in some strong ontic sense only constructions.

Porter articulates the dispiriting conclusion of such thought with respect to Said's notion of "Orientalism":

> As far as the representation of foreign places is concerned, the greatest problem to which a strict interpretation of discourse theory gives rises is the implication that there is no way out of cultural solipsism. . . . One may piously wish for alternatives to Orientalism, but how these would emerge in the context of a theory dominated by the concept of power/knowledge is by no means clear. (pp. 4-5)

In other words, the assertion—like many assertions of contemporary theory, which is devoted in large part to constructing systems which justify theory—is not amenable either to proof or disproof. This makes it, in my view, uninteresting, given that we can in fact leave our culture and perceive differences with another.

A related disadvantage attends those works which suggest a slippage between perception and reality on the part of Western observers of foreign cultures, suggesting not the strong position that conception equals reality, but the philosophically weaker one that conception frequently disfigures reality. Examples of this include Dorothy Hammond and Alta Jablow's *Myth of Africa*, chronicling the conceptualization of "the dark continent" in the nineteenth century, Christopher L. Miller's *Blank Darkness: Africanist Discourse in French*, which continues this chronicle with respect to Francophone writers, and above all, Said's overtly Foucauldian *Orientalism* that maps the canals in which Western thought about—and conceptions of—the Arab world have moved. Or rather, as Clifford points out, this is the case some of the time in Said. For, referring to Said's "ambivalence" in using the term "Orient" sometimes to refer to something which really exists and other times to refer to something merely constructed, Clifford observes:

> frequently [Said] suggests that a text or tradition distorts, dominates, or ignores some real or authentic feature of the Orient. Elsewhere, however, he denies the existence of any "real Orient," and in this he is more rigorously faithful to Foucault and the other radical critics of representation whom he cites. (p. 260)

Even if such books avoid the rigorously Foucauldian (or Kantian) conclusions Porter points to above, the unsettling suspicion we are left with after reading them is that prototypes like these do not come to be totally by chance. If a society can only take account of worlds outside in terms of such canalizations of thought, this is so because they offer the most efficient means of doing so. They are the line of least resistance at any given time. The result is that while we can make hay by criticizing any such conceptualization subsequently on the grounds of innacuracy—as is now fashionable with the conceptualizations of the nineteenth- and early-twentieth centuries—we are almost certainly caught in another such conceptualization pattern that will be criticized in its turn. I am reminded of those readers who congratulate themselves on having escaped the time period in which a *Moby Dick* could be ignored, or an Emily Dickinson unknown. Yet the liklihood is great that inglorious—if not mute—poets and novelists today are being ignored as well. We are no better than the previous generations; it is merely that we are in a position to see their faults, as others will come to see ours.

Moreover, there is always more than just a hint of what I would call cultural idealism about such thinkers. Rosaldo quotes Sollors, for example, on the subject of what Sollors calls "previously 'essentialist' categories (childhood, generations, romantic love, mental health, gender, history, region, biography, and so on)." The world is our own construction; nothing exists inherently. "Essentialist" must be written in scare quotes. To this idealism I oppose a form of geographical or inter-cultural "naive realism": the world outside exists independently of our perception; we can even perceive it (unlike Kant's noumenal realm). To be sure, we may not be able to write about it—as I will consider below. But this may be a limitation we ultimately come to accept.

Such insistence that the world is nothing but collective constructions reminds me of the princess in James Thurber's charming storybook *Many Moons* who wanted the moon, and was satisfied to get it in the form of a tiny golden disk the size of her fingernail. Clearly this was the moon, for, as she explained, her fingernail just covered the moon when she held up her hand. And when asked why, if she now wore the moon around her neck, the moon was still in the sky, she assured her questioner that the moon had simply grown back. The princess's logic is irrefutable; it is only the outsider who can see it as charming (if such an outsider is in a forgiving mood) or as self-serving and petty (if in an unforgiving one).

For if the world is constructed, the explanation of that construction is also itself constructed; more importantly, it is constructed-for-Westerners, just as the story of the moon only made sense to the princess. All of these theories—as well as works of contemporary ethnography such as Rosaldo's works, considered below—are works written for and toward a particular audience: ourselves. This guides and influences the content of these theories and reports, just as it determines the content of the Los Angeles Festival, or the fact of the Festival's existence. They are themselves part of Western discourse.

The attempt to subvert the theoretical distinction between ourselves and others by an insistence that all cultures are constructed ends up reinstating the difference at a deeper level than content, namely the level of whatever guides and determines content, our very Westernness—a commodity defined below. Yet only as long as it remains unenunciated and undefined can such a difference constitute a Difference. We must acknowledge our Westernness precisely in order that it not be essentialized in this fashion under the surface, from which position its power is absolute.

Under the present circumstances of intellectual discourse, this Westernness is unacknowledged, and so has come to form the bedrock of our projection of the Other. We may not be able to escape the initial fact of our Westernness, any more than we can escape the biological gender we are born with or the fact that our capitalist society gives us innumerable monetary advantages over people born into poorer societies. But this is not to say that any of these need totally determine our behavior. Enunciating what we are makes possible the expression of an alternative to it.

The assertion is much more easily provable that conception in terms of Otherness can be escaped, leaving aside the question of whether our Westernness can ultimately be, should we wish to do so. It is handy for my position too that this is relatively easy to convince ourselves of. We have only to go into the world without the mind-set which makes us see everything as something potentially-to-be-reported-on—which is, to say, the way we go about our everyday lives. I am thinking here of the alternative to the way Susan Sontag, in *On Photography*, suggests that tourists see a foreign country through a camera. Everything must be captured, everything must be mastered through the lens; to the locals, however, such tourists seem ridiculous. We can avoid being tourists and, appealing to the distinction Paul Bowles has one of his characters make in *The Sheltering Sky*, become travelers. In Porter's sense, we leave home with no desire and avoid the feeling of transgression. If we have no desire to leave home, we may not do so at all—but this allows us to see something important about the nature of conception in terms of Otherness.

One sophisticated example of this seeing-in-order-to-report is ethnography, which assumes that the ethnographer is at all times potentially writing a book or an article for the people back home, and so rests on such a positing of Otherness. The very presupposition that the ethnographer is in a "foreign culture" is the mark of primordial Otherness. All of what is seen by the ethnographer is of potential interest to the folks back home—precisely because they are folks back home, and the ethnographer is out there breathing the postulated air of Otherness. This is so even if what is reported, as so often nowadays, is that the people out there are just like the ones at home, that there is nothing to report. Thus, the contemporary ethnographer is a contradiction in terms: a live-in tourist. And from this contradiction arise the theoretical problems facing ethnography. In fact, we can operate under different assumptions, never knowing beforehand if what we are going to see will be foreign. What if we get to a distant galaxy and find Levittown? In this case we will decide that Andromeda is as un-foreign as New Jersey.

The ascription of inter-cultural Otherness is not a primordeal sin, something that we should avoid at all costs. As Porter's psychoanalytical analysis makes clear, the sense of limits is interesting to most of us. Crossing borders—of whatever kind—is highly pleasureful, holding out the lure of transgression and the thrill of the forbidden. (One work in which we get a sense of the thrill of the violation of borders which Porter does not consider is Graham Green's revealing travel book on West Africa, *Journey Without Maps*.) Such pleasure, while not illegitimate *per se*, does have its disadvantages. Conception in terms of inter-cultural Otherness is so widespread a means of conceiving the world that we cannot think about its elimination. At most we should work toward its elimination when it is based on illegitimate presuppositions, such as the equation of skin color or a mode of obtaining food—say cultivation with sticks rather than tractors—with inferiority or superiority. This is not Otherness *per se*, merely particular instantiations of it.

As an alternative relation with the world that does not bend back on ourselves in the projection of Otherness, we need only refuse to proceed from the presupposition that because a group of people lives elsewhere, they are, *a priori*, necessarily different than us. Of course, this frees us for a consideration of the specific ways in which a group of people can turn out to be different from, or be like, ourselves. Instead of positing Otherness as a rubric under which all other qualities are secondary, even if these qualities suggest similarity on some points, we need only refuse to posit anything at all, and see what we get. We need not lose a sense of being alien under these circumstances, nor should we adopt the view of "globalism." For this viewpoint is very hard, if not utterly impossible, to attain. Instead, we need only transfer the onus of alienness from the world around us, which is its location in conceptions of Otherness, to ourselves: we are the foreigners, not the country in which we find ourselves.

My enterprise is thus akin to Miller's consideration, in *Theories of Africans*, of both the necessity and difficulty of considering divergences between ourselves and others. Miller quotes Aimée Césaire in order to make the point that, as Miller puts it, "there are in fact two ways to lose identity, be it one's own or someone else's." In Césaire's words: "There are two ways to lose oneself: by segregation in the particular or by dilution in the 'universal'" (p. 24). Applying this to his analysis of Francophone African literature, Miller acknowledges, as I do, that

> no attempt to describe Africa's difference . . . seems immune from connotations and taints of ethnocentrism when seen in retrospect. . . . But [he asks] without some attention to the "difference" of the African past, how can we accurately read the African present? (p. 24)

In other words, Miller agrees that the nineteenth century's version of negative Otherness is not an option. At the same time he points toward a means of understanding the world outside that avoids the trap of universalism—or, I would add, the just as easy ruts of positive Otherness, the breast-beating primitivism of some contemporary Westerners. He is clear too that this kind of "looking to traditional African cultures" will not take place through the glasses of contemporary ethnology, engaged as it is in the "recourse to self-reflexivity" (p. 10).

Instead, Miller suggests this means of understanding the world outside will depend on a highly particular, highly sensitive look at this realm, which for him really exists (as I would say, exists outside of the constraints of Otherness). His conclusion is that

> the most fruitful path for the Western critic of African literature . . . is not to play it safe and "stay home," nor to pretend to "leave home without it" and approach African literature with a virgin mind, but to balance one impulse against the other: to reconsider with scepticism the applicability of all Western critical terms and to look to traditional African cultures for terms they might offer. (pp. 24-25)

Miller points out that his analysis "amounts to a defense of difference and otherness as inescapable armatures of reading and writing" (p. 10)—a defense to which I wish to contribute, though Miller's claim is only true exactly as he has written it, with these words in non-reified lower-case.

In concert with Porter, I understand the kind of Otherness considered here as a conception based fundamentally on an essentializing of place—as Chinua Achebe, whom I consider, perceived as well. Place is the common denominator in intercultural Otherness—though the common garden variety of contemporary interest in Otherness frequently fails to see this.

If asked, most of the audience members at the Los Angeles Festival would surely have said that they were interested in the markedly different people from wherever who danced before them, not the invisible places from which they came. Yet a differentiation of place alone—expressed in what Porter calls "cultural 'earth-writing' (geo = earth; graphy = writing)" (p. 3)—can explain why we see all of these individual people as having something in common. Their posited similarity as individuals, and hence their interesting difference from ourselves, is based on their origin in an equally posited Other place.

This essentializing of place is most easily explained in a negative fashion. Consider just how often we have the opportunity to essentialize place in this fashion and do not do so. I can go from Maryland to North Dakota (or the reverse), from Annapolis to Baltimore, from one side of the Yard of the U. S. Naval Academy to the other, or down the hall to a colleague's office, but at no point do I conceive of any of these movements as offering potential contact with an Other. At most, we can contact pockets of Otherness within our culture, such as Native Americans, or hard-core Baltimoreans. Yet it may be that for those the Germans call "U.S.-Americans"—to discourage those with United States passports from appropriating a term correctly applied to the entirety of North and South America—even a country as much like the United States as Canada presents a foreign Other, and Tonga an even more distant one.

Forms of Otherness based on other factors than place do exist, and I will devote a fair amount of space to a consideration of them: skin color, gender, sexuality, and so on. But a primary conceptualizing device in the world today is geographical Otherness, though this Otherness of place may be expressed in the related political and sociological terms of country and culture. I would guess that the ubiquity of conceptualization in terms of Otherness of place is the result of our widespread twentieth-century acceptance of the nation-state as a political organizing principle, an entity that captures the essence of a people. One has only to look at the United Nations definition of a sovereign country to be convinced of this. Somehow things that happen in Alaska are Inside for U. S. citizens, though things that happen in Toronto are Outside. In the United States, this extends to an essentializing of individual states as well. Hagerstown (which is set off from the rest of Maryland on a narrowly-joined panhandle) is Inside for Salisbury (east of the Chesapeake Bay), whereas Seaford, much closer to Salisbury but across the state line from it in Delaware, is Outside. Many Marylanders feel an interest in, and loyalty to Baltimore, the state's largest city, and a distinct disinterest in independent yet equally nearby Washington, D.C. — for the sole reason that Baltimore is, after all, Maryland. And because we in America talk of "Switzerland" (rather than, say, of Uri or Schwytz or Basel-Land), even the city of Basel — which sticks up into the German state of Baden-Württemberg — is permeated mentally with the smell of chocolate and the sound of cow-bells, in a way that nearby Konstanz, part of Germany though located south of the Rhine (that otherwise divides the two countries), is not.

Nothing is absolute about such mental maps of the world. When, in the early 1980s, I went jogging along the Teltower Canal in what was then West Berlin, I used to look with great interest across the water at the fences and guard towers in East Germany. That was Other. Yet after a trip to Potsdam during which I saw all these border installations from the other side, they lost their mystique. Thinking now of this dissolved border, I am once again reminded of Stein's phrase: there is no "there" there — which is to say, there is no longer an Other on the other side of the Teltower Canal. Similarly, someone who lives in the Washington, D.C. suburbs of Montgomery County, Maryland may feel a larger loyalty to the city he or she lives outside of than to the state of Maryland.

Proust, to take an example of one student of this sort of inter-cultural Otherness whom I mention a number of times, understood perfectly how this process of mental map-drawing created and destroyed our senses of Otherness. For him it was Venice that was charmed in his youth, yet came to lose its charge — and hence its charm — through a visit. Indeed Otherness generally fades into the light of common day through prolonged contact with the place that had been invested with it—unless we are there "on assignment," like ethnographers. This happens as the weight of individualizing detail over-whelms the postulated unity of the initial rubric; we no longer see "Switzerland" but this particular airport or border cross-ing, these streets, that high-speed highway. This disparation of Otherness has produced melancholy in many more writers—or ordinary people—than Proust.

Chinua Achebe was clearly concerned with the same issues when he noted, and criticized, the essentializing of place in Conrad's *Heart of Darkness*. For Achebe, individuality of people in Conrad was nearly completely subsumed to place. Yet not all relations with the Other subsume individuality to such a degree as Achebe thought Conrad did. Indeed, Achebe's chief objection to Conrad was that he was "a bloody racist," which charge he supported by linking it to place-essentializing. But conception in terms of Otherness of place *per se* is not responsible for the particular form and degree Conrad's racism takes. Otherwise many writers—and nearly all other people as well— would be as guilty as Achebe claims Conrad to be. And I do not think Achebe would be willing to claim this. Yet I concede Achebe's general point: Otherness of place does put commonality of place above individuality of people. That is its very nature. Hence, the conceptions of the Other offered to us as the only possible means of relating to foreign cultures do, at least to some extent, subsume individuality under the rubric of commonality—and this based on geographical distance, on cohesion of the Other culture in a place removed from where we are.

From this derives the thought-police aspect coloring contemporary thinking about the Other. For our thought concerning foreign cultures has been so channeled that we believe the world outside can only be touched through a conception of Otherness. Yet the very nature of such concep-tion makes the individuality of the people living there secondary to a commonality of place. Such commonality can be either honorific or critical; neither one is implied more than the other in the conception of Otherness. This is true because conception in terms of Otherness has no inherent valence; it is neither good nor bad. Whence the necessity felt by some on the contemporary scene to specify the acceptable kinds of Otherness, which (we are as good as told) can only be indulged in when it is to the advantage of those so conceptualized. In the same way, domestic Otherness may only be postulated if it is in a positive way, and by a member of the group involved, just as only a black person may nowadays claim that black people do make better musicians, basketball players, and so on. As a result many people feel, in a slang phrase admirable for its graphic nature, jerked around: they are encouraged to indulge in Otherness—only mind (they are told with a rap) it must be this kind of Otherness, not that one.

Though I have largely been speaking here in this introduction as if geographical Otherness were synoymous with the "primitivism" of the MOMA show's title, I am doing so only because the present work takes its inspiration from the current scene, where Otherness tends to take the form of primitivism. Yet we Westerners have been positing Exotics for quite some time, as consideration of literary works in the following chapters will make clear, and only recently has this taken the form of interest in what we nowadays call the "primitive"—by which we largely mean, scantily-clad non-white people from tropical countries. Or perhaps we have only had, over the course of time, to go further afield to achieve the same sense of strangeness: as Porter suggests, the Enlightenment found its limits in Greece and Rome; the French Romantics went to the "Orient" (that is, Egypt and what we call the Middle East), leaving to us of the twentieth century the aboriginies who appeared in Los Angeles.

Otherness is becoming harder to find nowadays. As I consider below, Charlotte Brontë's Lucy Snowe found it by crossing the English Channel, though it would certainly be difficult to find Otherness there now, and Ernest Hemingway's Robert Jordan found his Otherness among the partisans of the Spanish Civil War. Nowadays, we have to go further to get the same jolt of strangeness—and Lévi-Strauss, quoted below, would insist that we can no longer get it at all. A sense of how we as a culture exhaust the strangeness of the strange suggests an answer to the question that bothers many people today: why our grandmothers and grandfathers in the nineteenth century were so lamentably lacking in sensitivity to the "primitive" peoples we now find so fascinating. For if Belgium was already Other, Africa would logically have been quite beyond the pale. And what will follow our interest in the "primitive"?

Another way of acknowledging both the good news and bad news with respect to conceptions of Otherness based on place is to point out the benefits and dangers of such conceptualization. Much current discourse denies any dangers: looking at the Other is "fun." Yet looking at the Other can be dangerous. Not dangerous in an immediate, physical sense; instead it is dangerous in a more abstruse yet just as pernicious way. Once upon a time the Other that we are now most interested in today was immediately dangerous in a physical sense: a threat to life and limb. Our Western success in rendering this Other toothless has been so great that the danger of our interest nowadays lies in our very interest, not in the people who interest us. It is a danger inherent in Otherness, itself a conceptualization based on interest.

Our relationship with the Other is in fact more complex than its unequivocal partisans have suggested. Claude Lévi-Strauss, who believed that modern society had irrevocably destroyed traditional cultures, hinted at the complexity of this relationship in *Tristes Tropiques*, reflecting on his experiences among the tribes of the Brazilian inland.

> The fact is that these primitive peoples . . . are all, in their different ways, enemies of our society, which pretends to itself that it is investing them with nobility at the very time when it is completing their destruction, whereas it viewed them with terror and disgust when they were genuine adversaries. (p. 41)

It is not fashionable to admit that these societies ever were genuine adversaries to Occidentals, as for example white settlers in the American West in the nineteenth century would have said. This, as Lévi-Strauss points out, is so only because of the utter defeat of these societies by the Occident. In victory we can afford to be generous; our interest in what we have defeated is the interest of the zoo-goer in the caged lion, our relationship invested with the intimacy of an adolescent girl with a castrated stallion. Were such people still a physical threat, we would by no means be so interested.

Interest in the Other is fundamentally the result of a power relation—complex though it may be, as we see in the works of Hemingway. The quotation from Lévi-Strauss touches on this point that has been made loud and long by ethnographers and social analysts indebted to Marx and Nietzsche by way of Foucault, notably Said. Interest presupposes the quiescence and non-threatening nature of what we are interested in; when a potential Other does pose a physical threat, our reaction is not interest. Fear and interest cannot co-exist. Fear is a relation of someone on the bottom toward someone on the top, while interest is the reverse. We need look only at our current relations with the Arab world to find an example of this: the Persian Gulf war has rendered nugatory—or historical—an interest in the world of the *Thousand and One Nights*, or the Orientalism of nineteenth-century Europe. As another example, the United States has no interest whatever in contemporary Vietnam as an Other—for in this case those who were meant to follow our will defeated us—yet we indulge in nostalgia for the colonial days in Indochina, as evinced by the widespread interest among intellectuals in Marguerite Duras's *The Lover*, a recollection of an affair set during that time.

The conception of Otherness is a aestheticization of the social, in the sense that Terry Eagleton would speak of the aesthetic. This is the reason that so much contact with the Other takes place through arts festivals and literature conferences, and why it is a sport of the stay-at-homes, or of those who presuppose stay-at-homes as their audiences. For this reason many of the analyses in this study deal with aesthetic objects, largely literary ones. For a conception of Otherness to exist, the Other cannot be a real alternative—it must stay within its frame, firmly skewered under the gaze of the viewer, just like an art object. Like art, Otherness implies to-be-looked-at-ness; it exists as Other only in relation to ourselves.

The danger of playing with these caged lions is not that we may be mauled. For if such a danger exists, we simply fortify the bars. The danger that threatens us now is a more abstruse danger, but for all that no less serious. By confounding our interest in this impotent Other with a viable alternative to ourselves—which the Other can by definition never be, on pain of ceasing to be Other—we lose sight of the fact that precisely the system in which we live and with respect to which these are Other allows us such an interest, or produces it to begin with. We lose sight of the specificity of our own point of view in the vertigo of entering, if only briefly, into these captive Others' points of view. We come almost to believe that we are they, or could be they. Yet we are doing nothing but affirming our Westernness through the very act of this sympathetic identification with them. Indeed, *we* are making clear exactly why we can never be *they*.

What sets our society off from those which offer such "fun" alternatives—traditional, "indigenous," agrarian societies of the Third World, for the most part—is the very asymmetry of the relations between us: we can imagine being like them, yet we cannot credit them with the capability to imagine their being like us. If we do credit them with this capability they become like us, and so cease to be Other. The lure of traditional societies, conceived of as Other, is that they do not allow the possibility of alternatives. These societies, unlike ours, are not conceived of as contingent structures that people create and from which individuals can be detached. They may be so in fact, but only to the extent that we do not conceive them as such are we interested in them as Others. What makes us most uncomfortable is evidence that the looked-at are looking back, or integrating our culture into their own—or even more "corruptly," envying Western material goods and wanting to be like us. We do not want them to be like us; we want them to be different. That is the only way that they can serve as Others.

As Westerners, we are quintessentially the people-who-can-play-at-being-Other; what unifies us is the grid into which we plug our particular roles. But the grid itself is not valueless. It is the system of individual rights and responsibilities which we inherited from the eighteenth-century inventors of Western democracy, with all the alterations our post-Romantic mentality has wrought on these, and further modified by the inherent necessities of industrial capitalism. This grid includes such notions as that the people are the basis of the government, that the individual is the measure of all things, and the idea (which Americans take from our Declaration of Independence) that among our unalienable rights is something called the pursuit of happiness. This last idea is widely understood as implying that everybody has the right to valorization by the culture at large, a notion considered in Chapter Two.

I am not about to say that such ideas as these are the basis of greater Western "freedom," for the word is tattered beyond repair. The philosophical debates surrounding it remain unresolved. Degrees of freedom exist which make any generalization in absolutes useless; each of us is free or not free in ways which may come to the fore at different times. Yet the presenters of the Los Angeles Festival suggested that the alternative to our society is a traditional society that has not lost its "spiritual essence." If this is true, then it must also be true that central to our very nature is the tradition-destroying, rationalistic grid which demands of each of us that we define ourselves and decide what we will be, based on our own desires and situation—rather than merely accepting givens imposed upon us from without, such as nature, gods, or the interpreted will of ancestors. And this, in turn, has come to be as the result of our emphasis on the individual.

I hasten to acknowledge, to avoid being thought to paint an imperfect picture of Western thought, that the role of loyal opposition in this structure which places such a premium on individual self-definition has always been that strand of thought which insists that we are controlled beings. Its most celebrated representatives are Marx, Freud, social theorists of disempowerment based on sex and race, and—in a rarified form—Derrida, with his insistence that we are as much written by language as writing it. Yet in this strand of thought, an integral part of our Westernness, opposition from within rather than opposition from without can serve only as opposition rather than a party-in-power because each thinker in this vein is ultimately prepared to list the forces operating upon us. In a truly controlled world, by contrast, we could not even conceptualize the control, much less postulate its removal.

Marx and Freud, the high priests of this strand of thought, identify elements of control with the intention of removing these: in Marx, with the revolution; in Freud, with the re-establishment of psychic "normalcy." Even Derrida's post-structuralism, as a number of commentators have argued, presupposes both the prior movement of structuralism and the substantial literary object to be deconstructed.

The gravest danger inherent in our current interest in the Other is that we become dissatisfied with the grid that allows us the momentary fantasy of living outside of it, and so conflate this fantasy—made possible by and directed by our situation—with an escape from this situation. In another variant, our interest in the Other leads to the virulent defense of the ways of traditional peoples—as if these ways were ultimately desirable, save only as these tightly-controlled scenarios for wish-fulfillment. Yet few of us, even those who are fleeing most passionately our own alienation and rationality, would be happy as part of a traditional, non-alienated society that told us what to do to a degree unimaginable in our own, unless we could along the way drink from the waters of Lethe and forget our prior state.

The idea of becoming part of such a world has haunted Westerners at least since the Romantics, when Schiller made his distinction between naive and sentimental—and then had to all but concede that these were not really two categories but one. Both are the product of the sentimental, of those on the outside postulating an inside at which they were looking. Naivete is not a real state that we can identify with any historical time or period of our lives, Schiller had to admit; it is by nature a construction of the sentimental. Though when asked, those locked in the double-edged perception of the sentimental will say they want to go—or return—to this naive state, the state itself never existed. Instead, it is only a projection into the past of those who feel dissatisfied. Hence the melancholy of such poems as that by Klaus Groth, which Brahms set to music, on the impossibility of ever becoming a child again: "O wüsst' ich doch den Weg zurück . . . ." We want to be a child again, and recognize at the same time that the impossibility of ever becoming this again is what makes the idea so alluring.

The least defensible course of action is to use the undeniably therapeutic fantasy of escape from rationalistic societies to attack those things without which we could not have such fantasies to begin with; the intellectual sin here is a failure to acknowledge debts. This sin is at the same time comprehensible (sins always are). The easiest thing in the world to forget, in looking at the myriad of things we can see, is that the looker is something too. (Jerome McGann makes a related point in his *Romantic Ideology*, in his criticism of the mixed motives with which we post-Romantics look at Romantic texts.) The tendency to forget the looker doing the looking—or to deny that the looker is anything at all—is at least as old as the empiricists' realization that the "I" which unifies all perceptions cannot itself be a perception in the world. Kant seemed to go beyond this with his suggestion that the "I" was the form of things seen—but he had to begin by accepting the premises of the empiricists. In the twentieth century Heidegger has re-introduced this priority of the seen rather than the seer. Despite such thinkers, most people think that each of us is an individual in a world of individuals. We arrive at this conclusion by allowing ourselves to be convinced by the evidence provided by other people, or by mirrors, or by the pain of banging our elbows into a door jamb.

I am arguing for a political correlate to my "naive realism": because you cannot see yourself looking does not mean that you are not doing so. The height of intellectual dishonesty is to deny that the society to which these Others seem alternatives is what permits—and produces—our perception of them as attractive. Of course all of us tire of the endless dead ends of self-constructed goals to which our peculiar form of rationalist individuality condemns us; of course all of us dream of escaping them to worlds where we are so much a part of our liquid surrounding society that the "I" becomes indistinguishable from the world; of course all of us resent our eternal empiricist separation of ourselves and our subjectivity from the objectivity to which we can only aspire. And so we create philosophies which assert that the "I" is no different from the world; we play at interest in tribal communities that are still whole, unified, pre-lapsarian. Things become dangerous when we believe our own fictions, become so enraptured by our dreams that we forget the existence—and needs—of the dreamer. This conclusion is similar to Frank Kermode's point in *The Sense of an Ending* that the only pernicious fictions are the ones we end up mistaking for truth. Our society's nature makes possible our flights from it.

Rationalistic Western society is different from other societies in that it is to a great degree a mechanism for content, rather than a content in itself. The antidote to this current excess in the direction of the object of our perception is not, however, excess in the opposite direction, toward an obsession with the mechanism, with the conditions of this perception: the insistence that we wave a flag, buy into the lies of politicians, or enact a short list of actions that show our allegiance to this society. This mechanism has a content of its own, but the proportion of time spent tending the mechanism to the time doing what the mechanism is meant to make possible (action toward ends defined by the individual) is less in our Western societies than in any other. The choice here is far from being either/or. At worst, an obsession with the mechanism rather than with the things the mechanism makes possible leads to McCarthyism, or Fascism.

The other extreme—complete neglect or denial of the mechanism, the conditions of looking rather than the thing looked at—is equally undesirable. And it is this point which goes largely unseen. At this extreme the emphasis is to such a great degree on the individuality of the values that can be plugged into our societal function that the necessity of looking after the function itself is nearly forgotten. This results in a confusion of our interest in the Other with the existence of real and attractive alternatives to our society. The concomitant result is the conviction that nothing holds us together, or indeed at the extreme, the conviction that nothing should hold us together.

The ultimate effect of such a neglect of the looker in favor of the looked-at could be more serious, though I merely sound a warning bell against it. It is that we forget as a society how eminently possible it is to destroy our rationalistic, non-traditional Western societies, along with all the opportunities they offer the individual for what I can only call self-realization. The miracle is that such societies ever came to be; I am not certain that the course of Western history—with all its amalgamation of Eastern and non-Western influences, such as the absorption of Aristotle from the Arab world in the twelfth century—is continuous rather than discontinuous. (Here I am thinking more along the lines of a Stephen Jay Gould than a Michel Foucault: the discontinuity is perceived, rather than postulated.) This destruction can take place as easily by negligence as by the result of attack from without. If we speak slightingly of this society often enough, even if it is this society whose grid-like structure allows us to speak slightingly of it, we will neglect it, or allow it to collapse.

This may be an unjustified projection into the future of current trends which will reverse themselves or peter out long before they reach such proportions. My immediate hope is that some balance will be found between the reification of the grid and the enjoyment of the individualization that it makes possible. I suggest a more general understanding that the grid-like structure of our rationalism makes possible our sentimental odysseys into non-rationalistic, "naive" cultures. Western society is a real thing, one alternative among many—one that makes possible, and creates, those expressions of the individual that we call perceptions of the Other.

Even so critical a viewer of the pretensions of Western societies to exhibit "progress" as Stanley Diamond, in his unsettling *In Search of the Primitive: A Critique of Civilization*, takes for granted that Western society is in fact a real, substantial thing—an acknowledgement which comes hard to many people. He accepts that our Westernness exists, and that this sends us eternally in search of the Other—for him, the primitive. Diamond uses this last word without the now-obligatory scare quotes, because for him it is the positive pole; "civilization" is the negative. Indeed, for him the constant search of civilized people for the primitive is one of the few redemptive, or hope-giving, aspects of our society.

The West, in Diamond's view, is in dire straits: "our pathology . . . consists in our dedication to abstractions, in our collectivism, pseudo-individualism, and lack of institutional means for the expression and transcendence of human ambivalence"; "our illness springs from the very center of civilization, not from too much knowledge, but from too little wisdom. What primitives possess—the immediate and ramifying sense of the person . . . an existential humanity—we have largely lost" (p. 173). What is worse, the very things we prize most highly as the fruits of our society, such as individualism or romantic love, are themselves the most convincing signs of our plight.

Primitive society (which Diamond holds to be one of the identifiable forms of social organization), by contrast, exhibits such qualities as "the full and manifold participation of individuals in nature and society" and "the intensely personal socialization process through which individual qualities are delineated" (p. 172). Diamond's conclusion is that these qualities are "what civilization must selectively incorporate; we cannot abandon the primitive; we can only outgrow it by letting it grow within us" (p. 173).

Diamond is not a knee-jerk primitivist; he acknowledges the impossibility of ever attaining the Other. "It is not, and cannot be, a question . . . of 'retreating' into the primitive past. It is not a question of regaining lost paradises or savage nobility, neither of which ever existed in the manner imputed to their authors" (pp. 174-175). In addition he acknowledges that interest in the primitive can go in one direction only. Primitives are unable to conceive of our notion of "progress," and they are not, Diamond thinks, attracted to our form of society—we can think them, but they do not, and cannot, think us. Yet precisely because he distances himself in this fashion from the vulgar-primitivism so endemic to the 1990s, Diamond ends up sounding like a positive-valence version of the Joseph Conrad so infuriating to Achebe, a Conrad who conceived of the Congo as somehow metaphorically similar to an aspect of Europe's psyche. Diamond makes perfectly clear that his/our ultimate interest in the primitive is not for its own sake, but only insofar as we can use the knowledge this interest might produce to develop ourselves: "The problem . . . is to help conceptualize contemporary forms that will reunite man with his past . . . making progress without distortion theoretically possible" (p. 175).

Interest in the Other is on our terms only, as a means of developing ourselves; this is a conclusion with which I concur completely. Yet perhaps because Diamond is an anthropologist and, though skeptical of some of its methods and conscious of its presuppositions, a committed one, he—like virtually all writers on this subject—does not consider the possibilty of contact with the world outside that takes place without the constraints of Otherness. And this, I say, is possible.

Chapter Two

Kinds of Otherness

Our current interest in foreign Others is therefore intimately related to — indeed, the product of — our nature as Westerners in general, and as Americans in particular. At the same time this is the very source of muddled thinking concerning our interest. For interest in foreign Otherness is an offshoot of an even stronger current on the contemporary American intellectual scene: our dealings with intra-cultural, or domestic Otherness. Many people are quite aware of this, as seen for example in Rosaldo's clear linkage, in *Culture and Truth*, between his feeling of being an outsider as a Chicano in America and his interest in other cultures; indeed, this linkage is so clear that we tend to think of the foreign Otherness as an extension of the domestic sort. Yet the two are structurally dissimilar, and the givens of the domestic scene are completely inapplicable to the foreign one.

Thus we turn to a brief consideration of an emotion-laden subject: the nature of the contemporary American discourse concerning intra-cultural, rather than inter-cultural, Otherness. I hope that the generalizations I offer will be judged as generalizations rather than as fine-tuned descriptions of all of reality. Accepting such a generalization does not imply that we think no counter-examples exist, only that in the end they are less damaging than the examples which support the generalization.

The aspect of contemporary Western societies in general (and American society in particular) which sets them off from others is the language of self-realization and self-definition in which we Westerners express our most cherished goals. For Americans, "self-expression" is currently the highest good — with all the excesses this produces, such as the conviction that our individual opinion has intrinsic value just because it is ours. Western societies place a greater premium on the sensibilities and thoughts of the individual than do non-Western ones. One can be an individual in other societies, or feel joy or pain in the same proportions, but non-Western societies as a whole do not evince the same breathless interest in following the seismographs of individual sensibility as ours does, nor hold the belief that they are of general rather than personal interest. This may explain why we take failure of aspirations so seriously in the West—why a work like *Death of a Salesman* takes on the aura of tragedy in America.

What further characterizes Western societies with respect to non-Western ones is our belief in the efficacy of scientific or quasi-scientific discourse, involving an initial conflict between proposed answers and the arrival at one answer through a process of reasoning. Westerners believe that each person can, by scrutinizing his or her situation, understand if not change it. In the intellectual world, this belief finds expression in the insistence that each person make clear the individual elements of his or her ideas by silhouetting them against a background of others' ideas, defined through footnotes and citations.

This process of self-realization need not be automatic. Numerous factors work on us to prevent its achievement, and the "loyal opposition" strand of Western thought takes on content in pointing out such impediments. We are characterized as Westerners not by the extent to which we realize ourselves, but rather by taking this realization, however we understand it, as our goal. And part of this process always involves identifying impediments, shedding our outermost layer when we decide that it is not part of us at all, but instead part of the constraints of the external world.

In his interesting consideration of cross-cultural literature dealing with India, Richard Cronin—speaking of one of the characters in Ruth Jhabvala's *Heat and Dust*—echoes my formulation of the heart of our Westernness, and offers an explanation for it with Marxist resonance. (In contrast to Cronin, however, I do not offer explanations, and not much history: my intention is not to explain, but to characterize.) Cronin speaks of "the burden of individuality, of self-consciousness, that the West imposes on its citizens as the condition of the industrial society that secures their prosperity" (p. 96). He believes that many young Westerners once came to India to divest themselves of this burden — yet another example from the last thirty years of our attempt to escape from ourselves into non-Western cultures.

V. S. Naipaul puts it another way, speaking of the West (in connection with the Iranian novel *Foreigner* by Nahid Rachlin, where the Iranian progagonist returns to Teheran after a period in Boston) as the world "where it was necessary to be an individual and responsible; where people developed vocations, and were stirred by ambition and achievement, and believed in perfectibility" (p. 25): perfectibility, not perfection — process as end in itself, with all of the sometimes anguishing imperative to action that this implies.

This Westernness is easy for Westerners to ignore; it is like an odor in an enclosed space where we have lived for so long that we are no longer aware of it. Those who have never left the room cannot sense it. This is the reason that contact with other cultures is so therapeutic — it makes us realize what we are not, and hence what we are. Here I mean real contact, as opposed to the pseudo-contact afforded by Otherness. The first step in seeing what we are consists of seeing what we are not. And we may be encouraged to take this step by noting that most of the people on the earth find our strident claims for individual rights — or by extension, those of groups — ridiculous, if not incomprehensible.

Speaking of one of his experiences in India when an "urbane Indian businessman" spoke unapologetically of his dealings with an astrologer, Cronin expands on his perception as follows:

> I had stumbled over a radical difference between the Western and the Indian perceptions of human identity. Western identity is secured by difference, by a sense of the self as unique, the model of its association with others a contract, an agreement to cooperate to secure some end. But Indians know of another kind of identity, not grasped in an act of introspection by which the self becomes aware of its differences from all others, but acted out in all those customs and ceremonies in which the individual is assured of his place within the group. The Western sense

of identity is guaranteed by the individual's freedom, the Indian by the system of constraints within which the individualist is bound. (p. 95)

Abstract theories like these, dissatisfying though they almost always are, may well be the closest we can come to grasping what defines a culture. My attempts in this direction will probably be no more, but perhaps also no less, successful than they. (Another interesting example of such generalized theories is the attempt of John S. Mbiti to define an "African concept of time" — unsettlingly close, in its implications, to the American racist notions of "colored people's time" current until recently in some circles.) Such theories are tantalizing; at their best they help summarize reams of dimly-understood data, but under no circumstances can we draw much of a conclusion from them.

Whatever the nature of what unites us as Westerners, disagreements of content within this matrix will by definition be internecine. Our Westernness is found in a means of proceeding, a set of presuppositions concerning ideas of how to talk with one another and what the purpose of action should be — not a specific content. This leads to consideration of intra-cultural Otherness. For the fact that our Westernness provides only a matrix into which an individual's goals can be plugged has led to the paradox of the current American intellectual scene, namely that the most lively thinking nowadays is expressed in terms which seem at first glance antithetical to the assumptions on which such a matrix is based: instead of dealing primarily with the individual, the emphasis today is placed on the definition and valorization of groups.

A Rip Van Winkle of the intellectual scene who came back in the 1990s would certainly conclude that the notion of the individual had lost its ability to serve as the least common denominator in America; instead, the smallest conceivable unit is that of the group. This produces the discourse of intra-cultural Otherness which dominates the scene today — gay people, Native Americans, women, and hyphenated Americans of all stamps are asserting parity with a standard group, usually taken to be heterosexual white males. (In literature it is merely dead white males who serve as the standard group; sexuality does not seem to matter with the dead.)

In American society, of course, intellectuals are themselves such a disempowered or marginal group—which may be the reason why the causes of numerically limited Others are so appealing to intellectuals as a group. Indeed, this may also explain why so many members of marginalized groups defined by gender or sexuality frequently become committed academics and wield the weapons of academic discourse so tellingly: they can identify themselves with the marginalized position of today's professional academic to a much greater extent than "Old School" professors—usually white, straight males who don't see where the fire is. But this may be because such Old School types who (as is sometimes said) "just want to teach the literature" have no particular identification with the status of professor *per se* (they feel they could have been many other things in our society)—or come from regions or sub-cultures where this position is still honorific.

The terms of left and right can be applied to the spectrum of positions adopted with respect to domestic Otherness as well as with respect to inter-cultural Otherness. I do so in the interests of taxonomic shorthand, with the same understanding that governed earlier use of them, that they are non-pejorative labels for conveniently indicating whole schools of thought. In brief, "right" refers in this context to those who look forlornly for a center, "left" to those who gleefully proclaim the disappearance of such a center. Thus "right" refers to those on the defensive, "left" to those on the offensive.

Many of the current debates are carried on in this new discourse of groups, with (schematically speaking) the left supporting this discourse and the right against it. One such debate concerns the validity of making short-lists of recommended or required works in literature (as in lists of the "world's hundred great books," or in course syllabi). Those attacking the practice from the left are the more vocal group—logically so, given that they are on the offensive. Typically, they make the claim that such short-listed works by no means attain the universality ascribed to them by the right. Instead, so the usual argument goes, these are the products of one specific group, even if the product of that group still claimed to hold the reins of power in the world: straight white males.

Another result for literary studies of this conception in terms of groups is the demand from the left that we suspend any attempt to judge artistic quality. The criteria by which works would be called good or bad, according to this argument, far from being the universal standards they were once understood to be, are instead the standard of one group only, and hence not applicable to other groups. Groups are asserted to have their own ways of doing things, and that is that. In the realm of the performing arts, it is sometimes suggested that only gay people or people of color should review or discuss concerts by gay or non-white choreographers. Such claims are also perfectly logical under the circumstances: the most effective way of attacking an assumption of moral absolutism is by countering it with the equally big guns of relativism.

Such assertions from the left in turn call up from the right assertions of the necessity for a common fund of cultural givens to be transmitted by core curricula, reading lists of "great books," and so on, supported by the specter of cultural dissolution. When its joy at thereby having the right exactly where it wants it dies down, the left responds by saying that (1) dissolution of the repressive power-base of straight white males can come none too soon, and (2) such dissolution has (thank heavens) already occurred. And it is (2) which justifies the left in saying that those decrying such a development from the right are nothing but utopian reactionaries. In feeble response, the right asks plaintively whether art is not universal. No, responds the left with great decision. Does art not exist to remove boundaries rather than create them? asks the right. The boundaries exist already, responds the left.

Playing referee for a moment, I award the palm to this value-relativistic argument by the left, if for no other reason than that the right has had to accept the terms of its response from its opponents. (The left, in its turn, accepts even more fundamental assumptions from the right.) The right has largely responded to the onslaught from the left with that weaker position which the left mapped out for it: saying that many works by straight white males (1) are better and (2) can too speak to, say, Hispanic lesbians—as if the mere reiteration of its initial position could prove anything. The weakness of this argument lies is its appeal to the cooperation of the opponent: if the Hispanic lesbians don't feel spoken to, the argument goes up in smoke. The right, moreover, generally accepts the polarization of political vs. "aesthetic" responses to the work that the left has delineated; the right then lamely asserts its faith in the aesthetic pole and its lack of faith in the political one.

The polarization of our contemporary scene in intra-cultural Otherness is the result of conflation, by left and right, of divergences of content with divergences of form. The right, jealous of—or, as the left sometimes suggests, nostalgic for—the status quo, takes for granted the linkage of a set of characteristics with its ideal of "universal" values. The left, taking the right at its word, asserts this linkage in order to relativize it. If the matrix is identical with the morality of one limited group, then this may be discarded as useless for other groups.

Because this last argument is applicable to some of my claims, I pause to consider it directly. Such an argument would hold, for example, that the vocabulary of individual rights which I claim to be definitive of our Westernness was invented by and for the controlling group of white heterosexual males and makes sense only as the house jargon of such a group. What sense does it make, it is asked, to speak of self-realization and liberty for a 14-year-old non-white male whose only role models are pushers and pimps?

Yet such a position by the left does nothing in its turn but valorize the presuppositions of the right, rather than attacking them—in the same way that the right accepts the presuppositions of the left in the situation outlined above. Nowadays charges from the left consist largely of pointing out impediments to the achievement of this self-realization—the most egregious of which is the very existence of the group brought into existence by naming. The charge usually reads: access to power is limited for _____ (fill in the blank). This can only be an accusation—and hence a state to be put right—if the ultimate goal is assumed to be identical for all, namely equal access to power that the system said it guaranteed.

In other words, it only makes sense to articulate something held to be an injustice if the assumption is that those to whom we are articulating it will see it as unjust too. This is the reason that, according to many commentators, the civil rights movement was effective in the South in the 1950s and 1960s: white people rightly felt guilty. A second-generation example of such definition toward the middle was provided by the recent debate on the mechanism and implications of creating a museum of black American history in Washington, D.C. like the museum of Native American art that had just been approved. The issue revolved around whether it would be on the Mall, which no one contested was the most honorific position in town, whether it would have its own building, clearly more honorific than being a wing or an exhibit of a larger building, and so on. The form the argument took was of special interest groups against each other, and against the officials responsible for the apportionment of space on the Mall. Yet the very possibility of the argument presupposed a set of common values and goals. So too for the constant lobbying of groups to put up memorials on the Mall—of which the most recently approved is a monument to women soldiers in Vietnam. Every group, understandably enough, wants its individual valorizing monument in the most conspicuous of places. What we see as its expression is conflict, but this only expresses more fundamental commonality.

This is the nature of intellectual discourse today as well: each group (figuratively speaking) wants its building or monument on the Mall. This fact shows that the strongest claims from the left are unjustified. In a truly controlled world, such as the left sometimes claims ours is, it would make no sense to lament that we are being given the short end of the stick. If it were not recognized as generally desirable to be represented in a single-building museum on the Mall, no group would demand that it be so represented.

All such demands by groups which understand themselves as marginalized in our society are demands toward a center—

which means, practically speaking, in the direction of the right. Thus attack the mainstream though these marginalized groups may, their actions are unthinkable without it. Or better: their actions are unthinkable without the matrix that the group currently at the center is held to represent. If the response to this is what is frequently provided by the left, that the structure of quasi-scientific "proof" is part of the discourse being rejected—an argument structure that has entered contemporary dialogue through Heidegger—the right is justified in wondering just what the left is doing talking to them at all. Indeed, there is something self-contradictory about explaining as vociferously as the left does the thousand and one reasons why it need not explain itself. To whom is it explaining? Under such circumstances the only consistent course seems to be Wittgenstein's silence.

The discourse of groups is only provisional—even if those utilizing it do not realize this is so. How can the group fail to wither away once that group has achieved a status equal to that of the controlling group, leaving only the individuals of which the group was composed? Yet in the heat of polemical battle the admission that this is so comes hard, or is by definition impossible, like admitting in the middle of a war that our objective is less than the annihilation of the enemy: such an admission can itself help determine the outcome of the battle. In fact the whole world could be non-white, female, and/or gay and, barring problems of dwindling numbers, still function perfectly well within the same Western system; these groups are asking for nothing that those currently in power have not themselves asked for earlier.

Granting this means that the left must give up one of its most spectacular claims—spectacular because it is so annoying to the right—namely that the heart of Western thought is phallocratic racism. Instead, the left must acknowledge that this heart is located in the dream of self-definition that is being pursued so aggressively by marginalized groups. Such an ultimate vision of a "kinder, gentler" left is nothing but the state that most guerilla groups attain as they become mainstream: their efficacity as part of the subsequent government once they win depends on being able to abandon the adversarial thinking that got them where they are.

This is not yet the current state of affairs. For the moment, we find ourselves dealing with a polarized stalemate that results from several theoretical errors on both sides. The principal mistake of the left has been to forget that all of its reasoning is toward the center, so that it ends up attacking what it presupposes. The left courts the right more than the reverse—courting it, that is, through attack. The principal mistake of the right, by contrast, has been simple (after all, if you sit on your hands you don't trip over your feet). It has been to think that the left represents a threat of form rather than merely an alteration of content. In fact, it is playing by the same rules as the right—only the players are changing.

The failure on the part of the left to acknowledge that it is acting toward the center—and so valorizing the position of the right—takes flesh in the tendency of the left to deny as content what it affirms as act. The right, by contrast, sometimes affirms as content what it denies as act: it likes its power position and sees no reason to relinquish this to new groups. What is denied as content is the existence of that common matrix of Western rationalism which makes its claims possible and provides the only context in which these may hope to be effective. Many people in America are roundly unwilling to speak in terms of "we"—understandably enough, for this takes the air out of whatever attempt to achieve equality is being launched. Yet at the most fundamental level we are indeed a "we" in the West—which is proven each time the spokespersons for another group appeal to terms of justice and personal self-realization to show how their group has been disadvantaged. And precisely this commonality becomes clear when we compare Western culture with any other.

Other problems besides these are generated because of that substitution by the left which is at the heart of its theory: the insertion of the vocabulary of groups in the phrases hitherto reserved for the definition of the individual. For we can use such talk of group (self-) realization to refer to the individual, or to the group being conceived of in terms of the individual, just as we can use a collective plural as a noun—but not to relate the two. Perhaps we agree that, say, Hispanic Americans as a group have been disprivileged on the American scene. But does this mean that we should give special advantages to some individual Hispanics to compensate for this? Could an individual member of a group not so disprivileged nonetheless, as an individual, have been more disadvantaged than a more privileged member of a disadvantaged group? How in any case do we define the group to which an individual belongs, given that one person may simultaneously be many things—to each of which we may append the implicitly understood valance, whether positive or negative—let us say, white [+], male [+], gay [-], Arab-American [-], six foot two inches tall [+], a lawyer [+], and a poet [-]?

The result is a stand-off, with each side accepting an extreme willed on it by the other. Such a stand-off can only be mediated if each side clears up its conflation of general with specific, and content with form. On the literary scene, the right must admit that the claim of the left that works or types of literature speak to particular people, or groups of people, and do not speak to others, is true. For the appeal of literature is not universal; it is personal. And thus it can be personal for all the members of a group, if it speaks to the quality that defines them as such—which is the essence of the left's claim.

In the crudest examples of how we can be spoken to by literature, a reader may "identify with" the protagonist of a novel, or recognize an experience described in a lyric poem as largely identical to his or her own experience. The predominantly male students at the U. S. Naval Academy, for example, love the film *Top Gun*: how should they not? The hero is a young U. S. Navy officer such as they will one day be, a good-looking clean-cut athletic type (like many of them) who "gets the girl" (as many of them hope to do)—and a "classy" girl at that (such as many of them aspire to). They also like a novel called *A Sense of Honor* by a former Secretary of the Navy named James Webb who graduated from Annapolis, about the experiences of a plebe (freshman). The parallels between the situations considered in such works and the lives of the students are well nigh absolute; the result is that they "relate," as we said in the 1960s, to the work.

Yet this is precisely the reason that someone who understands himself or herself as most fundamentally Other with respect to the people or experiences considered in literature will have trouble being involved — and should not be forced to become involved. Students at St. John's College in Annapolis, the "great books" college whose campus adjoins the Naval Academy, are not in my experience similarly taken with *Top Gun*, and I have never seen any of them evince interest in *A Sense of Honor*. Yet nothing is wrong with this. Why force a conceptualization on someone who doesn't understand it? Far better to try another book.

Literature is — I insist with the left — an intimately personal encounter; we like better what we understand, and may well be repelled by what looks strange or antithetical to our beliefs. Literature has as its point that it helps us conceptualize the world and so come to terms with it. The practical problems that arise from this are because my world may well not be that of the person in the carrel next to mine, much less the same as that of someone two rooms, or two countries away.

On the other hand, it may be the same world in both cases — at least it may be if looked at under one aspect. The strange power of literature is to create such a common world by emphasizing an unaccustomed aspect of life. In doing so it creates similarity between people who, in most other situations, have little in common. The world of a literary work is a world seen through filters that enhance specific colors: some qualities stand out more in art than in "real" life, producing affinities where there were none before. Thus, even if literature is highly subjective and the point of literature is to show us something about ourselves, no one can say beforehand what aspect in a literary work will touch us — or fail to do so. We may end up responding most intensely to a character that shares with us none of the normally powerful type-definers (gender, race, sexuality, nationality, and so on). An American may learn more from a book set in Africa than one set in America; we may recognize as our preoccupations what preoccupies someone belonging to none of the groups we would list on our census forms.

Who, after all, says that the world is most fundamentally cut into groups defined by these normally-accepted type-definers? The groups we belong to are considerably more fluid, even in the social world, than the left would have us believe. In some situations I am most fundamentally the husband of my wife, in others most fundamentally the one professor of English on my hall with a fish tank in my office, in others the man with mycoplasma pneumonia in the hospital bed by the window. And literature is the field on which these other group-definers can be made to loom larger and last longer than they do in our hierarchical social world.

I pause to give the expected answer from the left: whatever else a gay black man—let us say—may be for briefer periods, he is undeniably also and always a Gay Black man, in a way that a straight white man is not similarly a Straight White man. Some qualities are essentialized in our world, and these become more important; no one can escape this fact. To which the response from the right should be: this is a fact that no one can escape, granted—save in the world of literature. The right might continue, what makes literature so interesting is that, within its admittedly limited boundaries, it succeeds in foregrounding individual qualities rather than typal ones. The pleasure of reading literature comes from understanding our commonality with sorts of people with whom we would ordinarily not come into contact—a commonality based on a foregrounding of these qualities that, in the social world, are subsumed and all but obliterated by the Big Ones of race, sexuality, and gender.

Thus, if the right must immediately concede the left's point that literature speaks to specific people under specific circumstances rather than speaking to all people under all circumstances, it need not concede the logically unrelated assertion that we can say how literature will do so. If the right must concede that works of literature written by dead white men may not necessarily touch all people, we have no reason for saying that works by gay men, Maoris, living women, and the homeless will do so either (or for that matter, works about

these people, which are also sometimes recommended).
Maybe they will, maybe they won't. In any case the battle can
be fought only on the footing of particular works—which
avoids the duality of individual people vs. groups of people. It
is something like this battle over specifics that I suggest in my
account of teaching in Rwanda as an alternative to a fruitless
battle of theory.

A book written by a gay man may well speak most directly to
gay men, but perhaps not—just as the Marxist Lukács found
Balzac a more appealing subject than Zola despite the fact that
Zola spoke more directly of the coming revolution. The left
cannot assume that it has identified a book that speaks to a
group just because the author, or the main characters, are of
the requisite persuasion. Similarly the left is wrong to claim,
as it sometimes does in the heat of polemical battle, that works
written by straight white men are useless to people of color, or
those of other sexuality.

The onus of clarification of claims in this battle lies on the
left rather than the right, given that the left is on the offensive: is it because a book by, say, a gay man will speak to gay
men that it is to be included in the syllabus? Or because it can
speak to all people? If the former, the right might eliminate
it—or at least, eliminate more than one or two such books
from any given course—by simply appealing to numbers; it
makes more sense to reach more people than fewer. After all,
this was the original claim of the right for the "canonic"
authors. Or is the purpose of canon expansion to make a
syllabus not intended to appeal as a whole to everyone (the
pretensions of the right) but instead where there will be something for everyone—so that each group is "allowed" one book?
This seems the worst of both worlds: instead of each person
getting in some sense the whole syllabus—which was the
intention of the right—each gets only one or two works.

Of course, this kind of clarification may not be to the point.
The sympathies of the left may instead simply be with people
alienated from mainstream culture; what it is asking may be
that works by and about such similarly alienated groups be
preferred—or at least, given equal space. Yet even if we

accept that this is the real motivation behind many of the demands of the left, it still does not allow us to determine a curriculum. For we can feel alienated for many reasons from America's brand of moralistic yet violent mass culture. We may be alienated because we diverge from the postulated mainstream sexually, ethnically, culturally, intellectually, or economically; the numbers of the potentially disaffected pile up to the point where we must wonder just who does not have the possibility for seeing himself or herself as an outsider. A poet may understand the frustration of a woman, a woman may understand the frustration of a black man, a black man may understand the frustration of a white man stuck in an unrewarding job, a white woman who has grown up feeling a disadvantage in being, let us say, of Polish origin may understand the frustration of gay men, and so on.

The complexity of this situation ought to lead left and right to talk to each other. This is the more so in that, while neither side can speak in terms of absolute certainty regarding the appropriate target groups of literature, there may be some justification for speaking in terms of probability regarding such target groups. A book about a midshipman at the Naval Academy will probably speak more directly to midshipmen than to students at St. John's College. Nonetheless, if midshipmen were its only audience, its commercial potential would be insufficient to allow publication, save perhaps by the Naval Institute Press. A book about a gay man's experiences may well speak more directly to gay men than to straight men — though this is only probable, never sure; perhaps a straight man has been in a generically if not specifically similar set of circumstances. Navigating in this world of grays requires cooperation, and as much information as we can get from all sources. What better way do we have to sense if work "X" is likely to appeal to group "A" than by asking someone who feels a part of that group to consider the situation on the basis of more than his or her personal feelings and give a response?

If left and right are willing to engage in discourse about the probable audiences for particular works, the right will have to accept a reputable opinion to the effect that work "X" captures the viewpoint of people to whom quality "Y" applies—group "Y"—better than work "Z," and that this speaks for inclusion of work "X." This does not mean that this work must end up on the list, even ahead of work "Z," or that yet other works may not well have stronger claims for other reasons. Still, the claim itself is reason to desire, if not effect, inclusion. In a world of such admittedly speculative dialogue, moreover, it may be that some consideration of aspects of works unrelated to questions of target groups will again play a role in the discussion for both left and right, rather than merely serving as a rallying cry of the right. The left should be willing to agree that features of form and treatment—which now are stigmatized as the refuge of the right—may also be allowed weight, as in: "book 'A' is well-written and insightful even if it does not champion gay rights."

This discussion of the intellectual scene in America nowadays may be summarized to show its relevance to the relation between the discourse of domestic Otherness and that of foreign Otherness: nowadays theory has become politicized. This is the converse of the claim that inter-cultural Otherness was aesthetized geography. Groups are using words intended to apply to the whole—which is to say, theory as it used to be understood (and as the right still understands it)—for the more limited purpose of furthering their ends. The justification for doing this is articulated by the left as part of the scene as well: all words, it is claimed, are inherently those of specific groups. Theory is not only now becoming political, says the left; it has always been so.

The application of this discourse of domestic Otherness to that of inter-cultural Otherness is made possible by the perception that the existence of alternatives to our society can serve as a powerful support to the point of view of those marginalized within it. Only people who are in some way alienated from their own world go seeking other ones— though there are many reasons to be alienated, and many degrees of dissatisfaction.

In the case of domestic or intra-cultural Otherness, someone from the marginalized group usually invokes Otherness, and the disprivileged term of the duality defines itself by reference to the privileged one. Thus, becoming Other on the domestic scene is progress: at least a member of such a group is not nothing. On the intra-cultural scene, however, the definition of Otherness occurs from the opposite direction, and has the opposite effect. Here representatives of the privileged term of the duality (the rich Western powers) attempt to define the disprivileged one, so that its effect is absolute: the inter-cultural Other is never integrated, but is essentialized forever as Other. Definition of Otherness on the inter-cultural scene is not toward a center, but away from it. Unlike definition of intra-cultural Otherness, the inter-cultural Other dangles off the side of the cliff, and hangs into space.

We tend to have positive feelings about the ascription of inter-cultural Otherness that are based on our experiences with domestic Otherness. Yet the relation of Other groups to the Western over-structure, expressed in the relation of intra-cultural Otherness, is the opposite of what obtains in the case of inter-cultural Otherness. This asymmetry produces the confusions and contradictions in Western treatment of inter-cultural Otherness which constitute the point of departure of this book.

The conception of the world outside ours usually takes place in terms of Otherness — for this is the kind of conception that valorizes ourselves in our discourse of groups. The more Other such worlds are, the better we Westerners like them. This is the paradox of inter-cultural Otherness. The result is that we bracket these societies off from any real contact with ours through our conception of them in terms of Otherness: their function, for us, is to be an alternative. This slot that we demand that Other cultures fill is a limiting one.

Moreover our capability to conceive of alternatives to the society we know is an expression of our Western belief in the inherent contingency of political entities, our belief that governments are constructed by people. This belief creates at the same time its obverse, leaves the space that, paradoxically, tends to be filled by societies whose characterizing feature is that they do not seem to have been constructed at all, but seem instead to be natural growths. It is Westerners, in fact, who conceive in terms of what we now call cultures, or societies (in the plural). To those in a traditional society, what we call the structure of society is to a much greater extent the structure of existence, and so cannot be conceived of as contingent at all.

This produces the paradox of inter-cultural Otherness: seemingly an objective expression of interest in the world outside, it is in fact an asymmetrical relation that remains fundamentally an expression of our Occidentality, condemning the worlds outside to the status of objects deformed to fit our conceptual matrix.

The illegitimate linkage of intra-cultural to inter-cultural Otherness leads to another anomaly. Those who perceive themselves as Other in the domestic arena become, for the purposes of the inter-cultural arena, mainstream. No matter how off-center a Westerner someone is, he or she is still in the last analysis a Westerner—and this becomes clear through contrast with other cultures. (Think of the black militants who left America to go to Africa in the 60s, only to discover that, for better or worse, they were Americans rather than Africans.) Thus the contrast of inter-cultural Otherness is established— largely by members of groups marginalized at home—by assuming as the standard just that mainstream culture which is so antithetical to them in a domestic context. Groups that are Them on the domestic scene taste the rare pleasure of being Us on the foreign one.

Moving beyond the nineteeth century's distain for naked savages, we are now encouraged to indulge in a longing for naked non-alienated peoples in touch with their spiritual essences. The valence in the first conception is negative; in the second it is positive. Yet both are conceptions for our own purposes; both condemn another part of the world to a role of Otherness. In the late twentieth century we have rejected the rampant nineteenth century of Cecil Rhodes and re-discovered the mid-eighteenth century of Rousseau—but still we are caught in a circle of our projections.

An alternative exists to the positive and negative versions of inter-cultural Otherness; the way out of this deadlock of conception in terms of Otherness is through proceeding deductively rather than inductively. We need only let experience—rather than an *a priori* decision—determine whether we have looked out, or whether we have merely looked around. We have no justification for assuming *a priori* that Angola will be different in any essential way from Arkansas, nor any justification for assuming that what we see there will be worth telling to the folks back home. Of course, we may come to the conclusion that some things we see are worth talking about. But we can come to this conclusion in Arkansas too, and the result is not necessarily Otherness.

The nature of the beast is that such a solid and well-defined world as the inter-cultural Other will be seductive—to the point where we are willing to play at entering a world ruled by such givens for an entire afternoon, by means of the sanitized intermediaries of smiling dancers or spotlighted objects in plexiglas boxes. Yet once having eaten of the apple of knowledge—the Western realization that it is the individual who must define himself or herself—we cannot put the fruit back on the tree. We can imagine being part of a traditional society, but a member of a truly traditional society cannot—by definition—imagine being part of ours. For the power of received wisdom is that it does not seem contingent. Once questioned, as Achebe showed in *Things Fall Apart*, it crumbles.

Traditional societies should be frightening rather than interesting to Westerners, being antithetical to many of the things we hold sacred. Traditional societies are not "fun." They are repressive, stifling prisons—or they would be for us, if we were forced to live in one. What they are like for people who take them for granted is another question. But the paradox of our situation is that we can never become such a person and so can never know what it is like for such a person. The only reason we do not find traditional societies frightening is because—as Lévi-Strauss would suggest—they are harmless to us militarily or economically. What could be more patronizing? Combining Hegel with Lévi-Strauss and perhaps Norman Mailer, we might say: the owl of Western desire only flies after the castration of tradition.

We are protected from ever having to think this relation out to its logical end because the version we get of other societies is so determined by our needs, so tailored to fit unobtrusively into our structure. This codification of the world outside in

the form of the intra-cultural Other—the essence of the
exotic—is the way we institutionalize and so nullify what
otherwise would be its threat. What cages the lion of divergence on the domestic scene is that the domestic Other is
defined toward the center; what tames the threat of the world
outside on the intra-cultural scene is its successful reduction to
this role of a spice for our main dish. The nature of Otherness
is inherently to be tame: if it is not, it is no longer Other but
merely a threat.

Because the lions of Otherness are exhibited behind bars,
we can never contact them. We can change place physically so
that we are surrounded by a world of Otherness, but we
cannot for all that enter Otherness. This impossibility is not
the same as a "thou shalt not"; we are free to adopt the
customs and lifestyle of those around us, wherever we are.
But we cannot become the Other, for we would certainly
retain some consciousness of being the person who was once
something else. If we do not, by some miracle, do so, then we
simply become these other people ("other" written with a
lower-case letter). It is the last theme on which both the exotic
fictions of Ernest Hemingway, considered in the following
section, as well as the book and movie *Dances With Wolves* ring
changes: we can go into the realm of the Other, but we cannot
become one with these Others—or if we do so, it is at the cost
of a loss of our identity.

II

Literature

Chapter Three

Otherness and Alienation: Hemingway with Wolves and Sky

It is not chance that inter-cultural Otherness is most often tasted through the medium of art works, for if domestic Otherness is correctly summed up as a politicization of theory, conception in terms of the inter-cultural Other is an aestheticization of the objective world. Such conception transforms a geographically discrete part of the world, casting over it a pall of subjectivity that is a version writ large of that more personal transformation of the lived world which the Romantics, most notably Wordsworth, thought was the *sine qua non* of poetry.

Inter-cultural Otherness is what we might (appealing to Sartre) call Romanticism in bad faith. The illusion of inter-cultural Otherness is that these places so transformed by subjectivity are not landscapes of the mind, but real places that we can visit. Thus, though the conception of inter-cultural Otherness appears in the world outside of literature and written works, art works—along with works that use some of the tools of artistic narrative, like ethnographic reports—are its privileged habitat, and such works are the privileged medium of its transmission.

Romanticism—especially in its later manifestations—included its own form of this reification of place; we might say, somewhat paradoxically, that this strain of Romanticism was itself Romanticism in bad faith. Yet this seems to have been more tightly a part of the entire spectrum of Romantic longing than its counterpart is of our sensibility today—a Romantic spectrum exemplified by Schiller's listing of all the possible sources of the "naive": children, nature, the Greeks, Shakespeare, and so on. By contrast, the world within our cultural borders seems to have lost this richness of conceptual possibilities. In our postmodernist world, we possess to a much greater extent only the two extremes of pure subjectivity — the "self-expression" so prized in our arts — and the pure objectivity of the science which rules our lives, exemplified for most people in the current elevation of medicine to almost divine status. We look with suspicion on the transfigured interior landscapes of the Romantics; gone too are the subjectivized worlds of the Modernists (Woolf, Faulkner, Joyce) where the objective world is refracted through the individual's sensibility. And acknowledging that science may be more subjective in its structure or genesis than we had thought does not diminish the power over us of its products; thinkers such as Feyerabend, Kuhn, and Koestler are certainly more interesting for literary theorists than for scientists. This leaves only the possibility of inter-cultural Otherness as an escape.

One of the most developed twentieth-century caches of conception in terms of geographical Otherness, and one of the most interesting, is found in the works of Ernest Hemingway. The names of other authors will spring immediately to mind too as constructors of this sort of Otherness: Graham Greene, say, or V. S. Naipaul. Yet Green's Haitis and Sierra Leones and Mexicos are still contemporary: we too see them as Other. And Naipaul's Kisangani still seems reality itself to an outsider who has set foot recently in Zaire. At the other extreme is Conrad, whose Other — as Achebe shows — is totally inaccessible to us, so that we can only find it offensive.

The Other worlds of Hemingway lie somewhere in the middle of these two extremes of accessibility, and are instructive for that reason. His bullfighters, big-game hunters, and fishermen inhabit or visit worlds whose Otherness is now all but lost, yet which still clings to them in tatters — victim, Lévi-Strauss would say, of our greater proximity to these worlds, made possible through the jet plane. Even if we can no longer believe in the exoticism of, say, Spain, such Otherness is recent enough in our cultural memory that we can imagine doing so. It is in a consideration of such half-distanced conceptions of

Otherness, rather than in those that we still believe in, that we can become most easily aware of the mechanisms of their construction. For in such cases, the Otherness is neither so close to us that we are unable to distance ourselves from it, nor we so estranged from it that it seems wrong. In addition, Hemingway's novels show the bad news about Otherness: its seductiveness lies in the impossibility of our ever achieving it—as all his heroes exemplify by their alienation from these Other worlds to which they are drawn.

Nearly all of Hemingway's major works rely, to a greater or lesser extent, on the essentializing of place in Otherness. To be sure, their ostensible point is frequently that the places in question are corrupt and the battles are only worth deserting, and the people in these exciting settings usually only make each other miserable. Yet without the setting of, say, "The Snows of Kilimanjaro," the hero's sentimental remembrances—in the Schillerean sense of sentimental, as well as in the more contemporary—of his lost youth in Paris would be merely pitiful. Instead, the reader is meant to see that if the hero has lost Paris, he still has Tanganyika—at least for a while—and so is worthy of interest. When Hemingway had another more concerted try at the vanished country of his youth in his memoir *A Moveable Feast*, he left the realm of essentialized place and inter-cultural Otherness. High Romantic rather than Decadent, he produced a far more coherent work.

One of the most fascinating of Hemingway's works from my perspective is *For Whom the Bell Tolls*. For in this work we can see clearly the process of production of Otherness in literature, worked out through the medium of a sort of dialogue. Indeed, this is a quality of the work that attracted immediate critical attention when it appeared in 1940. At the time, some critics remarked the fact that the Loyalist partisans among whom Robert Jordan was to spend his last three days on earth talked—well, funny. For some, this was a favorable quality. V. S. Pritchett, writing in *The New Statesman and Nation*, noted what he called the "astonishingly real Spanish conversation"—close, he thought, to the "literal Castillian phrase with its

Elizabethan nobility" (Meyers p. 348).   Howard Mumford
Jones asserted, in the columns of the *Saturday Review*, that the
dialogue, "carried over almost literally from the Spanish," had
produced a "combination of dignity, rhetorical precision, and
wild poetry unattainable in a Germanic tongue."

In addition, Jones thought that Hemingway had "solved the
important problem of rendering the profanity and obscenity of
the common peoply by using a device so simple and yet effective" that he felt obliged to "leave it for the reader to discover"
(p. 318).   Other critics were not so impressed — the Spanish
novelist Arturo Barea, for one;   Barea's points — made while
considering the "Spanishness" or "Castillianness" of the
dialogue — will be considered below.

The characters of this novel are, we understand, speaking a
Castillian dialect of Spanish.   Yet at the risk of playing the
child who saw that the Emperor had no clothes at all, it is
equally clear that what these characters speak is not Spanish,
not Castillian.   Instead, it is pidgin English.   Or rather — and
this goes to the heart of the problem — it is speech overtly
rendered as pidgin English.   For the language these characters
speak, peculiar though it is, derives its nature from a relation
to extant linguistic norms of high English, Spanish of various
sorts, and the peasant patois.

Its divergence from the norm is, however, of several sorts.
First, the English these characters speak is sprinkled with itali-
cized expressions in Spanish, as if they could not, momentarily, think of the word in the English language they normally
speak with such cockeyed fluency.   They utter the words
"desde luego" where we would say "of course" (as, for example, p. 93), and a machine gun is always a "máquina" (as on p.
27) — these examples are taken at random from many repeti-
tions throughout the book. Sometimes these phrases are
followed by other words we recognize as translations: the
characters utter the word "nada" — and seem to translate it
themselves after a comma with the word "nothing"; they
announce "me voy" and whisper to the uncomprehending
immediately after, "I go" (p. 30). "No hay derecho, mujer,"
Pilar quotes a character in her story as saying — then after a

full stop appear the words: "This, woman, you have no right to do" (p. 125).

This technique of peppering the dialogue with foreign language expressions, and even translating them, probably does not bother us unduly—the first technique is a common way of reminding us in literature of the nationality of a speaker in a country outside of the Anglophone world. As for the technique of "doubling" a phrase in English, we understand that it is the author who is doing the translating for us (though it seems to be Pilar in the example above), understand that the phrase would only have come out of the mouths of these "real" characters (whatever it means to speak of "real" characters) not twice but only once, and that in Spanish. The translations, it seems, are offered for our convenience, and we accept them gratefully. (In *The Empire Writes Back*, Ashcroft, Griffiths and Tiffin consider this technique in some detail— though primarily in novels that are written not by the colonizers but the colonized.)

Yet sometimes the translation ends up making the utterance sound more unlike our language than like it. For, were these Spaniards English speakers—whatever this means, given that they are characters in a novel where they speak at least a pidgin form of English—they would not utter the words "I go," but put the verb into the progressive. This is the technique of "literal translation," resulting in incorrect or faulty English—where the Spanish is neither one—praised by the writers quoted above. The effect of such incorrect English is to make these people seem strange, make them inhabitants of a strange place, make them Other.

Yet the people are not only Spaniards, who as a result say "nada" and "máquina" and "desde luego," they are Old Castillians as well. Hemingway (or Jordan, or an implied version of either or both) prepares us for this, and tells us it will be important, early in the book.

> The old man spoke rapidly and furiously in a dialect that Robert Jordan could just follow. It was like reading Quevedo. Anselmo was speaking old Castilian [sic] and it went something like this, "Art thou a brute?. Yes, Art thou a beast? Yes, many times. Hast thou a brain? Nay."

And so on, to include the phrases of: "I this and that in the this and that of thy father. I this and that and that in thy this" (p. 11).

If we assume that characters in a novel somehow exist in relation to or silhouetted against a "real" world or "real" people, this single short speech evokes a myriad of gradations of removal of the words on the page from the reality to which it is related. To what extent—we may ask—do the words we read diverge from those uttered, those that would have been uttered, or those that would have had to be uttered?

If Anselmo were speaking old Castillian, the likelihood of English speakers understanding him would be small indeed—unless we, like Jordon, speak standard Spanish and so manage to barely understand. Perhaps Jordan is translating for us; the likelihood of this being so is greater here than in the example with Pilar above, for it is also Jordan to whom, presumably, the speech "was like reading Quevedo." Yet on the other hand if it is the author, or his implied counterpart, who tells us that Robert Jordan could "just follow" this, the author may be the one who is translating, and the one who tells us it went "something like this."

For most of us, quotation marks indicate a direct reporting of speech. We may ask ourselves if this is a legitimate use of such marks given that someone, author or character, has admitted the divergence from what "was said" of what we read on the page. Again we may be inclined to brush this question aside, for we understand the necessity of translation, and accept too that translation can, in some sense, report the "same words." We can take the admitted margin of error and divergence written into the text as confirmation of the existence of a real norm outside of the text from which what we read diverges.

The next thing we may notice is a result of the relation of this language to forms of Spanish: the use of the archaic English "thou" form to render the contemporary Spanish "tu." And this rendering, a question of translation, brings us to the objections raised by Barea to the language. Such objections will undoubtedly already have occurred to all students of the art of transferring one language to another. "It seems to me," says Barea, "that poise and simplicity of language should be rendered by equally poised, simple and natural language." Barea continues:

> As a writer, I would be unhappy if Spanish dialogue I had written were to be translated into something as affected and artificial as "I encounter it to be perfectly normal", when all I have said in Spanish was: Lo encuentro perfectamente normal—"I find it perfectly normal"; or into "You have terminated already?" when I have said: Habeis terminado ya?—"Have you finished already?" (p. 358)

To Anglophone ears, "thou art" sounds comical, old-fashioned, perhaps Quaker, and thus a willful deformation of the normal Spanish "eres" or "estás." The problem is that while we may be willing to consider the Castillian dialect itself a divergence, so that we are not bothered by its being translated either perfectly or imperfectly, we tend to accept both English and high Spanish as norms in themselves. As Barea says, normalcy for one will be normalcy for the other. The problem arises with the particular norms the text accepts linguistically, not with the fact that it has such a point of view at all, which is inescapable.

The book is full of these comprehensible-but-strange sentences that the reader with the slightest knowledge of Spanish sees as "howler" translations, or as crude jokes. "What passes?" these characters are in the habit of asking one another (for example p. 119); people are frequently thought (as was Robert Jordan's—literal—predecessor) not "a bit strange," but "a little rare," translated—this time after the pidgin, p. 119—as "algo raro." Sometimes the strangeness in English results from an abnormal word order, explicable to the initiated as following a normal Spanish one. "I keep this always," Maria tells Robert of her razor blade (p. 170). Sometimes the sentences include all of the strangenesses enumerated here: word order deformation, "literal" translation, a verb tense incorrect for English, and a Spanish word untranslated. Anselmo, for example, offers the opinion of Pablo that, "since a long time he is muy flujo." This is followed by one of the repetition translations, itself a literalism: "He is very flaccid" (p. 26).

Amusing as the listing of kinds of such "mistakes" may be, we must deny it any taxonomic rigor for fear of doing violence to the extraordinarily haphazard nature of the appearances in the text of their instances. Sometimes the sentences include one kind of pidgin, sometimes another, sometimes all, and sometimes none—and these in almost dizzying alternation. Nor does any one such "mistake" appear consistently. Hardly have we begun to find all the thees and thous normal—for such usage grows on us, tends to seem unobjectionable as the result of sheer repetition—when the people start talking in yous. The sleeping bag scene from which the sentence about the razor is quoted above, for example, is conducted in a patternless alternation of thous and yous, both from the Spanish woman and the American man, both of whom are presumably "really" speaking Spanish. When Jordan is not speaking Spanish, we are told that he is not, and told in the same English of the rest of the page: the words "in English" are added after "he said" (as for example p. 27). One sentence complex enough in this vein to keep us amused for a while is the following (p. 180): "'Nothing', Robert Jordan said. 'I said "nothing" in English.'"

One sort of strangeness in the long passage quoted above fairly begs to be commented upon, for some of the words offered to us in quotation marks cannot have been spoken by any creature living or dead, real or imaginary, or—even in translated form—by the member of any identifiable linguistic group. I mean those words so highly praised by Jones, the substitution of place-holder words for the obscenities. In Anselmo's speech, these are the words "this" and "that"; elsewhere it is "obscenity" or "unprintable" that are used. "Go obscenity thyself," says Pablo. Augustin states flatly: "I obscenity in the milk of it all" (both p. 211), and tells Jordan: "Go to the unprintable and unprint thyself" (p. 45). Not even the explanation that the author is translating, or translating badly, satisfies us here, or tells us why we have these words rather than those "actually" said.

Of course, we know why—or think we do. We know that it is because of sensitivity to audience (or publisher) reaction—and this, particularly, in 1940—that this substitution is made. Yet the incantatory quality of these repeated words, rather than the slightly more various words they replace, makes the speeches sound more "poetic," and we may wonder if this effect is really not closer to what these often-used and thus partly unheard and ritualized curses must have for the Castillian peasants, rather than the "truer" but undoubtedly more shocking effect that so much obscenity would inevitably produce on the Anglophone reader.

All of these divergences from linguistic norms establish the people as Other. Yet such questions of fidelity or its lack to a postulated external standard of reality become relative when we realize that the most fundamental contrast in this book is internal to its language. It is between Jordan, who is the only character to speak "normal" English, and the partisans, who are turned into the Other through their language. The merciless pidgin of these partisans gives us at each moment a sense of their strangeness with relation to the English-language norm they constantly violate. This means that the taste of the exotic never leaves these people. They as individuals are not violating this norm, in the sense that Anita, the Spanish prostitute in Hemingway's hilarious *Fifth Column*, speaks abnormal English; they do so collectively. Their individuality becomes subsumed to their commonality—which we express, for lack of any better vocabulary, as that of place.

At the same time, Robert Jordan's pidgin is distinctly less comical for an English-speaking audience than that of the others, being limited essentially to the thees and thous and the occasional Spanish word. Moreover, his thoughts and mental monologues are all in normal English, so that we never lose sight of this contrasting norm. Jordan, the American, is speaking what for him is a foreign language in order to communicate with the partisans. Jordan is the only bilingual character among this group; they are limited while he transcends them. Thanks to the author's deformations of normal English, the reader becomes bilingual too—passing effortlessly, with Jordan, from pidgin (or "Spanish") to normal English. The constant friction for the reader reading this language which sounds abnormal—by being a variation of what he or she understands—is the equivalent of the strain someone experiences who is speaking a foreign language in order to communicate with other people of whose unlikeness to himself or herself that person is thus constantly aware.

This brings us to the other main point concerning this work, and virtually all of Hemingway's works: their implicit admission of what we may call the bad news involved in the construction of Otherness. Namely, that the more convincingly inter-cultural Otherness is evoked, the more inaccessible it is to us—or to the characters in the book who share our point of view—for whom it is Other. The language in this book throws a haze of strangeness over all the people save Jordan. For this reason Jordan remains irrevocably an outsider—a fact shown by his language—and so, consistently enough, is never required to come to terms with the world around him. Jordan remains the Montana college instructor on sabbatical who wonders whether he will be blacklisted on his return for having fought with Communists, who realizes that Maria will never fit into American life, and who is spared having to resolve these two worlds by conveniently being killed.

At first glance Jordan's "bilinguality" is what causes him to be at home in his foreign culture. Indeed, Hemingway heroes always speak the foreign language of their surroundings; Jordan and Lieutenant Henry are amused when they are spoken to in what we are told is, respectively, pidgin Spanish and pidgin Italian. Hemingway heroes all understand perfectly the customs of their countries that the outsider does not know. The most blatant example of this is the character Hemingway of *Death in the Afternoon* who explains it all to us. All the heroes preserve an attitude of laconic unsurprise towards their surroundings that shows us they are perfectly at home and nothing is unexpected. Only infrequently do they distance themselves from their surroundings by thought. As Pritchett notes, Jordan is the exception that proves the rule.

Yet their very bilinguality makes them outsiders to their monolingual surroundings. Hemingway makes the point explicitly: outsiders they all remain; the great truth Hemingway's novels reveal is that we can never become the Other.

This, I take it, is Hemingway's admission of the worm at the heart of his otherwise potentially so cloying evocations of Otherness: they are so seductive because we can never enter into them.

Frederic Henry, to take a less evident example than Jordan, introduces the story of his dead love by making clear to us that initially she was just another lay. Falling in love with her was unexpected, and since it is not shown in the work, it remains utterly unconvincing. When she is gone he reflects with tough-guy cynicism that this was sooner to be expected than not, as everybody gets it in the end; he withdraws again to the surface of his world. Jake Barnes, a stronger example, half-floats through the already foreign world of Paris from his position of shell-shocked impotence, and Robert Jordan's melodramatically pre-figured death ends his state as a tourist who somehow got involved. Colonel Cantwell is condemned to death and outsidership from the beginning, and knows it. His view of Venice is avowedly nostalgic, and thus is one of the truest of such relations in Hemingway.

Yet the most convincing Hemingway hero seems in retrospect to have been Hemingway himself who, according to Barea (who met him in Madrid), was "always a spectator who wanted to be an actor, and who wanted to write as if he had been an actor" (Meyers p. 360). Always wanted to be, always wanted to write as if: the phrases indicate the position of longing from which Hemingway wrote, the impossibility of ever fusing with a state of Otherness. Otherness, and alienation from the world that is Other: these are two sides of the same coin.

All literature, I argue, presupposes an inside and an outside; each work describes the outside from the point of view it takes as inside. In most cases—always, when the work has become a popular success—the position of this dividing line is identical to the situation of its audience, so that the unfamiliar is explained in terms of the familiar by someone who perceives from fundamentally the same point of view as its audience. Works that are not so popular or that require time for their digestion invariably require us to situate their point of view with relation to ours; they do not do so for us, or represent the same point of view. Though this is true of all literature, the problematic of inside point of view may, in particular works, become central. This is the case in *For Whom the Bell Tolls*, and it is present in virtually all of Hemingway's works.

The general situation of *For Whom the Bell Tolls* — the "inside" protagonist goes "outside" into a world with which he or she can have no real contact — is typical of many works where Otherness is constructed. We may see such works as marking the fruitful middle ground between the two poles of the evocation of inter-cultural Otherness. At one extreme, the outside is only dimly sensed in a world that is overwhelmingly inside. At the other extreme the point of view is so far outside that a sense of the audience to which this is Other is all but lost. We may exemplify these two extremes by, respectively, the Conan Doyle Sherlock Holmes stories, and many of the Kipling stories of India.

In the Holmes stories all the excitement comes from outside, while this is recounted from a position inside. The outside is glimpsed only through its momentary intrusions into the world inside, through the effects of misspent years in the colonies working themselves out decades after the fact, or through the effects of exotic animals or poisons unknown to the locals. The world at home is, for Holmes, a static and boring one: these intrusions from the more exciting, if more threatening, world Out There are necessary to draw him from his cocaine-fed ennui. The Other in the Holmes stories is sensed like a creature in the darkness just beyond the campfire: we feel its presence, but see only its products, to the point where its threat is indistinguishable from the darkness itself.

The point of view in the Holmes stories acknowledges the Other and its potential of threat. Keeping it firmly at bay is what makes it Other. Yet at no point is the Other dealt with directly. Indeed, it may be too powerful for this. In many of the India stories of Kipling, by contrast, the point of view is almost totally outside. Though such stories frequently take as their subject matter the actions of Britishers in the subcontinent, in the manner of Hemingway, the attitude of the narrator with respect to them is frequently one of bemused flipness regarding their pretensions to understand or control this so-strange land. In Kipling, it is as if the attitude of a Hemingway narrator had been pushed even further along the scale of acclimatization: all Kipling narrators, to a certain extent, are versions of Kipling's own Kim, Irish by birth but by upbringing more Indian than the Indians.

It is this, I think, which is the source of the discomfort many right-thinking Westerners today feel with Kipling, rather than the fact that sometimes he undeniably does turn into an apologist for Empire. (The times when he is criticizing Empire just as strictly tend to go unremarked.) The insoucience of his narrators, the way they take the outside so for granted (and thus at the same time their own presence in it), does not jibe well with our feeling that the Other should be treated seriously. If the Other is not feared, we tend to believe that it should at least be respected. Kipling's narrators frequently do not, in this sense, respect India: they take it too much for granted, whether the story is of "white" or "black." They are bemused, rather than solemn. Yet these narrators do still tell their stories; they too report on the goings-on in this exotic world, even if they seem to make light of its exoticism.

Works such as *For Whom the Bell Tolls* are in the middle between these two extremes established by the location of the narratorial point of view. They tell the adventures of one (or sometimes two) people from inside adrift in the world outside; characerically the audience is meant to identify with the point of view of the insider. *For Whom the Bell Tolls* stands out because, at the same time as it constructs the Other through language, it shows that the insider must remain alien to the outside, so long as the Other continues to exist as such. For this reason Hemingway's works seem more honest than other evocations of Otherness such as Durrell's Alexandria quartet, or the novel of Paul Bowles considered here, *The Sheltering Sky*.

Just as we sense the melancholy that lurks under the ceaseless search for distraction of Fitzgerald's Jazz Age fun-seekers, so the most profound thing about Hemingway may ultimately be something that his works suggest rather than express. Finally, only the exotic Otherness of place can speak to us who

are caught in the tasteless world of our   so-real lives.
Hemingway shows us both the reason we are so attracted to
the myth of the outside Other, and why it must deceive us
again and again. We may contrast this with the infinitely more
intelligent fiction of Virginia Woolf, which seems the attempt
to express this tastelessness of life "inside" directly—and so
ends by frequently being dull. Hemingway is the other side of
this coin, its logical contrary: the relentless avoidance of this
state of normalcy or reality through Otherness—avoidance of
the tasteless, dead center of all our lives.

We may pause before going on to Charlotte Brontë's *Villette*
to consider three works whose situations bear generic
similarities to Hemingway's novel, in that they all touch on
the impossibility of ever achieving Otherness. The first is
Bowles's *The Sheltering Sky*. The other two are a novel and film
pair, each entitled *Dances with Wolves*—the novel written in
amateurish prose by Michael Blake; the film, affecting despite
itself, directed by Kevin Costner, with a screenplay by Blake
that diverges from the novel in significant aspects. All three
works underline the lesson of *For Whom the Bell Tolls*: their
characters never enter a state of Otherness. (The recent film
by Bertolucci based on *The Sheltering Sky* is a watered-down
version of the novel, and I do not consider it here.)

The Bowles novel and the Costner film are cross-over stories
where the hero returns from a time with the Other where he
or she has willingly gone. The Blake novel is more complex
than either from this vantage point: the hero does not himself
return, though in a sense his story does. In the cases of Bowles
and Costner we have a positive-valence Other to which the
Western hero is drawn, along with the same bad news that
Hemingway gives us, that he or she can never achieve this
Other. This bad news is clearer in the Bowles novel, for
though the American hero returns physically to the non-Other
world (the Westernized city of Fez), she does so mad.

The actions of Kit, the main character in Bowles's novel—as
Richard Cronin would point out—are characteristic of later-
generation colonial novels. Instead of the European male
raping the female colonial (a typical Victorian scenario), a
female hero, such as Adela Quested in Forster's *Passage to India*

or Daphne Manners in Paul Scott's *Jewel in the Crown*, is raped, or desires rape, by more sensual darker-skinned men. Kit ends up the willing love-slave of an Arab. A precondition of this desire is the sexual lassitude of the West: Kit and her husband have separate bedrooms, and early on each seeks his or her sexual partners elsewhere. The husband does so initially with more satisfication than the wife, though this is comprehensible in the value system of the novel; he is shown coupling with an Arab woman, and Kit's first affair is with another white American.

Though the actions of these characters are formulaic, the twist in Bowles is that these actions seem to be utterly unrelated to the characters' thoughts and motivations, as if Kit and Port were two characters wandering about in search of an author who would make sense for them of what they feel impelled to do. We might say that this novel is a story of the search for Otherness as eviscerated farce. The characters do everything they "should" do, yet they are like sleepwalkers, doomed to enact a play they do not understand.

Let us consider this plot: a white man (Port, the husband) fleeing from New York (as a "traveler" rather than as a "tourist") contacts the Other sexually, yet the woman turns out to be a whore and a thief, and the encounter is without significance. Not too long thereafter the man dies, anti-climactically, of typhoid in a characterless city on the desert. He has gone in search of the Other, but has he achieved it? If not, why not?

The actions of the wife too seem, in their baldest outlines, formulaic to a novel of Otherness, and equally devoid of meaning. Unsatisfied by her sexual activities with white men, she leaves her dead husband to go into the desert, where she becomes the willing sexual prisoner of the young Arab whom she has met by chance. For a while she seems to enjoy the position of her bondage, and becomes attached to her dark-skinned captor. (Skin color is important here; on escaping she beds briefly with a black African whose color is dwelt on in some detail.) Finally she realizes that she would enjoy any Arab man as much as the one holding her prisoner.

Even so, it is not clear that her pleasure in sex with dark-skinned men is ever any more than hallucinatory (she seems half-mad from the beginning), or of any great import. Most of the time it seems as empty as masturbation, her mind elsewhere, her pleasure vague. To be sure, she exits the desert utterly mad, which seems to point to some sort of lesson—perhaps like that of Hemingway, that we cannot really achieve Otherness. Yet we are prevented from thinking this moral central by the fact that Kit was well on her way to becoming mad when she went into the desert, and the precise reasons why she becomes so, or becomes so here, remain obscure.

Finally we are left unclear, in *The Sheltering Sky*, as to whether anyone can or cannot achieve contact with the Other. Certainly neither Kit nor Port does so, but is this because of reasons peculiar to these characters or because of the situation? Chance or necessity? The Arabs may seem to be Other, but are they really so? If they are, then why is Kit mad when she leaves the desert? If they are not, why is she already so well on her way to this madness before? Is it herself she finds there? Or something else? And to all of these questions Bowles wants to say: "yes." The reader's reaction to the novel will surely hinge on whether this unwillingness to clarify the situation appears profound or lazy.

Thus, we may read *The Sheltering Sky* as a deconstruction —before this term became fashionable—of the myth of the Other, an insistence, like Hemingway's fables, on the impossibility of attaining that Other. At the same time, Bowles is banking on the power the Other possesses to make us interested in this process. He makes us voyeurs, then reprimands us for our prurient interest; he is counting on the fascination we still associate with the Arab—and here, particularly, the desert—world. He cannot escape the echoes of Rudolf Valentino and the "romance" of Lawrence of Arabia, nor should he want to, for purposes of audience interest.

We could legitimately aim at Bowles the criticism that Achebe aims at Conrad regarding *Heart of Darkness*: that he uses a region and a people (here Tuareg, there Congolese) as nothing but the "props for the break-up of one petty

European [American] mind." The echoes of Conrad in Bowles are unmistakable; there the jungle, here the desert, both as metaphors of psyche. The difference is that for Conrad the heart of the jungle parallels actions of Kurtz; for Bowles the emptiness of the desert parallels—if anything—only the lack of motivation in all the characters' actions. We might say that the plot in *The Sheltering Sky* parallels the story of Marlow but eliminates Kurtz. And what would *Heart of Darkness* be without Kurtz?

Neither the book nor the movie entitled *Dances with Wolves* is sophisticated in the way that Bowles's book is—though both try, in their fashion, to make clear the bad news implicit in the search for Otherness in a way similar to Hemingway. Unlike the revisionism of Bowles, Costner's revisionism in *Dances* is rather rudimentary: the film exhibits the principal characteristics of conventional cross-over story. The novel, from which the film diverges in several major ways, is more interesting for the present argument.

Book and movie tell the tale of a Union Lieutenant who is posted, at his request, to the prairie. He arrives at a deserted encampment; the book makes clearer than the movie that this will never be re-staffed, as it has administratively ceased to exist by the time the hero arrives. Gradually the hero becomes (in the movie) a Lakota and marries a member of their people who, conveniently enough —like to like—turns out to be a white woman raised since childhood (in the book, since adolescence) as a Lakota (in the book, Comanche).

That this is a fairly standard story of the search for a simpler life in a non-Western culture is made quite clear in the film; the screenplay goes so far as to have Dunbar, the hero, use the tell-tale word "harmony" with respect to the Lakota while the screen shows us luscious shots of autumn leaves and people sitting under trees. The Lieutenant's voice-over later tells us that when he was merely a Union soldier he had no idea "who he was." Finding self by entering a harmonious world outside: this much is familiar. The world of the frontier was a world outside at that point, rather than inside—or at least this is so as the film and book unroll. Dunbar is the only white person, excepting his future wife, in this Indian world. Though other white men are heard like distant thunder at the edges of things, they do not enter directly until the end where, for a time, they are vanquished.

Cross-over stories—where the inter-cultural Other is portrayed, as a result, with a positive valence—like travel books, are always written from the point of view of the world that the person making the crossing has left. From the point of view of those to whom he or she crosses over, this process is necessarily less interesting, representing a self-valorizing underscoring of values. We Americans, for example, are diverted to see people from all over the world come bobbing up on our shores in boats wishing to become American, but we are not particularly interested in their stories: it seems logical to us that they would wish to become like us. The more logical question for the crossed-over-to group is why it took the crosser so much time to do what seems perfectly normal; the first group will be largely uninterested in the twists and turns by which the person gets to this goal. (Another pertinent work from this perspective is Peter Schneider's *The Wall Jumper*, about a Westerner living in the two worlds of West and East Berlin.) *Dances with Wolves*, book and movie, is interesting from the point of view of the non-Indians, which is to say from the viewpoint of the white people at whom the film or book is aimed—or from the point of view of the Indians to the extent that they see themselves from the vantage point of the now-dominant culture.

The Costner film makes clear the lesson of Hemingway that the person living as a member of an Other group cannot ever become one with them. For the Lieutenant, who by this time has become "Dances with Wolves" (as in: "he who dances with wolves"), leaves the Lakota at the end with his equally crossed-over wife to tell his story to "those who would listen"—ostensibly doing so to protect the Lakota from retribution by the Army that is looking for him, and despite the fact that he would surely be tried and hung as a deserter. This is quite unbelievable for other reasons. How would these two people live among whites again, especially as the woman, in the film, has been taken by the tribe at an age closer to four than the book's fourteen? The book, by contrast, contains no such scene; the white man has become a red man, and remains with the Comanche, though they are doomed to captivity or extinction.

In the movie, we might say, the two white people bail out of a sinking ship and leave the Indians to their fate. For the film observes in a follow-up title on the screen that a mere thirteen years later the remaining Lakota "submitted to white rule," thereby causing a chapter of frontier life to "pass into history." The white people, that is, sojourn for only a time with the Indians, and bid them farewell at the end. The film is an example of the five-years-captive-with-the-Indian books that were common currency in colonial times; the only difference is that here the captivity of the man is willing.

Another divergence between the novel and the film script, intimately related to this alteration in ending, further underscores the point we saw in Hemingway. In the film, Blake adds a parting gift from an adolescent brave to Dunbar-Dances with Wolves: the latter's diary, which had been thought lost, that chronicles the process of his identity switch. In leaving the Lakota, Dunbar-Dances with Wolves is given back his history, the record of his alteration into his current state, as a necessary pre-condition of his leaving it to re-enter his original one. How much more daring the film would have been if the diary had remained lost in the stream where it had floated away! For a moment, in fact, as the hero's history disappears from sight on the water, the film viewer thinks that Dunbar will be replaced by Dances with Wolves.

It doesn't happen. Yet both of these things do happen in the novel. Despite its air of having been written by a slow fifth-grader—its dreadful strings of cliches, its one-sentence paragraphs and page-long sections designed to be easy on the reader's concentration—the novel takes more chances with its plot than does the film script. In the book, the Lieutenant becomes Dances with Wolves, and never un-becomes him. His white past is lost; the diary is not recovered. The book ends with the assertion by the tribal elder that if the white men come they will only find another Comanche brave, not a U.S. Army lieutenant who has deserted.

Though the film underscores Hemingway's lesson that we can never become the Other, the book seems to belie it. Yet it only seems to do so. For despite the much more daring ending of the book in which Dunbar actually becomes one with his Other world, it is written no less from the point of view of the non-Other than Hemingway's works, or the Costner-Blake film. It too, in its way, makes clear that Otherness cannot be achieved. Though something is achieved in the book, this something is no longer Otherness, either for the achiever or those looking on.

The novel ends with the crossing-over, just as comedies end with a marriage; the life beyond does not enter into the world relevant to the genre. Once Otherness is entered it ceases to be Other from the point of view of the crosser. Nor can the hero be followed any longer by the non-Other group, for this would be to individualize a member of a group defined by an essentializing of place. If the hero has become Other, he or she can by definition be no more interesting to the non-Other than any member of this Other group. The point of the story, from the vantage point of the non-Other group at which it must be aimed, is the becoming-Other, not the being-Other, a state about which nothing can be said—either from the point of view of the people looking on, or the person becoming it.

Though the book lacks within its story line those elements of distancing which the film includes, such as the diary and the decision to leave, the telling of the story as a whole fulfills this purpose. (In this particular it is similar to the most deconstructed contemporary ethnography.) The novel entitled *Dances with Wolves* itself serves as the recovered diary that becomes part of the movie's diegesis. The entire story, whether narrated in a microcosmic miniature in the form of a diary, or simply told, is still aimed at the non-Other group, and still cannot show the successful attainment of Otherness. What can? The nature of Otherness is that it stay Other.

Other elements of the film show its parallels to works referred to above. To begin with, it is as soaked in diegetic nostalgia, written into the script as well as implied by music and gorgeous nature shots, as *Out of Africa*. Indeed, the shots of endless prairie and tiny wagon give the first minutes of the

Western section of *Dances*—the movie opens in a blood-bespattered Union military hospital in a temporal reverse of the book's flash-back structure—the look and the sound of the opening shots of *Out of Africa*: the composer, John Barry, is common to both films.

Much of the nostalgia in *Out of Africa* is produced by the distance between the narrating voice and the events portrayed. Though *Dances with Wolves* has a narrative voice-over as well, its nostalgia is more overt. For the voice-over here is not separated temporally to any great extent from the events it narrates; thus the distancing the film offers us is felt not by the older version of the people we see, as in *Out of Africa*, but by them, as they act. Thus Dunbar tells the alcoholic officer who sends him to the deserted outpost (and who, in the film, kills himself shortly thereafter rather than—as in the novel—merely going mad) that he wants to get to the frontier "before it disappears." And the knowledge he keeps hesitating to impart to his Lakota hosts is that their world is held on the brink of destruction by the white men who are only months away from penetration of this world.

The Other world itself, like that in Owen Wister's strange and overtly self-referential late Western *The Virginian*, is already a sentimental one, rather than a naive one. This means that even if we are not shown Dunbar's physical leave-taking in the novel as we are in the film, we know that he will never have been able to fully enter this Other world. And it is for this reason that both of these elements are contrasted to an Other that, for its part, is fully as absolute as the negative Indian Other of the old-style Western: Dunbar seems more a part of this irrevocably Other world if both are unlike something else. For here, it is not "Indians" in general who are the bad guys, but one tribe—the Pawnee—conveniently enough the Other both for the Lakota-Comanche and for the white woman whom they have raised and whom Dunbar marries (Pawnee had killed her family).

The fact that Dunbar is playing at Otherness with the Lakota-Commanche all along rather than becoming something else also explains why he does not hesitate to use his store of rifles to help them defeat their common enemy: Were he really concerned with holding intact a viable alternative culture, he might have thought twice about using white technology in this way, even if for the short-term good of his hosts.   The encroaching world of the whites, his actions suggest, is good if it kills one's enemies, and bad if it kills one's friends—a cold-blooded judgment incommensurate with a situation in which the Indian Other is constructed as an absolute alternative to this world of white ways.

Ultimately the hero's crossing is more like sex in the head than real mingling, a masturbatory fantasy rather than the real achievement of identity that is hinted at.   Even his literal copulation is with a white woman rather than an Indian.   But this merely acknowledges the truth: all mingling with the Other is sex in the head.   Contact with the Other never really happens, so whether the hero leaves this people (as in the movie) or stays (as in the novel) may be irrelevant.

Chapter Four

The Coffee Grounds of the Labassecourien Housemaids or Inside and Outside in Literature

All literature, being utterances of one person that can be perceived by other people, presupposes a certain audience. And this fact makes it a fertile ground for the expression of inter-cultural Otherness. A work that wishes to create Otherness has only to portray all of the people living in a spot as strange; usually it does this most clearly if at least one character who does not seem so comes from the outside. In *For Whom the Bell Tolls*, Otherness was evoked by language spoken by all the characters save that one with whom the intended audience was, as a result, meant to identify. In Charlotte Brontë's *Villette*, it is evoked not by the language spoken by the characters, but more subtly, by the very things the narrator feels necessary to tell us about the world of those characters. Brontë's book is a rich source for studying the production of Otherness in literature, since this Otherness controls and determines the entire work: the establishment of inter-cultural Otherness is constitutive of most of the work's content.

From considering *Villette*, moreover, we see that while inter-cultural Otherness diverges from intra-cultural Otherness in the real world, in art both kinds of Otherness are part of a continuous spectrum. For art deals with individuals, while, in relation to individuals, all group characteristics are secondary, and are alike to this extent. As long as we are aware that the inter-cultural Otherness created in literature is only Other for the context of this work, we have no reason to not enjoy it.

After all, art is the legitimate domain of inter-cultural Otherness; there it exists as a conscious illusion.

One example of a work where the process of constructing Otherness is not constitutive, but momentarily and more intensely glimpsed, is Evelyn Waugh's *Brideshead Revisited*, whose most lyrical chapters are an evocation of a lost, unrecapturable youth in the manner of the Romantics or the Hemingway of *A Moveable Feast*. At one point the remembering narrator, John Ryder, tells of bringing an acquaintance, one Jorkins, home to dinner (pp. 68-70). Ryder's eccentric and manipulative father insists on treating Jorkins as if the guest were an American, though he is careful not to be caught in this game. The father carefully explains to the bewildered guest customs a Britisher could take for granted, in effect "translating" a way of life. The scene is amusing, since the evocation of Otherness is presented as a perverse joke. Nonetheless, it offers a paradigm for the techniques which *Villette* develops in greater expanse and detail. For in *Villette*, the narrator, like Mr. Ryder, feels obliged to explain. And it is the fact of explanation which shows us that we are dealing with an Other.

An examination of the techniques for establishing Otherness in *Villette* helps us see the way in which literature presupposes an audience: which is to say, who is meant to understand it, and how this is inscribed in the text. This explains why literature is not, and cannot be, universally accessible. In addition, it shows the connection of the novel's establishment of intercultural Otherness to the discourse of groups on the domestic scene: some groups within our society will be more spoken to than others as a result of the way inter-cultural Otherness is established.

We may better understand these techniques by focusing on an example of them, on a passage at the beginning of chapter 23 where the heroine, Lucy Snowe, has just received a letter from the handsome and vain young doctor with whom she is infatuated, Dr. John Bretton. She hides it, and, waiting until the girls' school where she teaches English is quiet for the evening, she goes first upstairs and then down, looking for a place to read her letter in peace. After rejecting the dormitory (which is inhabited) she thinks of going to the classrooms for this purpose, and tells why she is forced to continue her search for solitude:

> The classes were undergoing sweeping and purification by candle-light, according to hebdomadal custom: benches were piled on desks, the air was dim with dust, damp coffee-grounds (used by Labassecourien housemaids instead of tea leaves) darkened the floor; all was hopeless confusion. Baffled but not beaten, I withdrew. (p. 323)

Finally she goes to the attic, where we may leave her with her prize. For it is not Lucy Snowe who interests us most here, but the coffee-grounds dotting the floor of the room she abandons as a reading nook. Or, more precisely, it is the parenthetical remark which the narrator feels obliged to provide after this detail for the edification of her audience that is of greatest interest.

In this detail and its parenthetical explanation we have the clearest and most compact example that *Villette* provides, at the microscopic level, of a phenomenon present in all novels and even in all literature—a quality that can be effectively exploited for the construction of inter-cultural Otherness. The word "instead" is the point that draws our attention. For the reader of whatever era, or nationality, or creed—though distinctions of these sorts will be ultimately under discussion here—understands through this that a normal state of affairs is being referred to, and is being contrasted to an abnormal one.

Having the remains of beverage preparation on the floor is clearly normal to the narrator, for no attempt is made to explain or justify this, any more than the use of candles is justified, or the piling of benches on tables to get them out of the way. We could imagine a novel, say of a hundred years later, where the first detail would call for an explanation, such as that the electricity was out. We can also imagine a case in which, because of the great delicacy of the furniture, the second detail would be tantamount to an accusation of barbarism. Here neither of these is the case, and we under-stand this because of our general knowledge of the world that produced this work, and because the narrator does not comment upon them. What is not normal is merely that these damp dregs should be from coffee, rather than tea. And the source of this abnormality lies, we are told, in the fact that the housemaids are Labassecourien. This in turn evokes not only a geographical fact but the entire ways of life associated with (1) Labassecour and (2) the only other country treated at any length in *Villette*: England.

The parenthetical remark assures us that despite this culturally determined difference of substance, the function to which these substances are put is identical in both cases ("used . . . instead of"). And the generic similarity of tea leaves and coffee dregs, both the remains of hot beverage preparation, forms a second, implicit, point of resemblance, as if the products used for this common purpose were sought by all peoples in generally the same realm. Similarities do exist between the two countries.

Yet quite possibly a reader in the 1990s — or one from a culture unused to any but dirt and concrete floors, such as that in which the first draft of this chapter was written — Rwanda, in central Africa — may have trouble immediately identifying what this function is. It may not, that is, be clear to all readers that the word "darkening" is not merely a description of a visual effect, but partly a purpose as well. We must realize that the floors being referred to are wood, and that the coffee-grounds (or tea leaves) are spread across them to attract dust, as well as to give them a pleasingly dark hue, before being swept up again. And if we do not understand why wood should be clean or dark, the explanations must continue until we do understand. In other words, we may be obliged to continue for ourselves exactly the same kind of explanations as already begun within the text.

Yet the narrator stops here. The reason is obvious: more explanation is unnecessary; it did not occur to the narrator, or by extension the author, that all this required explanation. The theoretical point to which I am tending may by now have become a platitude, the assertion that all literature takes for granted the givens of a particular world, group, or society (what Riffaterre calls the "sociolect"); readers from another world, group, time, or society will have problems. This is the starting point of hermeneutics, from Schleiermacher to Hirsch, and it is the presupposition of much of today's more enlightened, that is, least mechanistic, semiotic analyses, from Greimas to Riffaterre.

Clearly a generation and a society brought up on vacuum cleaners will have problems when reading this passage, as will those from cultures whose floors are impervious to the aesthetic effects of either kind of dregs. For some critics this fact seems of primarily theoretical interest. For others, this is only an impetus to renewed scholarship, a question of pedagogy: let us learn about the world that produced these works, they say, let us write footnotes, let us provide supplementary information to our students. In either case the problem lies not with the different worlds or times, but with what we make of this fact, how we cope with it (or not), overcome it or are overcome by it.

This problem links our conceptions of Otherness in the real world with the conceptions of Otherness offered in literature. Otherness in the world and in novels is produced by adoption of a point of view. And the way we are asked to adopt a point of view in literature is the same way that Mr. Ryder established Britain as an Other to Jorkins, whom he pretended to think an American: through what needs to be said and what is left unsaid. This passage from *Villette* shows the realization on the part of the work's narrator, or author, of the necessity to draw a dividing line between these two realms, the "inside," which is defined by silence, and the "outside," which must be explained.

This "inside" in literature has gotten the greater attention from scholars, perhaps most meticulously in Greimas's binary configurations of elements forming the value matrix of a work. For though Greimassian analyses in terms of the square offer pairs of elements and so include contrasting poles of value, these are all descriptions of "inside," because, by definition, they are indications of what is included through reference in the work. Such analyses of inside answer the question, What is taken for granted in a work? However, questions fully as important as the first are, What is taken to be interesting by a work? What, that is, is outside? For on the outside rather than the inside we may find Otherness of all sorts; the Other is always found in what is interesting rather than in what is taken for granted.

Each work of literature has an inside and an outside. In order to have a point and even to come to be, it must offer something interesting—which is to say, interesting to somebody. It presupposes a point of view, or audience, that will find interesting (beause new), yet at the same time comprehensible (because old) what it offers. Whether it ever finds such an audience, and whether the audience will be what it presupposes, is another question. All literature is the relation of an outside to an inside—such as we see being overtly made in the passage quoted above, as well as in the novel as a whole. When this relation is consistently effected with respect to place, with many details relating to all the characters in a given place, or through reiterated details of setting, the result is an evocation of inter-cultural Otherness. In such cases this relation organizes that portion of the work devoted to its evocation.

In *Villette*, almost the entire book is so organized, and virtually all aspects of this book are arranged around this central evocation of inter-cultural Otherness. Indeed the very skeleton of this book is the contrast between England (Protestant, Anglophone, Anglo-Saxon, and, well, English) and Belgium (Catholic, Continental, Latin, and, well, Belgian). Pages at a time exist only because they describe, and thereby situate and render comprehensible this alien-looking and alien-thinking world, performing the same function of a book of travel reports to stay-at-homes. If we already know how a Continental girls' school works, we will see these passages as self-evident, forced, or naive; if we are Catholic we may see Lucy Snowe as tiresome and theologically all too predictable. And it is for a similar reason that Achebe finds so offensive Conrad's portrayal of the Congo.

The book itself is the delineation of the geometrical dividing line between inside and outside, here expressed in geographical terms as inter-cultural Otherness. Lucy Snowe, or again by extension the author, must explain about the coffee grounds of one culture to the tea-leafers she has left at home—or take for granted that no explanation is necessary. The girls' school cannot be merely referred to, for we would then assume it is the same as an English school; it must be described. If Madame Beck's peculiarly devious-but-not-evil character were a normal (English) one, the book could not contain all these pages of description situating it as being Continental and Catholic in contrast to the English.

Even Lucy Snowe's still-waters-run-deep quality is dependent on her being set in this alien world. For if this contrast between the individual and society were set in England (inside), Lucy would become more of a personal aberration, a misfit, unless she were alien to some segment of society itself strange to the mainstream. Because her surroundings are alien, her withdrawal from them can be extreme and yet appear normal to the reference group.

These descriptions of an alien clime play yet another role in the novel: they make clear Lucy Snowe's position as an outsider to her surroundings, as unseen and misunderstood, so that the contrasts of geography, language, religion, and mores that are insisted upon combine to give us a sense of her mental isolation. (This is another example of that Janus face of Otherness and alienation within it that we saw in Hemingway.) Yet if everyone in Britain had the same knowledge of Brussels that Lucy Snowe comes to have, neither she nor the author could use these details, as they now stand, to express alienation. Lucy Snowe or the author would have to present more alien details or *Stoff* that would be strange from the point of view of an Englishman or Englishwoman who knew Belgium. By the same token an England less suspicious of Popery, more sophisticated in its understanding of Catholicism, would fail to find even worthy of mention the half of Lucy Snowe's strange love-hate relationship with Catholicism that is presented as having to be justified.

Otherness is the essentializing of place, effected when we say that all the people in place X are alike in a way that we cannot explain otherwise than through ascribing this quality to geography. Just one person in this place who is different would rupture the relation of inter-cultural Otherness. In fact, this is precisely what happens in *Villette*, which is the source of its ultimate shortcomings as a novel. Otherness is first set up, then ruptured. Of course, to the extent that a reader sees the fundamental similiarity of the English and the Continental worlds (monarchical both, industrialized, bourgeois, and sentimental) and thereby rejects the evocation of inter-cultural Otherness, he or she may see Lucy Snowe as a structural misfit, the necessary outsider, because a woman and without money, in a society ruled by men with cash and capital.

A work evokes several such inside-outside distinctions. Lucy, like all of us, is at the same time a member of many groups: in her case women, schoolteachers, foreigners, Britishers, and sensitive souls, among other groups. At the same time, the work puts these groups in a certain order, making some more important than others. For example, the distinction between schoolteachers and non-schoolteachers is of minimal importance in this world compared to that between Protestants and Catholics. Of course, this ordering may diverge from that usually found in the world.

In a unified work only one such hierarchy is established; this is what we expect from something that presents itself as a single work. If it does not happen, we feel that the boundaries of the piece have been badly drawn and that we are dealing with two or more potential works, not one. Works, we may say, situate themselves with respect to life through their delineation of inside and outside. In life, the distinction of inside and outside this implies does not change, or at least not without a reason. If it does change with no reason, we have cause for criticizing that work on purely formal grounds. This is the germ of a separation of a formal criterion from the discussion of group relevance for which I argued above.

Villette does contain just such an unjustified alteration, just such a structural fault. The consideration of this fault shows us the relation between the inside and outside established in literature and what governs our lives. Numerous commentators concur in seeing such an alteration between the first two volumes of the book and the third, between the narrator's infatuation with Dr. John and her love for M. Paul. For only the first relation is based upon the distinction of inside and outside touched upon here. Dr. John is the ideal of an

English gentleman, with an idealized Anglo-Saxon physiog-
nomy—who, moreover, saves Lucy from two Labassecourien
mashers on her arrival in town. Similarly, M. Paul's impene-
trable shifts of mood are chalked up to his being a foreigner,
and one with Spanish blood at that—merely part of the
strange furnishings of this strange world that, collectively,
establish its Otherness.

Yet by the end of the book the hero is deeply in love with
this other man—a foreigner, a Latin, and a Catholic. She sees
his cruelty as only impatience with stupidity and his religious
creed as excusable if not acceptable. In order to make this
comprehensible, she must explain by relating outside to inside
(like the coffee grounds). In doing so she alters the inside to
which she is relating; the inter-cultural Other is made to
disappear before our eyes. Instead of our seeing as absolute
the divisions between England and things English on the one
hand and the Continent and things Continental on the other,
we learn that things must be seen from a more personal point
of view. Some individual non-English Catholics may in fact be
acceptable.

Of course, such alterations may take place in reality, and
could be made believable in the book. Inter-cultural Otherness can disappear in the world, as most of what Hemingway
relied upon has disappeared. For example, such an alteration
could be made believable if the story were told concurrent
with the events, say, as a diary, or by an invisible narrator.
The problem with the book as it now stands is that the Lucy
Snowe who writes has, even by the first page of the book, lived
through both relationships, and so her conception of
geographical Otherness that dominates the first two-thirds of
the book should have been ruptured.

Yet she narrates the first part as if the second part has had
no power to diminish, alter, or place into perspective the first.
Thus the reader concludes that it does not, and the first point
of view retains its strength. In a sense, Lucy Snowe remem-
bers too well her initial perception of Otherness; the reasons
behind her first relationship have not ceased to be valid by the
time she gets to the second. The question initially is not of two
kinds of love, or of two men—at least, not as it is initially

posed. Instead, the point of view governing the first relationship is so convincingly established as that of an Englishwoman in a strange world infatuated with the beauty and the very Englishness of a compatriot, the split between the inner world of the hero and the outer one so absolute, that we cannot later reconcile with this Lucy's subsequent acceptance of any other man at all, much less one with the qualities of M. Paul.

The final effect on the reader of being asked to consider this abrupt switch may therefore be to make him or her muse on the unpredictability of the human heart. If this is our ultimate reaction—which is to say a reconciliation at a meta-level of these two distinct configurations of the line between inside and outside—we buy it at the price of rejecting Lucy Snowe's assessment of the weight and meaning of her initial infatuation, based as it was largely on her alienated position among the Other. This makes the lengthy analyses of the first relation excessive, a mis-location of the line betweeen inside and outside, like explaining coffee grounds to someone who knows perfectly well what coffee grounds are used for. Knowing at the end of the book that the Otherness evoked at the beginning is an illusion, or being shown that it is an illusion, we resent ever having been taken in.

Gender criticism has had probing things to say about faults of construction, such as I take this switch to be, in works by women, including this novel. We would do well to consider such arguments, especially as they may challenge my assertion that each work should be based on a single primary distinction between inside and outside. Sandra Gilbert and Susan Gubar, for example, suggest that the novel's technical flaws (which they admit it possesses: "*Villette* is not meticulously crafted") are partly the source of its interest (p. 439, all quotations). They make a distinction between what they call a "literary object" (somehow male) and a "literature of consciousness" (somehow female), and assert that "the very erratic way Lucy tells the story of becoming the author of her own life illustrates how Brontë produces not [a literary object] but [a literature of consciousness]." Their conclusion is that "Brontë rejects not only the confining images conferred on women by patriarchal art, but the implicitly coercive nature of that art."

The argument of these authors is focused on the self-effacing nature of the narrative in its early parts, the way the story seems to be about all the characters but Lucy. Yet if we accept the assumption of the authors that the relation with M. Paul is a more healthy, liberating one than Lucy's infatuation with Dr. John, the position that this switch in affection represents a structural fault will seem at best a tautology and, at worst, the imposition of the criteria of a "patriarchial art" on the "literature of consciousness."

This argument rests on the fascinating but extremely nebulous notion of the French feminists of male or patriarchal form as opposed to content, an argument which has its correlate in the argument about culture, where the impulse is strong on the intra-cultural scene to essentialize differences between groups. Recent writers, including Linda S. Kauffmann, Frank Lentricchia, and most clearly Laura Claridge and Elizabeth Langland, have made the distinction between the products of biological women and "female" writing as well as between those of biological men and "patriarchal" writing. This seems the more productive line of thought, for the disadvantage of asserting essentialized differences is that the realm where communication between these groups is possible is reduced commensurately. What, it has been asked, is the status of the discourse in which this essentialized difference is asserted? Far better, it seems to me, to acknowledge that such distinctions are heuristic to begin with and clear some space in which we may continue to talk.

The more interesting result of Gilbert and Gubar's analysis of the novel is to call in question the assertion that a work adopts a single world-view which can be objectively determined and which allows us to guess at its probable audience. The case could well be made by someone sympathetic to their position that the primary line drawn between inside and outside in this novel is not between countries and their corresponding life-styles, but between male and female; the novel, they might well say, does not evoke geographical Otherness at all.

The assertion that it does evoke Otherness can be justified through a distinction of personal interest and constitutive structure. For though the portrayal of a female sensibility may well be the most interesting facet of this novel for many readers, this is not the same as its being the most fundamentally constitutive. The narrator's complex (female) psyche can only be expressed in the terms it is because of the geographical contrast on which it is based. In fact, I imagine Gilbert and Gubar would agree that the novel as written is aimed not at women, but at male-dominated society. Most of their arguments regarding women's fiction concern its deformation in the attempt to be palatable to this society. The psyche that so interests us comes through the cracks, rather than being directly expressed. Faults remain faults, and interesting is not the same as formally successful—though it is frequently more productive of our own considerations.

Literature only tells people what they do not know, or else there is no point to it, but it does this by relating what they do not know to what they do. It is this relation which is exploited by Brontë to result in geographic Otherness. We may best consider this assertion by developing the implications of what at first glance may seem a minor strangeness: the fact that the narrator begins her journey in England, a real country, both now and in the nineteenth century, whose capital is London ("really" so, then as now), takes a boat—as one must still do to remain on the surface of the earth, rather than over it or under it, and leave Britain—to end up in "Labassecour," a country whose capital city is called "Villette."

For us late in the twentieth century, it is difficult to see any reason short of satire for having one member of the European Community called by its real name and another by an invented one, as if we were not supposed to notice. And we rule out the thought that satire is intended in giving Belgium the name of that part of the farmyard where the geese are kept, or calling Brussels only a minor or small city, for at no time is it suggested to us that the city is boring or provincial or the country ruder than England. If anything, quite the contrary is shown. In *Villette* we have a better example than

Hemingway's works of the construction of an Other that we can no longer see as an Other at all.

Tony Tanner, in his introduction to the Penguin edition of *Villette*, side-steps the question of inter-cultural Otherness by suggesting that in re-naming these so-real places the hero creates her own subjective psychological landscape: "Charlotte Brontë hands over to Lucy Snowe the right to re-name her actual environment" (p. 50). He suggests, in other words, that inter-cultural Otherness is not being evoked. Yet England is not re-named, nor France, nor Germany; the world is the real one we know. The only conceivable explanation for this "fictional" name is that, for the Victorian Englishman or Englishwoman, the Continent was sufficiently general, seen as a large and suspect Other, to make more palatable the use of such "typalizing" names than they are to us—in the way that we might invent and give a fictional name to a south German state of the eighteenth century. For someone who knows exactly what south German states existed, of course, this level of generality seems ridiculous.

In the same vein, we can well imagine a novel about China in 1953, a hundred years after *Villette*, that invented city and province names without a Western audience's ever knowing, or if knowing, being in the least bothered. (The country name of China, however, would be difficult to invent.) This is what we call poetic license, or the freedom of fiction. It makes fiction fiction. The reason why we do not object to a hero named Lucy Snowe is that we do not know the names of all the Britishwomen who lived in the middle nineteenth century, and so cannot say that no one of that name existed. We can accept frankly invented names, such as the characterizing names of seventeenth- and eighteenth-century literature even up to Fielding, and in *Villette* the heroine's name seems, with its hints of primness and coolness, to mirror the personality of the woman who bears it.

Each of us, like Lucy, belongs concurrently to many groups, and the establishment of a hierarchy of groups through a distinction of inside and outside determines the world-view of the work in question. In this work, Englishness-Protestantness is an essentializing quality; skin color is not. In each view there are several prominent and defining features, a large gray area where the drawing becomes schematic, and a vast area that could well be labelled "out there." They all turn out like the celebrated Saul Steinberg cover for the *New Yorker* of "The World from Tenth Avenue," where the other side of the Hudson River is already only "Jersey" and points beyond in Europe are basically blank. And we don't know which world-view is being evoked by a work until we look and see. This is why the question of groups in audience, the subject-matter of the discourse of domestic Otherness so central on the current scene, must be subsequent to the study of artistic works, not definitory of them. The enunciation of the world-view in a work can define the group spoken to, and so cause it to come to be.

The initial world-view necessary for the establishment of an inside is evoked, not reproduced. Enough of its essentials are given that we know what is being talked about. We never, for example, have any description of what Lucy's pedagogic techniques were, or what kind of underclothing she wore. Though these were extant in the "real" world of an English teacher in Brussels in the nineteenth century, the book's leaving these out does not show a rejection of the "real" or an excessive prudery. They may be left out because they do not evoke what is peculiar about the English, Protestant world-view central to the book; they do not distinguish for us inside from outside. It is not with the entirety of the real world that a work of literature is compared—despite claims of theoreticians as diverse as the Naturalists and the Russian Formalists—but with a particular hierarchy of group-membership, which can be evoked perfectly well with limited means. We may feel the lack of specific details, but we never feel the lack of all details.

Yet such a standard state of group-membership can be incorrectly evoked for a particular audience. No one today, for example, can write a novel in which a Western European country is innocently typalized in this fashion. For this to be possible the country must be lost in the mists of time or imprecise geography, in a way that Belgium is not for us. In a contemporary American novel about New York, Fashion Avenue cannot be located between 2nd and 3rd Avenues, unless there is some joke, or the New York of the story is not "our" New York, or the audience possesses little contact with America. The city at the top of the Chesapeake Bay is not Cleveland, and cats do not have stomachs like cows. If the work in question is correct about Akron and Buffalo but incorrect about Baltimore, if it correctly describes dogs and squirrels but shows ignorance on the subject of cows, we justifiably conclude that these features are simply wrong. This assertion makes clearest my divergence from Nelson Goodman's notion, in his *Ways of Worldmaking*, of discrete worlds in art.

If we have a novel about the queen of England who ruled most of the nineteenth century, in other words, she must be named Victoria, or the book is a satire understood with constant reference to something else, or else this England is not the England we know and the world portrayed in some fundamental way is not our world. (Kafka's *Amerika* includes an "Oklahoma" that is by no means our own—but its unreality is consistent with the rest of the work, and we accept it as an invented realm.) These options hinge on the establishment of a set of givens, an appeal to an inside familiar to the audience. This in turn delineates an outside, the realm in which things may be invented. In relating these two in new ways, literature creates groups, at least for the duration of its consumption.

In some works, as a result, features like these would not be an error. Indeed, they may not be so for some audiences of this work. We are not, as the hermeneutic theorists are sometimes taken to suggest, helplessly caught within our own perspective; we can be conscious of the perspective of others. This is the reason we do not call the re-naming of Belgium in *Villette* a "mistake"; instead, it is an understandable, historically-determined establishment of "out there." Yet we arrive at such conclusions based on real knowledge of the real world. There is no point in gratuitously inventing such other audiences in thought—the postulated audience, for example, that lives in a world where the dogs and squirrels are like ours, but not the cows. We come to know about such other situations, and we can say, if only in as tentative a fashion as any other assertion, whether they exist or not. And one possible conclusion is that the work in question is simply wrong.

By this point we are well into the discussion of the questions of truth and verisimilitude in literature whose consideration stretches from Aristotle to John Searle. Sidney, drawing on Aristotle's claim that literature referred to the possible rather than the actual, defended poetry against the charge of lying by saying that it didn't assert anything. Modern speech-act theory has played a variation on this, trying to figure out just what made an assertion in a play different from the "same" assertion on the street. And, in *Languages of Art*, Goodman has tried to preserve the honor of literature against the encroaching power of science by saying that literature provides another kind of information. The more interesting theories in this vein offer answers somewhere between the extremes the questions of whether literature is true in the way other things are, and whether it is an objective entity in the world. Neo-classical theories are endlessly interesting, for example, in their attempt to refine Aristotle's notion that literature offered the typical or ideal reality in contrast to the quotidian.

My position is that we can reasonably say of certain aspects of a given work of literature that they are true or false. Of course, nothing guarantees that we will not subsequently change our ascription of truth or falsity, any more than we have such guarantees when we make a similar assertion in the world. We do the best we can at a given point. There will, however, also be things in works of which it will not make sense to say that they are true or false; this is the category of possibles—which is to say, things which fall in the realm of "outside."

"London" is a correct name for the capital of Great Britain and "Lucy Snowe" is a possible name for the hero. And were we not able to explain it through differences of time and geography, "Villette" would be an incorrect name for the capital of the (partly) Francophone country that is not France yet separated from England by water. Thus, Aristotle's claim that poetry is more philosophical than history means that, having evoked a world-view whose only givens are types of personalities or actions, or specific actions of proper-name historical persons, the poet is free to fill in the undefined areas of those views. A Shakespeare, for example, can fill in what Brutus said to Cassius because the exact words are unknown to us. Caesar's last words to Brutus, on the other hand, have been preserved and are a given. We may go further and say that Shakespeare must fill in what Brutus said to Cassius, for this is the blur left to him to exploit. The particular world-view evoked determines the extent to which this filling-in can be done in any one case, not some abstract quality of "poetry."

Our world-view need not be identical to that adopted by the work; indeed, we are most able to identify that world-view when it is not ours. This means that arguments may erupt over whether what is found to be false for one reader is not, after all, possible for another, not with what is taken to be true.   One way of identifying this world-view is through placing it in space and time in a position alien to ours. Yet we can only do this if we (1) have a reason to do this, a perception of the work as strange to us, and (2) knowledge of the real world which suggests this is appropriate. We do the best we can with the knowledge of the world we have. Yet there is no reason to assume that our knowledge of the world is always deficient; if it were always so we should be similarly reticent about judging a similar statement in the world outside.

We could in each case save the text by postulating an audience or a world in which this was not so, let us say by postulating a possible world in which the Queen who ruled "England" for much of the "nineteenth century" was not named "Victoria." But what is the point of this? Literature is not written for Martians; it is part of an actual world. The distinctions of time and place that we may make as caveats to any statement are distinctions within the real world. As an alternative, we could suggest written forms in which such a variation would be justified. But this is beside the point: is it justified here? At this point we may begin to speak of error.

Few Americans, to take another example, would accept even as sophisticated fantasy a contemporary biography of John F. Kennedy—that is, a work based on enough correct details for us to assume that it was trying to have all its details be correct—that had him dying in his bed. If enough other things in the work were "incorrect" in this fashion we would cease to call them incorrect, and instead we would speak of having a different world-view and hence a different delineation of inside and outside. Indeed, in a few centuries, or even now in Tibet, this one detail may well be lost in the blur; under these circumstances such details may fall into the gray area in which a writer is free to "invent." Poetry, or literature in general, is not inherently probable or possible in a way that the world outside is not. Some of it is capable of being pronounced right or wrong, based, as all such pronouncements, on our knowledge of the world, while some of it merely takes advantage of the blur in the conception it evokes.

The problem of interpretation or subsequent readings is a manifestation of the fact that a work of literature presupposes a line between inside and outside. If we do not accept this line, the work seems wrong, dated, too particular, wordy, or trivial — and these, if not explained by one of our means for expressing essential difference (always a possibility), can be a judgment of literary quality, just as our opinion that someone is a bore, a windbag, and self-contradictory (if unmitigated by circumstances or consciousness of our subjective situation) can be a judgment about the person himself or herself. The passage of time does not, in and of itself, produce divergent reations of this nature, nor does contemporaneity assure their absence. Nor need variations of geography, or class, or education produce such variant readings. It is not, for example, because we are of "another age" that we have problems with Dante's notion of inside and outside, but instead because we have such problems that we conclude that we are of "another age," which means, we do not accept the work's premises. We can only say by looking what groups we belong to in our own world (intra-cultural Otherness) or what constitutes our world (inter-cultural Otherness).

The bone of contention between readers regarding this matter can be articulated as the distinction between the true-false category and the "possible" category. The line is between inside and outside, with some readers (or groups) wanting to call some things false while others insist that they are possible. This need not be so between any two groups we may identify.

Even when differences of this sort arise, we can always attempt to explain how these different reactions are arrived at; we are not caught in our hermeneutic prisons of groups. The very existence of groups allows us to mitigate between them, through an articulation of their presuppositions. The achievement of unanimity is not possible with literature, but only a relating of the variations through explanation.

This in turn raises Eliot's "problem of belief," and the question of reading "as": reading as literature, or as content. Let us say that a reader of *Villette* in the 1990s, a non-Englishman or Englishwoman and a non-Protestant, does not accept the point of view taken as inside. The problem of belief arises to the extent that we see a paradox in the fact that we can get anything from the work at all. Yet for such a reader, to whom distinctions between England and the Continent, Protestantism and Catholicism are minor, the division must be all the stronger between this one individual woman and all society or, for a Marxist reader, all industrial society. Thus, the novel is read in a way that would have been unacceptable to that world which the novel takes as inside. Yet it is not a paradox to acknowledge that this is possible. This reading of the novel, which may lead to different drawings of the line between the realm of the true-false and that of the possible, would have been unacceptable because the boundaries determining inter-cultural Otherness have shifted, or are seen as mutable. Precisely this is what we can become aware of. The clearer the initial distinction of inside and outside in the work, the greater the certainty that those who accept other distinctions will produce their distinct views of the work.

Grasping this situation from the wrong end leads to the assertion, so common in the discourse of intra-cultural Otherness, that we can only read works that directly speak to our group. The fact is that we don't know what works will do this until we try them and see. Only by noting differences in actions (or reactions) do we arrive at the definition of groups at all. Perhaps someone as close as next door is of a different group, as someone far away may be of the same; we don't know until some particular set of circumstances, such as a reaction to a work of literature, establishes or questions this difference.

New information is transmitted in the blurred area of the particular world-view, where literature can begin to change the world. For the English, *Villette* provided information about the Continent; for the social world it gave information about the inner life of an outwardly unprepossessing woman. This last perspective almost falls outside the gray area of the world-view on which the book is based, and into the much larger, totally uncharted one. I do not know if we can say that the extraordinary world of Lucy Snowe's psyche is even probable for the world of the patriotic English subject dedicated to Queen and Country; her psyche seems instead to be that part of the world overlooked by such an intensely social group definition.

The information in the book is neither true nor probable, given the initial world-view; it merely is, as when a friend tells us of far-off lands. We may believe him or her because that person is our friend, but otherwise we simply register the information as told to us. Any individual is unknown territory to the intensely nation- and religion-defined world-view at the center of this book. Only a single individual, moreover, can be so developed in the book, and this may be why Dr. John remains so flat a character. Even two such developed individuals within the same social world-view would destroy the primarily social nature of this view, by showing us that contrasts between individuals can exist as well as between the individual and society.

The most fruitful question to pose at the beginning of the consideration of a novel or work of literature is: What is supposed to be interesting in this work? For this separates the "outside." Then the next question is: For whom is it supposed to be interesting? or more fundamentally: For what point of view? This gives us the "inside." In answering these questions we bring into play whatever knowledge we have of the world, of history, perhaps of people in general. If we wish, from these questions—imperfectly answered though they may be—we can derive subsequent questions: What most interests me here? What is the point of view this implies? Can this point of view ever be that of a group in the world that understands itself as such? By encouraging this query the potential of literature to change the world, in which it nonetheless must follow the rules, is manifested.

Chapter Five

Brothers under the Skin:
Achebe on *Darkness*

If a consideration of Hemingway shows us some of the disadvantages of the construction of inter-cultural Otherness (we can never actually attain it), and a consideration of *Villette* shows the shifting nature of the relation between ourselves and Others, in turning to Chinua Achebe's now-famous lecture-essay on Conrad's *Heart of Darkness*, entitled "An Image of Africa," we can see the disadvantages of Otherness from the point of view of the Other and see these disadvantages as inherent in the construction of Otherness. For at the same time as we acknowledge the justice of some of Achebe's particular charges, we may use his reaction as exemplary of something larger than he intended, drawing more general conclusions regarding Otherness than those at which he was aiming. Otherness is neither so easily avoided nor disposed of as Achebe imagines.

Achebe's most pointed charge in his passionate and witty lecture-essay, delivered first as a Chancellor's Lecture at the University of Massachusetts and subsequently printed in the *Massachusetts Review*, was that the Conrad of this novella, despite his liberal veneer, was nothing more or less than a "bloody racist": obsessed with blackness, denying speech to people whose undeniable likeness to himself he could only find "ugly," and convinced that the inhabitants of Africa were what he called "rudimentary souls."

Achebe's charges of racism against Conrad are, I believe, well founded. Yet the very fact of their truth leads us to an alternative point of view on this debate. Achebe suggests that Conrad is racist not just because of the specific content of his portrayal, but because of its general nature. Conrad uses another people as a means to an end rather than, as we might say in Kantian terms, an end in themselves. In the terms adopted here, we would say that an inter-cultural Other is evoked, only to be used as a definer of the primary group of reference. The way this works out in Conrad, according to Achebe, is through the denial of common "humanity" to the Africans, and through an essentializing of place. Conrad's Africa is bereft of individuals and is evoked only as a monolithic, undifferentiated whole.

Yet this essentializing of place is the very nature of the construction of inter-cultural Otherness. It is indulged in not only by Conrad but, as it happens, Achebe too, as for example in his most widely-read novel, *Things Fall Apart*. Indeed, countless novelists utilize these methods of definition of one group through unequal reference to another which result in an essentializing of place. Though Achebe, therefore, is justified in attacking the uses to which these techniques are put in Conrad, he goes too far in implying that they can be simply eliminated. The problem is that inter-cultural Otherness can have either of two valences. Achebe is objecting to the negative charge of a specific example, yet he does so by way of attacking the general phenomenon. Through this attack, however, we can consolidate our understanding of how inter-cultural Otherness is constructed.

This is a substantially new way of viewing Achebe's essay. It stands apart from those of the stream of commentators who have written to defend Conrad against Achebe's charge of racism, such as Cedric Watts, or—in the most interesting case, that of Patrick Brantlinger—both to defend him from and convict him of it. It also takes a different tack from a recent article by Mark Kinkead-Weeks, which gives an interesting twist to the defense of Conrad against charges of racism. As other commentators have done, Kinkead-Weeks distinguishes between Conrad and Marlow, arguing that the entire narration by Marlow is comparable to the obsessive narration of Coleridge's Ancient Mariner, the attempt to expiate his own lie to the Intended through which he begins to be as corrupt as the Kurtz whose story now obsesses him. Nonetheless Kinkead-Weeks's argument, dependent as it is on a modern understanding of colonialism (Naipaul and Ngugi are discussed as well), is less than convincing as an understanding of the Victorian Conrad.

At any rate, Achebe spends most of his essay substantiating, by references to Conrad, the two points noted above, which turn out to be one: that the people of Africa are portrayed as fundamentally different than the Europeans, and that this is most clearly seen through the fact that Conrad denies them normal speech. This echoes my analyses of *For Whom the Bell Tolls* and *Villette*, where we saw that Otherness was established in the Hemingway precisely through the denial to the Other characters of "normal" speech, while the explanations of *Villette* have as their effect the "making strange," by acknowledging the necessity of making familiar, of all of the non-English characters.

One of Achebe's prime exhibits in pursuit of his argument is Conrad's contrasting portrayal of the two women of the novella, Kurtz's mistress in the Congo and his Intended back in England. The first, Achebe reminds us, quoting Conrad, was

> wild-eyed and magnificent . . . . She stood looking at us without a stir and like the wilderness itself, with an air of brooding over an inscrutable purpose. (Achebe, "Image," p. 785)

This woman may strike the reader today as considerably more interesting and powerful than the second, that self-deceiving flower of a European emotional hothouse, who has always seemed to me like a figure on a droopy Victorian gravestone, or a figure from an Edward Gorey cartoon:

> She came forward, all in black with a pale head, floating towards [Marlow] in the dark. . . . She took both [Marlow's] hands in hers and murmured, "I heard you were coming." . . . She had a mature capacity for fidelity, for belief, for suffering. ("Image," p. 785)

Achebe, for once missing a nuance, sees no impatience in Marlow-Conrad's description of this woman, no suggestion that the entire civilization which she represents is being faulted for being too fragile to accept the truth.

What bothers Achebe the most about the two portrayals he contrasts here is that the African woman never speaks. This is what he calls Conrad's "bestowal of human expression to the one and the withholding of it from the other." For, as he explains, "it is clearly not part of Conrad's purpose to confer language on the 'rudimentary souls' of Africa" (p. 786). The years that have elapsed since Achebe delivered this lecture have made common currency the vocabulary for expressing this point in technical terms: Conrad denies Africans the phallic Word, denies them subjectivity (in the sense of being a subject) and hence condemns them to a state of silence.

Achebe acknowledges that this silence is not absolute; the Africans do on occasion speak. Yet the only times Conrad allows them speech he makes sure that they express themselves in a caricature of English even worse than the pidgin of Hemingway, as when one of the men on Marlow's boat, who are cannibals, suggests that the captain procure them food in the form of a prisoner.

> "Catch 'im,' he snapped, with a bloodshot widening of his eyes and a flash of sharp white teeth—"catch 'im. Give 'im to us." "To you, eh?" I asked; "what would you do with them?" "Eat 'im!" he said curtly . . . . ("Image," p. 786)

And Achebe quotes at this point what he calls Conrad's "famous announcement" to the effect that "Mistah Kurtz—he dead."

This quotation of Conrad's "famous announcement" must have been one of the most unforgettable moments of the entire speech. An eminent man of letters delivering the Chancellor's Lecture at the University of Massachusetts, a multi-lingual internationalist whose most well-known works describe and explain the life of one people to another: how witty the audience must have found this pidgin English on Achebe's lips. The irony of the situation is thick, and Conrad cannot, and should not, come off untarred by it. For the unspoken example of Achebe himself on the podium that day certainly provided the strongest reason for condemning

Conrad's denial of speech to the Africans of his novella and made this pidgin English in his mouth seem embarrassing.

Yet Achebe's use of this quotation as a dramatic high point of his lecture helps us see why Conrad *would* seem so exasperating to someone like him. For once we accept, as Conrad did not, that Africans can be comprehensible to Europeans and Americans, even to the point of explaining their own culture to these outsiders, we too find Conrad's refusal to provide the characters in his novella with this capacity infuriating. The lack of articulate speech for the Africans—which is to say, speech articulate to the Europeans—is clearly what upsets Achebe. For *Heart of Darkness*, this means the absence of an African character as articulate in the European tongue as Achebe himself. *Darkness* lacks, for Achebe, what he calls an expression of "the human factor" in the Africans.

In Achebe's response to Conrad we see the effects of an alteration on the configuration of the world to which the inside-outside distinction of the work is meant to appeal, and a difference in geographical perspective. Achebe finds unjustified the division between inside and outside that Conrad establishes partly because he comes from the place considered "outside," and partly because time has passed so that this division is no longer as absolute even for the "inside" group as it once was.

In doing this, Achebe is offering a parallel, in his reaction to Conrad, of our own reactions to the Other world of Belgium in *Villette*, and to the melodramatically exotic worlds of Hemingway—namely that they aren't so Other. Achebe is the Other talking, or as we now say, writing, back, and so denying its Otherness. But he enters our discourse in just the same way that we take account of the dancers at the Los Angeles Festival: all are enough like us to communicate with us—they have learned our language, and know what a microphone is; they hold our attention, play our game sufficiently by the rules to be understandable. This is always the way communication takes place. The response must presuppose the two groups, as well as the possibility of mediating between them. In responding to Conrad, by "writing back," Achebe is necessarily

playing the same game as the person to whom he is responding. And this is so by logical necessity.

A bit later on in his lecture Achebe quotes a Scottish student
who assured him that Africa was "merely a setting for the
disintegration of the mind of Mr. Kurtz," as if giving the
reason why Conrad did not have to portray the Africans as
"human" (p. 788). Achebe finds fault not with the observation
itself, but with the fact that the Scotsman intended it to excuse
Conrad.   For Achebe this is precisely what is wrong with
Conrad's treatment of Africa.   Conrad uses "Africa as setting
and backdrop which eliminates the African as human factor";
he treats Africa "as a metaphysical battlefield devoid of all
recognizable humanity."   The larger effect of Conrad's denial
of speech to the non-Europeans is "the dehumanization of
Africa and Africans," made possible by a "preposterous and
perverse kind of arrogance" which reduces Africa "to the role
of props for the breakup of one petty European mind" (p.
788).

As Achebe points out, a perusal of other reports on Africa
contemporary with Conrad's work would lead us to the
conclusion that the Africans of the time "must have had other
occupations besides merging into the evil forest or materializ-
ing out of it simply to plague Marlow and his dispirited band"
(p. 79l). As an example of such other activities he gives the
mask-making capability of the Fang, a people whose art — not
coincidentally, for Achebe's argument — was seminal in influ-
encing the course of Western painting in its march toward
Cubism. We should consider this example in detail, for in it
we find a paradigm of the way Achebe thinks one people can
be made comprehensible to another, avoiding Conrad's fault
of making one only a backdrop to another. Yet this alternative to Conrad turns out to have its own set of problems.

The Fang, Achebe says, are "without a doubt among the
world's greatest masters of the sculptured form" (p. 79l). This
is something Westerners can understand.   However, this
understanding is the effect of the precise words Achebe
chooses to describe them, words which express a quality at just
the right level of generality to be comprehensible to Westerners. "The sculptured form": this is applicable even to Western

creations of marble and bronze. The result is that we see the "common humanity" of the Fang and Western sculptors.

Had Achebe instead referred to the same products by saying that the Fang make wooden masks whose content is determined by the particular ceremonies of which they are intended as a part, that the life of these masks is not intended to be long, and that by and large the object itself is discarded when its ceremonial use is exhausted, he would have had a considerably more complex situation on his hands. Are these objects in fact the equivalent of Rodin? the audience would have asked. I do not say, the equal of, for the question is a Pandora's box, and perhaps uninteresting as well. At any rate, current thought on the matter suggests, in contrast to Achebe's 1970s formulation, that enough differences exist between the functional, directed integration of carved objects into African societies, and our notion of the art object as something which is supposed to inspire only disinterested contemplation, that Achebe's own quoting of Frank Willett's bombastic phrase concerning the "world's greatest masters" is disingenuous at best and at worst, hopelessly accepting of the primacy of Western standards (p. 791).

In other words, the language in which Achebe expresses his example of the Fang shows that the example is something-to-be-seen-by-Europeans. The very choice of his words is determined by the necessity to subsume individual variations under a generic commonality, a necessity because these words are used for rhetorical, communicative, purposes. The choice of words establishes or destroys equivalences between facts, through the level of generality at which they settle. After all, no two things are really alike, and we can only see them as such if we subsume both under a larger concept that contains them both. Western guns and chemicals on one hand and spears and sacrifices on the other: it is a *choice* on the part of the person who articulates these to subsume both under the rubric of "war" rather than insisting on the differences between them.

Such creation of equivalences between one people and another through words is at the heart of Achebe's own most widely-read novel, *Things Fall Apart*. Achebe presupposes as a contrast-definer a European point of view to which the doings of the Ibo people must be explained. This necessitates the very language of his book which emphasizes the "common humanity" of these two groups through the appeal to the generic over the specific; the Europeans in *Things Fall Apart* are no less backdrop to it than are the Africans in *Heart of Darkness*. In saying this I am not re-invoking the charges that have been habitually leveled at Achebe to the effect that he was unable to make "believeable" European characters; perhaps this is true, but if so it is only a symptom of the larger, more important issue.

The method by which the doings of the Ibo are "explained" to this presupposed external point of view is the same as that which Achebe used in his example of the Fang masks. Language establishes equivalences between what the Ibo do and what the Europeans do by settling on the level of what, in English, is the common genre. Achebe assures us that the Fang are "masters of the sculptured form" because this phrase can be applied to Rodin as well. If the Ibo "wrestle," so do Europeans, and this is therefore comprehensible without further explanation—so too if they "go to war," for so do Europeans, when they "prepare food," or when they "die."

Now, it may seem the very basis of enlightened common sense to take for granted equivalences like this. All people, we might say, cook, and die, and exercise their bodies—and something like this is suggested by Achebe's reference to the "human race." But my point is that this is the perception of an equivalence that must be created on the page by language. Earlier, less "enlightened" writers did not see the equivalance as primary, and so did not use these words. Instead, for them, Africans rolled around naked on the ground instead of wrestling, slit each others' throats over trifles instead of going to war, and, instead of preparing food, cooked up a revolting mess of leaves and roots.

Such formulations as these will of course strike us as insulting. The point can be made more palatably by returning to the example of the Fang masks and asking whether in fact all people can be said to "make art," that is, make art in the Western sense. Perhaps African masks are not "art" at all, but some other kind of object. And why should they not be? It is pride which leads Africanists to insist that African objects are art. For Westerners, this is an honorific label, and it seems akin to racism to deny it to other people's objects while assigning it to our own. Yet even if we are unwilling to deny this formulation to the Ibo, we may be willing to say that, in throwing away twins, the Ibo did not practice religion, but merely inhumanity—even *Things Fall Apart* suggests as much. A yet stronger example is the so-called female circumcision, that is, clitoridectomy, still, in both Black and White Africa; for it may be that even the most value-relativistic observer will be unwilling to accept the local description of this as initiation rite and find it, instead, sexist barbarism.

Things Fall Apart is comprehensible only if we understand it as the conscious attempt to transcend differences of specifics by an appeal to a level of abstraction accessible to the European point of view. Virtually every page contains examples of such an appeal to the generic; we may list some of them from the book's opening passages. The first sentences give the first example:

> Okonkwo was well known throughout the nine villages and even beyond. His fame rested on solid personal achievements. As a young man of eighteen he had brought honour to his village by throwing Amalinze the Cat. (p. 3)

We are told first that his fame is the result of solid personal achievements, a notion familiar to a European. We are prepared therefore to accept that a wrestling match may, for this people, provide evidence of such achievement, though this is likely to be a more dubious notion for Europeans.

> It was this man [Achebe continues] that Okonkwo threw in a fight which the old men agreed was one of the fiercest since the founder of their town engaged a spirit of the wild for seven days and seven nights. (p. 3)

Fights with spirits are therefore like wrestling, something itself known to Europeans; we know this because of Achebe's use of the word "fierce" to describe them both.

The next example comes as soon as the following paragraph: "Unoka [Okonkwo's father], was, of course, a debtor,
and he owed every neighbour some money, from a few cowries
to quite substantial amounts" (p. 4). Achebe does his work
skillfully here: he gives us first the generic comprehensible to
Europeans—the "money" that Unoka owes—so that the subsequent divergent specific, the fact that this money is a substance
which seems inherently worthless to Westerners, becomes
secondary. Achebe, that is, uses words which suggest to us that
what these people do is generically the same as what we do,
even if it is different in particular form.

Once he has established generic similarity, however, he is
free to acknowledge, even celebrate the specific divergence
through a non-essential, decorative description of those
specific differences. Just such descriptions of non-essential
difference provide the bulk of *Things Fall Apart*. Chapter Six,
devoted to the wrestling match, is an obvious example of an
extended description of non-essential difference. For, once
having established that this is comparable to the athletic activities of other societies which have "wrestling matches," Achebe
is free to paint in the particulars of individual variation.

For an Ibo the lengthy descriptions of their customs would
be pointless, for they would know them already. So too with
the implied explanations of actions by putting them into
equivalence relations with Western actions. Translated back
into Ibo, this book would only have interest as a book translated from the English.

Richard Cronin makes something of the same point as this
last one, in *Imagining India*, in the context of contrasting
Salman Rushdie's *Midnight's Children* with Balraj Khanna's
Nation of Fools. Rushdie's book, Cronin suggests, "must be
written in English." His reason is that "only in a foreign
language . . . can India appear whole." *Nation of Fools*, by
contrast, being what Cronin calls an "Indian novel of India,"
"is written in English only by chance," and "it is only possible
to write it in English at all if, somehow, English . . . can be
transformed . . . into a vernacular" (p. 23). Using this distinction, we may say that *Things Fall Apart* is a book that must be
written in English rather than one that is written so by chance,

even if the reasons this is so are different from those Cronin gives for his example.

Things Fall Apart takes Europe and things European as no less of a backdrop than *Heart of Darkness* takes Africa and things Africans, and is therefore "guilty" of using precisely those techniques for which Achebe condemns Conrad in his lecture. The only difference between the works is in the valence of the inter-cultural Otherness that is constructed, not in the nature of that construction. Achebe's work, of course, is a written novel — which is to say, a Western form on both counts. More fundamentally, however, both books presuppose an Other in relation to which the people with whom they are primarily concerned are defined. This is what I mean by suggesting that Conrad and Achebe are in fact brothers under the skin. The specifics of the relation between two peoples in their works are different, but generically they are the same.

Of course, this may seem a peculiarly cold point of view to adopt with respect to these books. The differences of specifics may in fact not be something we will wish to transcend through this appeal to their generic similarities. After all, Achebe's intentions seem to be to allow one group to understand the other; Conrad's intentions are much more limited and perhaps more selfish. Achebe looks at the group he takes as primary from the point of view of the other; Conrad is capable of no such dislocation, and looks at the other from the point of view of his own group.

Yet we can say without paradox that of the two, it is Achebe's work which presupposes the Other to a greater extent. The very evocation of the world he presents depends on its constructed likeness to this Other, whereas Kurtz and his fascination with what he takes to be Africa and its lessons are the exception for his people rather than the rule. Without Marlow *Heart of Darkness* would not have much of a plot, but without the presupposition of the European point of view that would find interesting this evocation of a lost life in *Things Fall Apart*, there is nothing at all. This is true even if it is contemporary Nigerians who are, to this extent, adopting such a Europeanized point of view. Achebe is turning the Ibo into an Other the way an anthropologist would do so, by assuming that their customs and doings are of themselves worthy of comment. In *Things Fall Apart* a whole world is evoked, and evoked for someone who does not "understand" it, even if those who do not understand it are urbanized, Anglophone Nigerians.

The case of *Things Fall Apart*, in fact, allows a few generalizations regarding the nature of literature that "writes back." Cronin's point is once again relevant: there exist novels necessarily written in the language of the outside group, while other novels are so by chance, and make this the language of the group inside. I extend this distinction to form, including that of the novel. The mere fact of a work being in a form originally foreign to the country of origin of its author does not mean that the work is condemned to aim, as *Things* does, at that outside society. A work can possess qualities in common with works of an outside group without being co-opted by or aimed at this group, as the use of American English is not, or at least is no longer, an act of speaking or writing back to Britain. Conversely the use, say, of a non-European language does not ensure that the work is aimed elsewhere than at the world outside. It is only because Ngugi is now famous that he can afford to write in Gikuyu, itself the language of the dominant people in Kenya, knowing that he will be immediately translated into English.

Contrary to what many pugnacious theorists suggest, writing back is not the most effective escape from colonial hegemony. Instead, the most effective escape is individual selective appropriation of aspects of the Western matrix, making the outside part of the inside. The problem with what seems the direct mode of attack of writing back is that such writing must, in order to make itself comprehensible to the world at which it is aimed, define itself with respect to that world. Writing back presupposes an Other to just as great a degree as the worst kind of colonialist, racist clap-trap, and it does the Other point of view the honor of considering it worthy of refutation.

The works that escape conception in terms of Otherness, by contrast, are those that instead of attacking, refuting, or questioning the presuppositions of the world that for them is outside, merely go about their business of chronicling individual sensibilities, even if these individuals are determined by qualities of the group. I believe that Achebe's *Anthills of the Savanna* is just such a book. As in *Nation of Fools* which, for Cronin, treats English as a local dialect, things taken from the outside — such as language — are simply appropriated. Or they are not; in either case this relation is not the issue. It is always the individual that breaks the mold of Otherness.

Yet even if literature effects the more thorough act of deconstruction on Otherness, appropriation, it cannot escape being defined by the intersection of the point of view it takes as inside and what it takes as outside. The fact that a work of literature may begin to create such groups is the source of literature's potential not only to mirror the world, but to change it. Every work must make its obeisance to the world, but what it says after that is up for grabs. It enunciates something unseen and unknown — which is to say, unknown by someone. At the very least this unknown thing is the artwork itself, which the artist had to make.

All of this is not intended to accuse Achebe of somehow having sold out to the Westerners, either by becoming the so-eloquent "child of two worlds" he is, to use a phrase of the East African writer Mugu Gatheru, or by writing novels that put one civilization in the terms of another. My point is ultimately more abstract than this. The construction of inter-cultural Otherness is merely one possibility for literature, though it is a thoroughly logical one implicit in the nature of art, a particular use of the fundamental distinction all works must make between inside and outside. Because this construction of inter-cultural Otherness is only one possibility on a variegated scale, all novelists, and perhaps all artists, are brothers and sisters under the skin. After all, literature necessarily delineates a group from others, a group it takes as "inside."

Because of this close similarity between the techniques employed by both Achebe and Conrad, the larger claims made in Achebe's essay are less justified than the attack on the specific case of Conrad and the Africans. When Achebe widens his sight from a consideration of Conrad, he advances the claim that essentializing of place in literature can never be anything but an attempt "to set people against people" (p. 789). He even goes so far as to make the comparison between Conrad and Nazis or slave traders. Yet let us think of the way the American South is essentialized as steeped in nostalgia and the past by many Southern writers, or frigid, twisted New England by Edith Wharton's *Ethan Frome,* or the verdant California evoked for the sake of bitter contrast in *The Grapes of Wrath.* All of these give the sense of coherence of one place by implicit contrast with another: the North, let us say, or more temperate climes, or Oklahoma. The novels of Walker Percy essentialize the South as well, through more explicit contrast with another place. Percy's heroes are forced to artic- ulate the South rather than merely living as Southerners. All of the so-numerous works of fiction which evoke place as an entity in itself essentialize and so, in Achebe's sense, they dehumanize the implied Other which is necessary to the construction of a sense of this element of place.

To be sure, Conrad's denial of English speech to Africans will seem ludicrous to an African who has such speech, espe- cially one like Achebe who has shown, in *Things Fall Apart,* how a novel can give such speech to Africans without thereby becoming improbable; the secret is simply to translate it with- out comment into a language that the group of reference understands, rather than demanding that the characters them- selves "really" speak this language. Yet no one from what is now Nigeria would, at the time Conrad wrote his novella, have been capable of doing this, and only few people today of any country enjoy the literary prestige of an Achebe that makes everyone pay attention to his utterances or gives him the possibility of speaking ironically with some hope of making an effect.

I suggest, in fact, that it makes no sense to castigate Conrad for establishing the particular inside-outside distinction he does. It may even have been perfectly appropriate for his world. Our world, however, is different, and we may say that it is inappropriate for us, while still acknowledging that it may have been appropriate for Conrad. It is the illusion that liter- ature exists in a timeless realm apart from the real world — the notion that it is not true or false in the way other utterances are—that leads to the feeling that we should be able to go back and re-write the works we don't agree with.   The more productive means of dealing with our disagreement would, however, be to distinguish our world-view from their world-view.   In fact, it is precisely in doing so that we come to the conclusion that the world has changed.

In the same way that Achebe criticizes Conrad's essentializing of Africa, moreover, a Venetian could well find ridiculous the similar essentializing of Venice in *Remembrance of Things Past* by the character "Marcel."   Indeed, a meeting with a Venetian early in the young Marcel's life might have popped his bubble of the solidity and beauty of the Serenissima well before a visit to it by the middle-aged Marcel did so.   In this example, the valence of the essentialized place is positive, so that the worst we will probably do is to shake our head with respect to the ignorance of the essentializer rather than "defending" Venice against this too-positive view.   In the same way, we wink nowadays at positive-valence inter-cultural Otherness such as that of Durrell or Paul Bowles and fire both barrels at its negative-valence counterpart, all the while speaking as if the fault lay in the construction of the inter-cultural Otherness *per se* rather than the particular value put on it by the author in question.   How much more honest it would be to say simply that we do not approve of this picture, and then say why.   Indeed, this is yet another example of the politicization of theory that is so endemic nowadays.   We reach immediately for the cannon of abstraction to deal with partic-ular flies.

All inter-cultural Otherness is based on falsity, even if it is frequently flattering falsity.   The possibility that someone will object someday to its evocation is written into the technique. Anyone who confounded the characters of a Faulkner Gothic with the real inhabitants of the American South, or Scarlett O'Hara with the Atlanta where we change planes would be in store for a rude shock.   Of course, frequently we do reject such essentializing views which purport to be about situations we know are more complex.   Baudrillard's view of America in his book on the subject seems a caricature to some people, for example, or that of Andre Konchalovsky in his recent film

Homer and Eddy, or Conrad's view of Africa in *Heart of Darkness.* I for one do reject Conrad's view of Africa, having seen nothing of the world that Conrad constructs during my two years in central Africa. And, as it happens, I taught *Heart of Darkness* at the National University of Rwanda in order to make many of the points that Achebe does in his essay.

Though we may reject any particular essentializing of place as unreal and inaccurate, we cannot, as Achebe wants to do, reject all such essentializiang processes. For the construction of inter-cultural Otherness, based on the essentializing of place, is only one use to which the necessary split between inside and outside in literature may be put. This split always essentializes the outside, even if it is not put into the geographical terms which characterize inter-cultural Other-ness. For this is the world that is not being spoken to. We must finally accept the fact that all art deforms "reality," and this by definition, because it offers only one person's view of things. Some art, such as Proust's, acknowledges this situation more freely than other; most art merely exemplifies it.

Yet this is not a fatal flaw in literature. The "reality" it deforms is only that generally accepted social world of common definers, which itself can be changed. Art creates new alliances and definitions through playing with the line between inside and outside. The alliances thus created, as for example between gay men and straight men, white women and black men, Hispanics and Eskimos, may last only for the world of the work. But who says that their creation was for that reason illegitimate? Someone might be inspired by such a limited re-alignment to change the world, even succeeding so well that this re-alignment becomes the new social orthodoxy.

This allows us, in closing, to consider the following defini-tion of art: art is that expression form capable of expressing "incorrect," not generally shared, views of reality because of the possibility of other people seeing this view on their own. This does not exclude non-Romantic art: at the very least, what a more socially integrated artist like Bach "saw" in his work was a particular arrangement of tones that had been hitherto unknown. In the delineation of an inside from an outside new information is given; this is the personal aspect of a work of literature.

The result is the work of art, in which the artist makes others see as he or she did—at least for the duration of the work. There is no art, Achebe's included, which is totally free from the presupposition of a backdrop of people who, if they appear in the work at all, remain silent—or far more often, are excluded from representation within it entirely.   The unpleasant truth is that no art is "humane" in the sense that Achebe means this word. Art does not—indeed, by definition, cannot—give equal time to the "other side."

We may grant Achebe's charge that Conrad is racist, but if we go on to criticize the general techniques through which this racism becomes manifest in Conrad, we are on the same dangerous ground as Achebe.   In the confrontation between Achebe and Conrad, therefore, we must be sympathetic with both sides—for each is expressing, in his fiction, a uniquely personal point of view. We may place these two side by side, teach them together, understand the objections of the one to the other. Yet we must acknowledge that neither can hope to win such a confrontation. Because they are fellow artists, Conrad and Achebe are in the deepest sense brothers beneath the skin.

III

The World Outside

Chapter Six

Reflections on Rwanda

The opening chapters took the position that an alternative existed to conceptualization in terms of Otherness for contacting the unfamiliar. Like the novelists here considered, I take an example from my own experience, which involved teaching English and American literature in 1985-1987 at the National University of Rwanda, central Africa, a country changed since my time there from an oasis of calm to one torn by invasion and the threat of civil war.

To set the scene: Rwanda is a country the size of Maryland, or Albania, lying east of Zaire and west of Lake Victoria. It recently achieved a degree of name recognition in the West through *Gorillas in the Mist*, the popular film about the primate researcher Dian Fossey. Rwanda calls itself, with justice, "The Country of a Thousand Hills"; it is composed of ridge after ridge of sloping, finger-like folds covered with patch-work farm plots and dotted with banana trees. With neighboring Zaire it shares the highest lake in Africa, Kivu, one of the chain of great lakes that extends along the Rift Valley from Uganda to Malawi. In the northeast of Rwanda begin the chain of volcanos which are home to the gorillas; yet further to the north, between Uganda and Zaire, lie the Rwenzori, or "Mountains of the Moon," where the Egyptians thought the source of the Nile was to be found.

It can only be the lakes in Rwanda, and perhaps its mountains, that have prompted the national tourist office to advertise the country as "the Switzerland of Africa." Aside from its landscape, size, and its landlocked situation, Rwanda is the very antithesis of Switzerland: pre-industrial, isolated, and its population predominantly illiterate. Life in the hills goes on largely as it did hundreds of years ago, with the exception of the fact that the Tutsi, who once held power under the monarchy, are now only another tribe, while the numerically superior Hutu rule the country.

The overthrow of the monarchy took place in 1959, well before independence from Belgium was attained in 1962. An invasion occurred in October of 1990 by Tutsis of Rwandan origin who had been exiled to Uganda. The subsequent months have made clear that the problem is not merely tribal in nature, but may well involve Ugandans not of Rwandan origin. In addition, the government of Rwanda appears to be using the troubles as a way of ridding itself of Tutsi opponents within the country. And at this writing, in spring of 1991, the country seems headed for inter-tribal civil war.

Yet in my example we are back in 1985, a time of peace for Rwanda. The university had asked for an American professor, a request seconded by the government. Despite this official approval of my function, I had gone to Rwanda as the representative of a culture still quite foreign to it. Though the university was run by and for Rwandans, it too was a Western institution — and a recently-imported one at that, set up by the Belgians after independence and largely paid for by the Canadians. The language in which I taught, English, was foreign as well; the local Bantu language is Kinyarwanda, and my students had added French (the country's second official language) only in high school. Before coming to the university they had some instruction in English; after graduation from the "second cycle" (five years in all) most of them would return to these schools to teach English themselves. Some few might, with luck, become bureaucrats in the capital, Kigali, or enter the diplomatic service if they had the proper connections.

Sometimes the gulf between the world represented by my neatly-dressed students, sitting in our brick classroom talking of Michelangelo, and the world of the peasants who plodded barefoot in the dust along the unpaved road outside, seemed so large as to induce vertigo in me. My students represented a minuscule proportion of the country's population of over six million, and the entire university had a student body of only about 1,500. Yet my sense that the students and I were in the same boat set adrift from the rest of Rwandan society was deceptive as well. For their reactions to the literature we read suggested that, in many ways, they were more a part of the world of the little boys driving cattle along the unpaved road outside than they were of the Westernized, English-speaking world we called into being in the classroom. And why should they not be?

During the time I spent in Rwanda, that is, I was forced to reflect on the reactions my students had to the literature we read. My position as the foreign professor demanded that I explain to them my point of view — which, in most cases, I held to be the point of view of the world from which this literature came. This required explaining their reactions to myself. The easiest of these reactions to explain, first to myself and then to them, were cases where the students interpreted events described in the English-language text as if they had occurred in Rwanda. For example, they informed me that the narrator of John Updike's little 1960s fable *Of the Farm* was weak and unmanly because he did not immediately beat his wife for calling him a "bastard" (which, I had explained, was closer to the French "salaud" and did not question his legitimacy), and that he was abnormally involved with his mother because he allowed her to hug him. They were univocal as well in telling me that Sister Carrie was a bad woman — something they knew from the first line of Dreiser's book onwards, since only bad women move to cities alone, abandoning their families in the country.

This sort of reaction-out-of-context provides the subject matter for one of the most entertaining essays we have on culturally divergent reactions to literature, Laura Bohannan's piece on "Prince Hamlet in Africa," a reflection on the author's experiences re-telling Shakespeare's plot to a group of West African tribesmen. (In the *Norton Reader* in which this essay last appeared, it was paired, divertingly enough, with another example of working at cultural cross-purposes, an account of teaching the Romantic poets at the U. S. Naval Academy, where this is being written.) Bohannan left for Africa, she tells us, with the presupposition that "human nature is pretty much the same the whole world over," and that "at least the general plot and motivation of the greater tragedies [of Shakespeare] would always be clear—everywhere." Furthermore, she "was sure that *Hamlet* had only one possible interpretation, and that one universally obvious" (p. 498, both quotations). When, however, she tried to entertain her African hosts during a rainy afternoon by telling them the story of the play, she encountered problems. Her audience of village elders thought that Claudius had done just the right thing in marrying Gertrude (brothers of dead men should always marry the widow), and they were firmly convinced that Laertes had secretly drowned Ophelia to sell her body to the witches. Hamlet, moreover, had done wrong in killing his father's brother; he richly deserved his fate of being bewitched, as he clearly was. Why else does one go mad?

Bohannan's initial presupposition is what I would call the old-fashioned paradigm for literary study: the assumption that "canonical" Western literature is universal. Yet when she rejects this viewpoint she goes to the other related extreme, suggesting that literature is not universal, but particular to a culture. Her conclusion, with respect to literature, is one of cultural relativism; this ends up essentializing Otherness, creating an Otherness of place. That the culture is Other for her is never in doubt: Bohannan translates haltingly into the language of her audience, and is constantly at a loss as to how to render certain ideas or relationships to them. And this is the point of view that informs anthropology, even the self-reflexive, self-questioning sort of ethnography, the branch of anthropology based on the acquisition of data about other cultures in the field, that is nowadays undertaken. I reject both of these alternatives, and propose that a third possibility exists for contacting the culturally unfamiliar: what I call naive realism.

Let us pause for a moment in the consideration of Bohannan to look at the nature of contemporary ethnography, which many people see as able to contact the culturally unfamiliar on its own terms. Though this brief look at ethnography takes us away from the subject of Rwanda, it ends by clarifying my reactions to it and supports my claims for the necessity of a third way for achieving direct contact with the outside world.

Ethnography is nowadays in a state of theoretical upheaval, fleeing from an acknowledgement of postulated Otherness that condemns the looker to permanent outsidership with respect to the perceived culture. Yet such postulated Otherness is at the basis of ethnography today to no less an extent than it was in ethnography's most embarrassingly patronizing days. Contemporary ethnographers like James Clifford and Renato Rosaldo reject what they perceive as the overly-magisterial pronouncements of the founding generation of post-Victorian anthropology (Boas, Malinowski, Benedict, Radcliffe-Brown, et al.). They even seek to go beyond the second thoughts of Lévi-Strauss, beyond the yet more self-conscious subjectivizing of observatorial position seen in the work of a writer so important for the current generation, Clifford Geertz. In doing so they favor a more participatory "dialogic" ethnography where the subject Others frequently speak directly to the record rather than being described by the ethnographer, and where the onlooker makes as clear as possible the specificity of his or her position and the limitations of that person's point of view.

Contemporary ethnographers seek at all costs to avoid any hint of the frisson of fascinated horror on the part of the observer that was the stock in trade of the founding generation of ethnographers. The result is frequently that the ostensible subjects of the study end up seeming just like us — and so, are boring. (A parallel is provided by the way some feminist film-makers influenced by Laura Mulvey's theory of the phallocratic viewer's gaze resolutely refuse to construct characters we are interested in or desire. Such film-makers demand instead that we find our very boredom before the result interesting.) A concomitant development of this trend toward acknowledgement of subjectivity is the demand that the ethnographer stay for a longer time with his or her hosts than was normal in the early years of ethnography, and acquire a more profound acquaintance with their language. The work of Margaret Mead, to name only one star of the founding generation, has been attacked in recent years for being deficient on both counts; and the fact that the relation between observer and observed is conceived of in terms of host-guest is itself indicative.

Clifford and Geertz, in interviews with the academic journal *Lingua Franca*, have named Rosaldo's *Culture and Truth* the most provocative contemporary book in their field. In fact, Rosaldo's book contains a succinct summary of this shift in ethnographic paradigms:

> In contrast with the classic view, which posits culture as a self-contained whole made up of coherent patterns, culture can arguably be conceived as a more porous array of intersections where distinct processes criss-cross from within and beyond its borders. Such heterogeneous processes often derive from differences of age, gender, class, race, and sexual orientation.
>
> This book argues that a sea change in cultural studies has eroded once-dominant conceptions of truth and objectivity. The truth of objectivism—absolute, universal, and timeless—has lost its monopoly status. It now competes, on more nearly equal terms, with the truths of case studies that are embedded in local contexts, shaped by local interests, and colored by local perceptions. . . . Such terms as *objectivity, neutrality,* and *impartiality* refer to subject positions once endowed with great institutional authority. . . . Social analysis must now grapple with the realization that its objects of analysis are also analyzing subjects who critically interrogate ethnographers. (pp. 20-21)

The intention of this new conception of ethnography is to break down the analyst-subject power relation, just as contemporary psychoanalysis questions the power relations implicit in the Freudian model of analysis. This is meant to give the people in question direct access to what is called "the word," the capability to address directly the Western public who are primarily the consumers of anthropological studies. In pursuit of these goals, current ethnographic thought democratizes the access to discourse and identifies the point of view of the ethnographer as one among several possibilities, rather than the only authoritative one. At least, the observer's point of view is made to coincide to a much greater extent than in earlier generations with that of the people being written about, as almost an apologia for their ways.

Rosaldo is explicit about this convergence of point of view between host and guest. In *Culture and Truth* he speaks in great and moving detail about the grief he felt at the death of his wife, which caused him to understand for the first time something of the meaning of the Ilongat practice of hunting heads, a practice which the headhunters themselves explain as an expression of grief. Rosaldo's point is that only his personal experiences allowed him to understand the more general practice of the Ilongat. And this is a subjective fact of perception that must, in his view, be opposed to the Victorian pretenses of objective inter-cultural seeing. His stated aim is thus to substitute personal understanding for sensationalism, to render quotidian the exotic.

Yet even Rosaldo's sort of ethnography postulates Otherness, and does not fundamentally end up by un-postulating it. The Exotic remains exotic, even if now it is an Exotic that we have had "explained" to us. Though Rosaldo can use his personal grief to understand that the Ilongot may feel similar grief, at no point does he question whether this similar grief should be expressed in the way it is: by headhunting. After all, Renaldo himself didn't hunt heads, though he may have been tempted to. By refusing to subject this difference to scrutiny or refer it to an explanatory principle, he takes it for granted, and thereby creates an Other. The Other remains Other in its actions, if not in its motivations.

None of this softening of the tone of voice can alter what must by definition be the fundamental presupposition of the ethnographer: that the people in question is fundamentally Other, and hence different in some essentialized way from the person doing the perceiving. Among ethnographers of the new generation the need to create Others is strong, given that frequently the genesis of their interest in inter-cultural Otherness is a perception of its intra-cultural version. Rosaldo, once again, makes this clear, citing the link between the break-up of our domestic American "melting pot" and the new spirit in anthropology: "For me as a Chicano, questions of culture emerge not only from my discipline, but also from a more personal politics of identity and community" (p. xi). Because he senses intra-cultural Otherness, he does ethnography. But the move from internal to external Otherness is illegitimate. Rosaldo is creating an identification with mainstream domestic culture at the expense of turning a foreign one into the Other;

though he is Chicano at home, he is Anglo with respect to the Ilongot.

Moreover nothing can change the fact that whatever language is used to establish communication, the audience for the final report will be primarily of the researcher's world, not the world of the researched. And the presupposition of the researcher is that whatever he or she finds will be of interest, even if it is expressed in terms that are fragmentary, self-reflexive, and dialogic. Whatever the content of the report, even if it denies that the people are fundamentally different than we are, the fact that we report at all on this other people as a group marks them as Other. We may let Them talk, but the result is offered to an audience of Us and makes sense only in the context of Our culture; the only possible end product of ethnology is reports to stay-at-homes. Ultimately it is this world which defines their nature, just as we fit the dances of the Other into our structures in contexts such as the Los Angeles Festival, and the cult objects of Africa and Oceania into the Modernist white-walled museum.

George Stocking considers the same constraints on contemporary ethnography from a historical perspective. Speaking of ethnographic anthropology on the eve of its development, which he centers around the Crystal Palace exposition of 1851, he writes:

> The historical unity of the tradition which in the Anglo-American sphere is called "anthropological" has been defined primarily by its human subject matter which—allowing for differences of terminology and attitude—has for the most part been essentially that of pre-Darwinian ethnology. Although the questions asked of this subject matter have changed, the dichotomy between the European civilized observer and the culturally distant (and objectified) "other" has always been central to the anthropological tradition—as indeed current attempts to surmount it testify. . . . What unifies the scholars we retrospectively include in the anthropological tradition is the fact that they studied peoples who were once called "savages." (p. 47)

Whether these "current attempts to surmount" the dichotomy between Europeans and Other could, in Stocking's view, be successful is unclear. However the suggestion is strong that as long as contemporary ethnography remains sufficiently within the parameters of the anthropological tradition for its activities to be identified as part of that tradition, it will be defined by these parameters—even if, like the Derrideans who question substantiality, this takes place through a questioning of some of the tradition's most egregious excesses. All contemporary ethnography can do with respect to these givens is put them in question, not reject them entirely. If it did so, no one would be able even to identify another people as an Other people sufficiently to go out and live with them, much less have an idea in advance how to go about reporting on the experience in a coherent manner. Ethnography presupposes a relation of Otherness as the precondition of its very possibility: Otherness is a condition of form, not of content.

It is curious that an approach to ethnography such as Rosaldo's produces works which, bereft of the claims put forth by the glory days of early twentieth-century ethnography to "objectivity," approach more closely those avowedly personal travel literature or accounts of life in the colonies that fed the curiosity of stay-at-homes in the nineteenth century. "Scientific" ethnography was meant as an alternative to books like that parodied by Graham Greene in his *Heart of the Matter*, an imaginary work entitled *A Bishop Among the Bantus*. By giving up pretenses to objectivity and science, ethnography is once again becoming anecdotal and subjective.

Though this way of doing ethnography is in tune with the intellectual mood of the times which engenders a pleasing intellectual modesty and makes scholars more hesitant to offer unqualified pronouncements, more unwilling to speak for others, the result is what I can only call ethnography in bad faith. Ethnography today continues to presuppose the postulated situation of Otherness at the level of the group, even if we subsequently come asymptotically close to claiming it is not so situated. We do not conduct ethnography on what we see as our own world, save only in a mediated fashion by adopting the paradigm of foreignness, and with the intention of distancing us from it, as Thorstein Veblen did in his *Theory of the Leisure Class*.

Christopher L. Miller points out in *Theories of Africans* that if contemporary ethnography does achieve its apparent goal of shifting its focus "from observed to observer, then its use value as an interlocuter for the criticism of . . . literatures will have been lost" (p. 27). And I would add, for the understanding of societies as well. Ethnography is playing with fire; the paradox, at once the good news and the bad, is that ethnography cannot really self-immolate. The goal of contemporary ethnography can only be achieved in content, not in form; Miller's point is valid, but his fears, for better or worse, are ultimately exaggerated.

Rosaldo's conclusion with respect to culture is similar to that of readers of literature like Bohannan, who, brought up on the notion of a universally comprehensible literature — say, that of Western white males — go to the opposite extreme on realizing that understanding literature is much more personal than they had thought. They conclude that reading is purely personal, just as Rosaldo argues that truth and objectivity in ethnography have had their day as the expressions of a monopoly position competing with local interests. In both cases the reaction is that of someone who still takes initially for granted, if only to reject it, the notion of objectivity and universal truth.

For Rosaldo does not question whether a foreign culture should be conceived of as an object of study at all; his only point is that, once having decided that it is, we must be willing to cope with polyphony in its reporting. In the same way, Achebe takes literature as just the universal, timeless realm its proponents in the nineteenth century claimed it was. For this reason, as if with the acrimony of the disappointed lover, he criticizes Conrad for having written in the way Conrad did, rather than saying that it is inappropriate for us, or for Achebe himself, to do so. The desire to draw a general conclusion unites both the absolutists and the relativists, whether this position is applied to literature or to culture. In opposition to both, I propose a pragmatism in dealing with the unknown. And this brings us back both to Bohannan and Rwanda.

Though Bohannan ends up in the same value-relativist position as ethnographers like Rosaldo, she does not go as far in letting the locals do the interpreting as Rosaldo claims ethnographers should do. To be sure, he still reserves the final explanatory position for himself; if nothing else, he votes to take as true what the Ilongot say about their own practices—he accepts that they are in fact an expression of the rage of grief, rather than mere barbaric murder. Yet it is precisely the agreement of the Africans with the old-fashioned belief in absolutist values that is Bohannan's point of departure which ultimately causes her to reject it. The village elders are quite convinced that interpretations of literature are universal: namely, just the way they say they are. In fact this is perfectly comprehensible, for the definition of our non-traditionalist society is that we can articulate others' points of view. The definition of a traditionalist society rather than a rationalist one, by contrast, is that it accepts its tenets as given. Bohannan never articulates to the elders her conclusion, nor suggests to them that something can be learned from reflecting that each culture thinks this is the case. Instead, she interprets this evidence through the assumption of cultural Otherness, and ends by throwing up her hands. She might, by contrast, have explained to her audience why Gertrude, living in Medieval Europe, should not have married Claudius, and explained that Gertrude's second marriage could not be justified, as the elders thought, on the grounds that she needed someone to hoe her fields.

We should note too that Bohannan was not dealing with a printed text, but with a story transmitted orally, lacking the independence and rigidity of print while being amenable to interruption and even re-formation by the audience. This audience, moreover, was composed of the elders of the tribe with which she needed to get along, rather than of people who had come to her for information.

My situation in Rwanda was different from Bohannan's on all these points. And this permitted a relation different from hers with the world outside. I was dealing with printed texts, which were independent of both me and my students, and to which I could appeal when it seemed to me that something was being missed or misunderstood. Furthermore, my inter-locuters were people who had come to me for something; I did not have to underplay differences between us, as Bohannan did in order to be the polite guest, nor did I have to give in to what seemed misreadings out of a sense of social obligation. The job I was being paid to do was to mediate differences as best I could, rather than simply noting them as insuperable barriers.

My conclusion from this experience was that we can deal with perceived differences in groups of people without resorting to conceptualization in terms of Otherness, essentializing in terms of place. This means, first of all, that we leave open the question of whether or not we are dealing with Otherness; we can refuse to postulate absolute difference merely on the grounds that we have changed place. It also means that we look for specific causes to specifically perceived differences. We can mediate differences, as Bohannan did not, by searching for a general explanation of our specific divergence.

From such a point of view, the people among whom we find ourselves and our own world are particular instantiations of a more general principle. This avoids both of the valence possibilities for Otherness, which implies in each case the opposite valence for the non-Other. The first step in the process of mediating differences is thus the articulation of what was causing the problem; the second step is the appeal to a principle that relativized this difference, putting into relation the two specifics as types of a single genre. (This is always how we "explain" something, by relating it to something we know.) In the case of Updike's *Of the Farm*, this generic relation was easy to find. I simply assured my students that physical contact of this sort was normal between mother and son in the West and that men nowadays had to accept a great deal more than merely name-calling from their wives but did not, by and large, feel unmanned as a result.

Another set of reactions among my students that I found anomalous was almost as easily explained. During a discussion of the successful harvest that led to the first Thanksgiving in the Bradford *Plymouth* journal, the students were puzzled by the weight Bradford placed on this event and uncertain why it should lead to such an outpouring of gratitude on the part of the settlers. I reflected that Rwanda, despite its burgeoning population, had until that point managed to feed its people. There are four major harvests a year. The hills are dotted with banana trees, a good source of nourishnent—though most are used for the production of the national drink, a banana beer called *urgwagwa*. The last large-scale famine was in the 1950s, nearly beyond the memory of a society where the average life expectancy is below 50 years. The next class period, I arrived prepared to explain that this was the only harvest of the year for the Pilgrims, and that it would soon be followed by a period of cold in which no food-growing was possible.

Yet it did not occur to me, newly arrived in Rwanda as I was, that my students lacked more fundamental knowledge relating to this literary passage, namely a sense of the cycle of seasons. Rwanda, after all, is only a few degrees from the equator, and is small enough that it knows only one climate, called equatorial mountain. In this climate, the diurnal temperature variation is greater than that between seasons, which at any rate are designated by amount of rainfall rather than by temperature.

I noted this lack of understanding for the seasons more sharply in our reading of the English Romantics Shelley, Keats, and Gray. This poetry is heavy in descriptions of the "vegetable universe," usually correlated to mental states. My students did not see that poems set in autumn were inevitably about melancholy and loss, that those set in winter inevitably had to be meditations on death, that spring poems were associated with hope and re-birth, and summer verse with idyll. Nor was the season the poem was set in always clear to them; references to falling leaves did not evoke autumn, much less produce in them the sympathetic sense of sadness such a reference would evoke to a Westerner. After all, leaves do not fall in Rwanda unless the tree is dead, though chances are it will have been cut down long before in any case. Wood is scarce and the evenings are cool.

Other problems arose in their encounter with Thomas Gray's "Elegy: Written in a Country Churchyard." To most of them this seemed only a literal description of an everyday scene, while to others the churchyard was already a sign of

civilization, like the occasional missions in the otherwise
remote Rwandan hills. In other words, the poem seemed
anything but the sentimental appeal to the power of nature
and a rejection of life in the urban fast lane that it appears to
most Westerners. I explained this, first to myself and then to
them, by noting that Rwanda is almost completely agricultural
and non-industrial. Even Kigali, the capital, is little more
than an overgrown town, rather than the bloated urban sprawl
of many African cities, so that the notion of fleeing the city is
foreign as well.

These were divergences that I could explain to my students
by putting certain aspects of their lives in relation with aspects
of the lives of others. In some cases I was reticent about
communicating to them the explanations I came up with,
largely because I was unwilling to take up any more of the
available time with explanations. And this acknowledged the
particularity of my position as observer, in a way Rosaldo
might well approve, far more than a wooden adherence to the
principle of "getting the view of the locals" would have done.
The assumption that another's sense of things is always better
than one's own is part of an essentializing of place. Why
should we make this assumption?

My students almost inevitably took what the majority of
Westerners would regard as a moralizing stance with respect
to the work, something we tend to identify with the Victorian
period. How could I make this clear without being insulting?
For I was not completely free of the social constraints
operating on Bohannan, and that she should have acknowledged more openly. In a class of seven students, six (all the
men) admitted that they had not liked *Moll Flanders* because it
did not sufficiently punish the protagonist, who was not only
clearly immoral but somehow doubly culpable for being
female.

The lone woman, on the other hand, voted it among her
favorites of the works we read. The university-wide representation of women in Rwanda is only ten percent, about the
same as at the U. S. Naval Academy. Though educated
women fetch much higher bride-prices than do others, their
presence at the university appeared to be resented by most of

the men, who echoed reactions common among male students at the turn of the century in England and America: that the women students were there because they could not get a husband, that they were unattractive, and so on. Incidentally, the fact that the direction of money flow in a Rwandan marriage is the opposite from that common in Europe up to the twentieth century caused them to arrive at our discussion of the opening of *Pride and Prejudice* in great puzzlement. What an enviable situation it seemed to them for a father to have so many female children who would have to be bought!

If the students' overall reactions to the works seemed somehow moralistic, the form this took was heavily Christian, specifically Catholic. The White Fathers did their work well in Rwanda; most of the members of the educated classes are Catholic, and the Church occupies a special place in the government's heart due to its support of the revolution which overthrew the Tutsi. Any hint of relation to a Biblical situation or to Christian teachings in a poem or story tended to be remarked to the almost total exclusion of any divergence. I think of a class where the students insisted that Anne Bradstreet's hymn to the worldly, "On the Burning of My House," was a perfect parallel with Job. This tendency on their part to see such connections as primary where the Westerner would be conscious of divergences from the religious paradigm possibly arose because Rwanda relates culturally to the West through Christianity, so this is perceived first of all in a consideration of Western literature.

On the other hand, a consciousness of matters religious helped their readings of works that, in today's more secular West, go largely unappreciated. *The Scarlet Letter*, for example, received a more understanding reading than I had ever seen it get in the West. The notion of sin and an awareness of how it destroys the soul was something the students understood; they were surprised when I told them that the notion of sin was not currently in fashion in many circles of Western Europe and North America.

These qualities of their reactions were more personal than those caused by geography or climate. The explanations for yet other reactions, in turn, lay somewhere between these extremes of personal and impersonal characteristics.   For example, the students picked out parts of works for attention that to a Western reader seem incidental: scenes or descriptive passages that gave them a picture of life in England or America, like those glimpses of Chicago at the end of the last century which dot *Sister Carrie*. They were also, perhaps as a correlate, roundly uninterested in the few excursions we made into non-descriptive literature.   I reflected that there is no television in Rwanda, and none of the plethora of throw-away print and visuals that glut the West and that we take for granted: posters and billboards, picture magazines, flyer advertisements, and junk mail. These novelistic descriptions, I thought, played a role like that now played by travel in the West which Lévi-Strauss so deplored.

This lack of visual and textual throw-aways in Rwanda, where everything is endlessly re-cycled that is made of plastic or that comes from the West, produced a greater intensity of reception of all texts when compared with the reaction of students in the West.   I have never heard such sincere laughter as when we went through the jokes in *The Adventures of Huckleberry Finn*, the total absorption in the reading out loud, and the sudden explosion when they "got it," whether this was before my explanation or after.   Indeed, one of the most striking of the things I saw in Rwanda was the extraordinary power of the written text on these readers, members of a society still largely oral save in the tiny educated class. (Classical Rwandan poetry, which consists of court epics about battles and pastoral poems on the beauty of cattle, has only recently been written down.) I reflected as well that the Bible was the first introduction of these people to print, and this less than a century ago.   Some of the status that the printed word possessed for my students, I reflected, must be the result of this still-recent experience with Christianization.

This attitude of respect for the printed word *per se* took concrete form among my students, though this may appear paradoxical, in academic plagiarism whose incidence seemed higher, or at least whose exercise was more guilt-free, than in the West.   Indeed the notion of plagiarism itself appeared foreign to Rwanda.   In the most flagrant case of this I was asked to deal with, an undergraduate turned in, as his senior paper, an analysis of Hemingway's *A Farewell to Arms* identical in every particular to the analysis I had offered in a graduate seminar. He had been told that I would be one of the readers of his paper and apparently thought I would be pleased to see his successful assimilatation of what he took to be my transmission of brute fact.

I decided that this was, in fact, an expression of respect for the word, rather than, as in the West, an expression of disrespect. If something was printed or transmitted by an authority figure, the assumption seemed to be that it was by definition true, whether it had to do with the surface area of Kenya or the analysis of a poem, and thus was the legitimate quarry of citation without acknowledgement. And the confusion that might have occurred because any three given articles on a particular literary work will probably present three divergent views was obviated by the deficiencies of the library.

This respect for the printed word may have been an effect of the society's still so-recent orality, a phenomenon visible in Western peasants of the last century. For there are no bookstores, in a Western sense, in Rwanda; what few books do exist for sale are prohibitively expensive because they are imported. Students in Rwanda do not buy their books; they borrow them from the library, which is stocked with foreign donations of paperbacks in multiple copies.

The corollary of this respect for the written object was an equally great respect for the word of the Professor, as its adjunct and explicator, even its high priest. The obvious parallel that came to mind was with Medieval Europe, where the words of the explicators of Holy Writ became themselves part of the subsequent editions of the text and partook of its privileged status. The concrete form this took with my students was their prodigious note-taking. Most of them wrote down every word that came from my mouth, producing perfect transcripts of my lectures, as (a gratifying comparison) the works of Aristotle and some of Wittgenstein's have been passed on to us in lecture notes.

Another aspect of the works we read to which my students were more receptive than their Western counterparts was the role played by class differences and the struggle for material possessions that literature stressing these differences frequently portrays. I think of their acute sympathy with Miss Julie's abasement in sleeping with her servant in Strindberg's play, and their complete identification with Sister Carrie's urge to "make it" in the world.

Rwanda is an authoritarian culture, and rigidly hierarchical. Everyone with a little money or a few possessions has a servant, and the servants, who have risen in the hierarchy with respect to the day laborors on the fields, usually have servants themselves. When all else fails, the men of whatever social position have their wives, who do the domestic work for them that they do for others. Servants in Rwanda are, by Western post-Enlightenment standards, ill-treated, and the notion of human value regardless of societal status is foreign.

This acute materialism of Rwandans seemed linked to and hence at least partially explained by the extreme limitation of resources. Robberies, for example, almost always result in violence to the owner, if that person is present and defends his possessions — as he invariably does — or to the robber, if caught. (Female victims of robbery would get help from male relatives.) If this happens the least violent result is likely to be the slashing of the soles of the robber's feet with a panga knife so that he cannot get away; it is not unusual for the robber to be beaten to death by friends of the victim, and such occurrences are treated leniently by the official justice system. Europeans, who always have more goods to protect than the majority of the Rwandans, fit well into the system, since wealth is respected for its own sake. The Rwandan guards whom the Europeans hire defend the possessions of their employers with great energy against their compatriots.

I did not try to articulate this difference between their society and mine to the students, pleading the necessity of getting on to the next work. Furthermore, it seemed part of another, more fundamental feature of the life in Rwanda that struck me repeatedly, and that I would have had a harder time communicating to my students. Namely, the ubiquity or at least high visibility of death and everyday carnage in Rwanda. (In order for them to see this as striking, I thought, they would have had to experience for themselves a world in which this was not the case.) Death of any sort is an everyday fact in Rwanda, perhaps much as it was in the European Middle Ages: highway fatalities—since the people prefer the level roads to the hillsides, malaria, AIDS, polio, and infant mortality from diarrhea or from unknown causes.

It was this, I thought, which explained the fact that my students did not understand the mystery with which modern Western literature invests death, or our twentieth-century reluctance to talk about this subject. Sex, on the other hand, is as tabu in Rwanda as it was a hundred years ago in the West—so that the students' attention was immediately caught by the slightest sexual reference in the text, which set them off laughing. I recall especially their giggles at *A Farewell to Arms*, with its soldier-talk about masturbation and its tough-guy references to sex.

It was this inversion of the roles of sex and death, I think, which produced their reaction to Ibsen's *Ghosts*. An entire group of students came to the discussion period convinced that what Oswald wants his mother to do is fornicate with him, not kill him. And it was, I decided, precisely the air of hushed mystery and unwillingness on Ibsen's part to spell out what was going on which had led them to this conclusion. The evidence they offered as proof positive of the validity of their reading was the horrified line of Mrs. Alving as she refuses Oswald's (unenunciated) desire: "I who gave you birth!" In fact, I had to concede that this interpretation is nowhere contradicted by the text. It does, to be sure, leave unexplained or unclear in purpose a number of other lines in the play. But not all of the remainder of the dialogue contributes to the "right" interpretation, either. In this case I found myself forced to look for substantiation in a given of the genre rather than in the text, suggesting to them that mother-son incest could not have been portrayed in this manner in a nineteenth-century play, even by Ibsen.

This example, one of the most striking of my professorial experiences in Rwanda, may serve as paradigm for all of the divergences of reaction between the way my students saw the works of literature, and the way I, as the resident foreigner, read them. For in each case I felt I could take a stab at identifying, even if I did not feel free to communicate, the differences of situation that had produced these divergences. In some cases the differences were those of climate, in others those of religion, in still others, a lack of information. Yet in all cases we could transcend these differences by putting their situation and mine into relation at a higher level of abstraction that we as individuals could comprehend and share. Identifying, for example, what I took to be an inversion of sex and death in our societies did not deny the divergence of our reactions to the literature, though it did deny these cultural differences the capability to divide us as individuals.

This suggested to me that another way of dealing with the world exists than offered by the points of view which assume all people everywhere to be alike, or which erect the walls of Otherness—even the porous membranes of contemporary ethnography. We can live a real alternative to both: we need not postulate the commonality which is Bohannan's point of departure; on the other hand, we need not assert Otherness, which is her conclusion. Instead, we can set our primary focus on something to be achieved: on personal understanding, even if this understanding is of group differences. For in understanding we do not transcend differences; instead we put them into relation.

Understanding between people, moreover, is not a postulate, but something that must be achieved. And this gives value to our presence in and action on the world. Understanding is something we must work for; it is a vector arrow rather than a static state. It builds human endeavor into the world, which is something that neither the patronizing assumptions that the Western standard is valid for the entire world nor the alienating Otherness of a Hemingway, a Conrad, or a Rosaldo can do.

Though I have questioned the methods of writers like Rosaldo, my position is nonetheless closer to his than to writers who assume the universality of Western standards. However such an assumption of universality is not so moribund as we may think, nor is its expression confined to the extreme right. In subsequent chapters I offer two examples of such an assumption from a position closer to that of the left. The purpose of these examples is to show how we may succeed in mediating specific differences, namely by postulating commonality on an abstract level. Both examples involve the way we react to concepts or works we bring into our culture from outside, and they may thereby be of more immediate practical interest to the majority of Westerners than the situation of the present chapter.

The first example concerns the fact that when even more "enlightened" Westerners talk about AIDS, we largely do so with the assumption that the world outside our cultural borders is identical to that within. The paradox is that this is an assumption of which the Victorians, from whom many progressive Westerners feel so alienated, would have been proud. Chapter Eight concerns, in a related situation, the problems we Westerners encounter in coming to terms with what is referred to nowadays as "world dance."

Chapter Seven

AIDS — Moeurs de Province

One of the sessions at the 1987 convention of the Modern Language Association of America, set in a San Francisco not yet ready to wake into spring, was entitled "The Literature of AIDS." At that point, I had just returned from Rwanda, the buckle, we might say, of the African AIDS belt. With my lingering hang-over concerning many things Western, above all the boundless arrogance of our belief that we are the measure of all things, I found the talk of Susan Sontag and Harvey Fierstein, the evocation of a "golden age" of free sex before the deluge, and the words of one of the audience members who spoke of those "dying in the AIDS trenches" like another manifestation of what, in another context, we might call the last death-cry of a decadent bourgeois society. All this seemed evidence of the utter self-involvement of the pampered creatures who populate the West, of the conviction that our own version of something is equivalent to the situation as a whole. What struck me, in short, was the provincialism of our North American view of AIDS. And how was this different from the boundless self-assurance of the Victorians that their criteria were the only possible ones?

To be sure, it was as nothing more than an amateur observer of AIDS in Africa that I had these reactions in the over-crowded conference room of the San Francisco Hilton. I was neither a doctor nor a researcher, though I knew the doctor sent to Rwanda to do research by the city of San Francisco. What right had I to express an opinion? But at least, I thought, I had had one experience that all but a handful at this huge convention had not. I had *been there*, had seen a reality in contrast to which all this talk about talk seemed as self-enclosed and claustrophobic as the stifling and aurally dead room around me. I had spoken with my students at the University and with people in Kigali, read the articles in the Rwandan party newspaper and the editorials in the neighboring *Kenya Times*, and handed out photocopies of *Time* magazine's "AIDS in Africa" article to those I knew, waiting for their reactions.

For the fact is that what one of the earnest young presenters at this MLA session called, using my candidate for the most ubiquitous word of the 80s, "the discourse of AIDS" (meaning how we *in the West* speak about AIDS), is different in Africa — where the problem is incalculably more serious, numerically speaking, than it is in the U.S. To a great extent, of course, this "discourse" is different there because in Africa the disease apparently strikes both sexes equally and affects primarily the urban well-to-do, thus hitting the very center of societal power. This is a clear contrast to the situation in the U. S. where primarily groups that are seen or see themselves as marginal, or excluded from power, are affected. And this seemed yet another example of a perception of intra-cultural Otherness being writ large and used as a matrix with which to view the world.

A deeper difference between the way we conceive of AIDS in the West and the way it is conceived of in Rwanda, in Africa, and perhaps in the agrarian Third World as a whole is revealed by reflecting on the extraordinary resistance that the governments in many African countries and their people showed initially to attempts by the industrialized world to convince them that AIDS presents a problem at all. This resistance was the tip of an iceberg, an index pointing to what I came to see as the fundamental difference of sensibility between the way death and disease in general are conceived of in the industrialized, post-Romantic West, and the way they are seen in those countries that have not been subject to the changes which have so determined our life in the last two centuries. In coming to this conclusion, however, I am not creating Otherness. Far from reporting a difference and taking it for granted, I am attempting to explain it. And it is the explanation that mediates difference, prohibiting it from achieving the status of an Other. The implication is that we would be the same as they if we lived under these circumstances, to the extent that it makes sense at all to speak of a "we" and a "they."

Until recently, the official reaction of most African governments to the Western insistence that AIDS presented a problem for their populations has been flat rejection. Many highly placed Kenyans, to take one example, seemed to conceive of the attempt by Western doctors to identify the incidence of AIDS there as the creation of the disease — not identification, but contamination. To be sure, some of this fear of AIDS talk was caused by the government's readily understandable love of the tourist dollar (pegged to the Kenya schilling, and gushing into the country in post-*Out of Africa* waves), or by the equally understandable disinclination of African nations to have foisted on them the image of being the source of yet another planetary ill, after over-population and political chaos. Westerners reading about the speeches of African diplomats at international conferences on the subject in the last few years could only laugh, as they did at Soviet claims that AIDS had been invented in the racist and imperialist laboratories of the Americans or the South Africans.

Even the recent announcement that Kenyan researchers had developed an effective anti-AIDS medicine, called Kemron, merely exhibits this resistance in another guise. While wanting to keep all options open, most Western researchers have been extremely skeptical of the efficacity of the Kenyan product, for which extraordinary claims were made. Indeed, the very suggestion that this was the hoped-for wonder medicine produced skepticism in the West, as too clearly an expression of a desire on the part of the Kenyans to pronounce the problem solved and remove it from the public spotlight. To this skepticism some of those Kenyans involved reacted by saying that the West was jealous of its success, and did not want to acknowledge that a Third World country could have found so easily that for which so many had been looking for so long.

More recent reports from Kenya, as for example an article by Steve Rabin in *The Washington Post* in November of 1991, have suggested that in the last few years, African governments have not only acknowledged AIDS as a problem, but have done more to educate their people of the danger than have most Western governments.   If so, then an about-face of attitude has occurred in a relatively short period of time in Africa.   Yet it would be indicative for its very intensity and abruptness: AIDS has suddenly been added to the list of maladies that must be addressed, as if the inevitable had suddenly been accepted. The point is that for the longest time Western pressure to acknowledge its presence was resisted; both the resistance and the about-face tell us something.

This initial resistance was not, I think, merely the result of governmental attempt to paper things over for as long as possible so that revenue would not dry up. Even pecuniary motives could not explain the fact that nearly every time I opened the *Kenya Times* there was another letter to the editor about how the source of the contagion was the West, and how the only way to halt its spread in Kenya was to stop all white people at the airport and give them an AIDS test. This may have been an instinctive reaction to talk of giving Africans an AIDS test in the West, a kind of protest in advance. After all, I sensed the same rejection in Rwanda, which, until the Fossey film came out, had basically no tourism at all.

Instead, the motivation behind a rejection of Western attempts to identify the spread of AIDS in Africa appeared an almost instinctive understanding on the part of the Kenyans of what I take to be Foucault's point in *The Birth of the Clinic*: that the presupposition of curing a disease is a kind of invasion of individual privacy, the conceptual separation of the disease from the individual who carries it. The naming of the disease does indeed create it. Prior to such naming and identification, it was the person who was ill; after the act of naming the person becomes the carrier of the disease. From my perspective in Rwanda I saw what it means to create a problem by talking about it rather than, as this earnest young man at the MLA suggested was the case in the U. S. reaction to AIDS, creating, or worsening, a problem by *not* talking about it. For those Americans interested in AIDS, primarily those groups most threatened by it who see themselves as marginal to mainstream society, silence may indeed equal death, as the ACT UP posters point out to us. In Africa, on the contrary, speech seems to many to be the opposite of this, to be tantamount to the invention of the disease.

Why, Rwandans asked, this interest of the West in this one disease? The answer is, of course, that it has affected us, and so we are interested in them. The AIDS problem exists as a problem in Africa, the Africans rightly see, to the extent that it exists as a problem in the rich North. Why, they wondered, so much interest in this form of sickness and death, chosen as if at random from among so many that affect people outside of industrialized countries? Death is omnipresent and polymorphous in Rwanda. While four children out of five now live to be five years old, fully 200 infants out of 1,000 die before their fifth birthday, carried off by the ubiquitous diarrhea or by other diseases, made worse by undernutrition. As far as that goes, Rwandan peasants are better at curative medicine than preventive. Preventive medicine, based on the notion of hygiene, depends on a belief in physical things that cannot be seen. In Rwanda it is the vaccine, given with a palpable needle, that has won a large measure of trust; indeed a shot is sometimes held to be a cure-all as long as it is given by a foreign doctor.

In Rwanda the average life expectancy is in the upper 40s; there are a few very old people and many very young ones. Death on the highway is common at all ages, and not, as in the West, as the result of accidents between cars, which are luxury items in Rwanda. Of course, the over-loaded taxi-busses routinely cut blind corners along the twisting Chinese-built north-south highway; every few days one ends up in a tangle of metal with another car. Yet most accidents are with pedestrians. The peasants use the one paved single lane highway as a footpath through their densely-populated hills, even at night when they become invisible, wrapped in dark cloths and leading brown cattle, and do not seem to understand the power of several tons of hurtling steel. The polio victims who survive hop and crawl along the roads; malaria, though less serious here at Rwanda's mile-high altitudes than on the coasts, nonetheless kills those infected by it who have not been carried by their friends in the straw litters one sees along the roads to the far-away hospitals to get shots of quinine.

Starvation is less of a problem in this fertile country, to which the West has given massive agricultural aid, than elsewhere in Africa. Yet is not unknown at certain times and in certain parts of the country. Malnutrition, on the other hand, is endemic at all times and all places — for the people live largely on potatoes and beans. Meat costs money, and a lot of it. The fact that it must be bought in cash, rather than by barter, already assures its inaccessibility for most people.

Thus death and disease, I would say, appear to Rwandans in a much larger and less differentiated spectrum of forms than they do to Westerners, as well as a spectrum more integrated into their daily lives. The heritage of the Enlightenment makes us believe that any disease is at least conceptually curable, and causes us to see the menu of woes as being divided up into neat compartments of separable maladies (Foucault's point again). The Western, and especially American, assumption, in fact, is that the normal, conceptually neutral state of the human being is one of the absence of disease. Disease thereby takes on the status of the Other. This has produced America's cult of youth and our total refusal to integrate death and dying into our lives. For Westerners, each divergence from this ideal state of perfect health, exemplified in those paragons that people Pepsi-Cola ads, is a sullying of perfection that must be removed — named, isolated, and eliminated. If this is not possible, as in the case of death itself, we ignore it, or banish it. Any such divergence from a state of perfect health is shocking, as AIDS was a surprise for the West. For this disease to which we have no remedy was seen as something that *should not be*.

Rwanda has been more open to Western talk of AIDS than many countries, certainly more than its neighbor, Zaire, whose lacerating colonial past has bred suspicion of Western values. The educated, or Europeanized Rwandans, those most accustomed to the way the West separates impersonal diseases from the people suffering from them, accepted Western interest in the disease sooner than others. Yet the mood I saw was of patronizing tolerance, or resignation rather than real interest.

Let the West be interested in AIDS if it liked, was the attitude of my university colleagues — as well this as something else. We can't give up sex, one colleague told me, and if we don't die of one thing it will be another.

I do not think that AIDS was a surprise for Rwandans — even the educated ones. Instead, it was yet another example of something that is merely a fact of life in so many Third World countries. Thus, the Western panic at AIDS, its conviction that this *must not be so*, appeared inexplicable: an over-reaction, strange and silly. Probably everyone has heard that for a while the joke in Kinshasa was that "Sida" — French for AIDS — stood for "Syndrome Imaginaire pour Décourager les Amoureux." Some jokes were involuntary: it was also about this time that hundreds of t-shirts were distributed as publicity for the Swedish International Development Agency that boasted "SIDA, c'est moi!"

Even a limited solution to the problem of AIDS, such as use of condoms, takes on the aura in Rwanda of being part of the problem. For birth control is not in vogue in Rwanda, and the association even the educated men have with condoms is of uncleanliness. They are by and large unwilling to use condoms even with prostitutes, for this is to admit that what they are doing is tainted. The result is that large numbers of students and soldiers do contact venereal disease. Since most are not incapacitated, they see the attempt of the West to encourage their use of condoms as yet another attempt to brand them as sufferers from a disease they do not perceive themselves as having, whether this is syphilis or AIDS.

Brought up without the Western assumption that disease is alien to the pristine clarity of the ideal body, in a world where access to a hospital cannot be guaranteed for everyone, and where the treatment, because rudimentary, will not cure everyone, Rwandans do not conceive of life as the perpetual motion machine we imagine it in the West, but instead as something that goes on until it falters or stops for whatever reason. Nor, for that matter, do the Rwandans seem to want to look as closely at these reasons as we do. For their vision of the conceptually neutral state of the body already seems to involve the possibility of illness, the certainty of death. We

Westerners would say that these people are more fatalistic than we are — which under the circumstances perhaps means, more realistic. In the African context where illness and death are more quotidian than in the West it is impossible to expect the sense of urgency we feel with regard to AIDS, the same sense of disbelief we have in discovering something we cannot control. Only in Western society, and perhaps most of all in North America, is the point of departure for thought that anything is possible. When we discover that in fact everything is not possible we still express this in terms of particular circumstances, rather than revising the postulate.

Society in Rwanda is one that T. E. Hulme would have called classical rather than romantic — one that does not believe that all things are open to human control. Before the Enlightenment, even the West may have been a society of this sort. But of course, once enlightened — once having realized that the very nature of knowledge and control lies in naming, isolating, and separating from ourselves — we cannot become un-enlightened; we cannot return the apple of the tree of knowledge to its branch. I am not suggesting that there is anything remotely approaching nobility in the lack of interest shown by the Rwandans or other Africans in the Western attempt to identify and perhaps some day eradicate this one part of their continuous spectrum of disease. How many Rwandans, a half-century ago, would have approved of an anti-malaria campaign? But I think there may be at least food for thought in the capability of these people to accept, at least in theory, the fact that death, disease, malfunction, and dissolution are also part of life rather than the excluded Other that they have become for us in the West.

A story may make this distinction clear. Shortly before I left Rwanda (July 1987), a European friend of mine fell on his video box while filming the hippos in a nearby Zairian national park and ruptured his spleen. His wife was able to charter a private plane to get him back to Kigali, where a Belgian doctor removed the pulverized spleen. The next day, however, the doctors found themselves unable to control massive blood clotting in his legs. They did not, more precisely, have the machine to monitor the dosage of the medicine used against clotting, which by chance they did have, so that Hans would not be in danger of being killed by the medicine itself. Yet my friends had insurance against just this sort of emergency, and Peggy arranged for a private medical jet to be sent from Germany to evacuate him. At the last minute, however, it could not take off from Frankfurt, and the next one could not leave for two days.

Peggy spent the afternoon on the telephone (reasonably dependable telephone connections with Europe had only existed in Rwanda since the previous spring) to find another plane which could come immediately if this should be necessary. At a Swiss clinic, she found one. Cost, 80,000 Swiss francs, for which the insurance would not pay. However, the doctors assured her that Hans could survive another day; she took a chance on their word, and the second German plane arrived in Kigali on schedule. Doctors on the plane began treating Hans as soon as he was loaded on board, while it still sat on the runway in Kigali. He was cured in Munich; now, without a spleen, he is back in Rwanda. And the three of us had a lovely visit together the following fall in Annapolis.

The moral of this story is surely something like this: Hans lived because each fragile link of a long chain happened to hold. What seems miraculous is that the chain might easily have broken at any one of many points and yet it did not do so — or Peggy did not allow it to break. Had there been no plane to charter from the game park, no treatment at the hospital, no phone connection, no money, or no available medical jet, Hans might well have died. If this had happened, we Westerners would have said: it happened because the phone was inoperative, because the plane could not come, because the hospital did not have the necessary machine. We would have blamed the lack of something that was not there to prevent this happening.

But what of a Rwandan whose world does not contain the possibility of $60,000 jets whisking him or her off to Swiss clinics? If the Rwandan ruptures a spleen, he or she merely dies. A Rwandan under such circumstances dies not because the plane doesn't come, because such a plane would not have been within the realm of possibility to begin with. Similarly, in our world people die of AIDS because our doctors have not yet found a cure. In Rwanda they merely die.

There are differences between our two worlds, even those we may be willing to articulate as differences of "mentality." But these are perceived, and can be explained: they are not taken for granted as in the evocation of Otherness. It is differences of this sort that constitute our "Westernness"; an acknowledgement of them is necessary to understanding our own limited place in the world. Difference, in other words, is not the bottom line, and need not be essentialized; indeed what I have attempted to do here is to mediate these differences. In the case of AIDS, the mere possibility of articulating the Rwandan view of sickness as a particular view like our own particular view provides this mediation. Both are views of sickness, even if they are divergent in their particulars.

An acknowledgement of real and perceived differences should not be confounded with essentializing Otherness. Because frequently so confounded nowadays, and because Otherness is itself confounded with only its negative-valence instantiation, it is considered bad form in some circles to suggest that there are any differences at all between ourselves and others. But this is the greatest arrogance of all. For whose criteria will we use for expressing this lack of difference? Certainly not that of the others. And the result is the assumption that the world is like us, an assumption that usually fades only when the person making it actually gets outside of the Western hothouse of talk.

We need not accept such ridiculously appropriating assumptions, nor the false modesty of those who go to the opposite extreme and say that, caught in our own worlds as we are, we cannot begin to deal with others. An alternative to both is to treat the world outside as just another particular like our own set of particulars. These may be identical in some circumstances, and divergences be explained by an appeal to a common rationally constructed matrix. This very act of mediation through identification of commonality, of course, uses the Western matrix to come to terms with the world outside. But what else could we use? This is the only matrix that can include other options than itself. It is in fact the defining characteristic of our Western rationalism, indeed what makes our world-view a matrix rather than a set of absolutes.

Chapter Eight

An Evening at the Kabuki: Bringing the Outside In

The interest of the American dance world in non-Western dance and theater—what we now call "world dance" and exemplified by the Los Angeles Festival—offers another test case of how we deal with perceived foreignness, the flip side of the case of teaching in Rwanda. For it suggests that, in the case of those bits of the outside brought inside as well as when we take ourselves outside, we can articulate differences between ourselves and others without resorting to Otherness. We can, that is, develop a more individualized and fine-tuned mechanism for articulating perceived differences in the imported products of foreign cultures than that involved in the explanation of these differences by the *a priori* presupposition of Otherness.

Even perceived differences expressed in collective terms do not necessarily lead to the ascription of a negative-valence Otherness. The frequent assumption that any perception of difference is equivalent to the ascription of such negatively conceived Otherness means that, paradoxically, involvement with works of art from other cultures rarely goes beyond respectful boredom. And the theoretical underpinning of this is the "anthropological" point of view that leaves unenunciated its presupposition of difference. The paradox is that what this point of view expresses is the opposite of what it presupposes. What it expresses is something quite different: the position of cultural relativism, which suggests that all cultures are fundamentally alike, and that our own point of view has no more justification than any other.

Cultural relativism is the explicit thrust of one consideration of dance from an anthropological point of view, Joann Kealiinohomoku's article "An Anthropologist Looks at Ballet as a Form of Ethnic Dance," anthologized in Roger Copeland and Marshall Cohen's *What Is Dance?*. Kealiinohomoku turns the analysis of ethnography back on Western dance, and comes to the conclusion that ballet too is rooted in its culture. Now, conclusions arise in specific contexts, the circumstances under which they are worth making. The context in which such a conclusion as Kealiinohomoku's is worth enunciating is what Bohannan also took as her point of departure, the assertion of universal art, comprehensible to all cultures. And given that this is Kealiinohomoku's context, it is not surprising that the contrary assertion by the culture-relativists is that art is not universal but local, so that it cannot be appreciated by members of other cultures. Such a position can be defended either by showing how an initially incomprehensible art form from another culture can be made comprehensible, or how a comprehensible art form (ballet, our own Western form) is somehow strange.

Kealiinohomoku's enterprise is the latter, a version of "making strange" with respect to our world, the description of things we take for granted in alienating ways, so as to make them worth noting. Her analysis, however, is based on a construction of Otherness. Far from contributing to the creation of one happy family of people, as we may suspect her purpose to have been, her analysis instead divides us along lines of what we in the West call divergent cultures. (It is already a mark of our Westernness that we speak of cultures in the plural.)

Let us imagine a viewer led blindfolded into a performance: he or she looks at what is going on, has trouble with it, and has to ask—Is this foreign? Or is it postmodern? And the reaction of that person will depend on the response. We can see how essentializing the notion of "another culture" is by realizing that we approach dance works with different perceptual expectations when we are told that they come from a "foreign" culture than if they are from ours. In this case, we offer them the reaction of uninvolved, respectful attention that is currently in fashion; we give what we see (so to speak) the benefit of the doubt, assuming that some explanation exists for the things we see to which we are not privy. This is why a whole festival of such dance forms defined as coming from Other cultures, like the Los Angeles Festival, can flit across our mental screens with little effort and fit so well into our daily routine. Our seeing can in a sense be effortless seeing.

Far from being more difficult to comprehend for most people, foreign dance forms are usually much easier. The average viewer of dance from "another culture" simply ascribes the things he or she does not understand to the absent context summarized in the notion of "foreignness," and goes on to the next event. We feel that real comprehension of foreign art is not expected of us; mere perception will do quite well, the way someone ignorant of the rules of baseball can still perceive a Dodgers game as a series of unrelated or only partly organized visual stimuli, or a tone-deaf concert-goer can see the black-clad orchestra on the stage as an interesting visual phenomenon. This may be a perspective unavailable to someone who understands what is going on.

If we are assured, while looking at a dance performance, that we are not missing any rules, that our perception of what we see is all there is—that what we are seeing is domestic "creativity" rather than foreign dance—we can at that point begin to order our perceptions the way someone going to a baseball game might well produce a fascinating description of motion and patterns, or the way we make sense (or not) of an equally incomprehensible dance performance. Yet with dance products labelled as "foreign" we cannot do this; they are not ours to judge. And this leaves us with the other alternative to dealing with such performances, namely attempting to learn something about the culture that undergirds what we see, trying to fill in the gap which the information that this is from a foreign culture creates for the perceiver. Yet this alternative too has its own set of problems.

We can arrive at an understanding of these problems by considering a 1989 appearance at the John F. Kennedy Center for the Performing Arts in Washington, D.C. of a Japanese

Kabuki troupe led by the celebrated actor Ichikawa Ennosuke III. This was an art form unfamiliar to all but a handful of those watching it; the result was an "information gap" between the audience and the stage. If the performances had been taking place in a museum or an ethnic society auditorium, this fact alone would have acknowledged the need for something to fill this gap. The audience would have come expecting explanations to fill it, perhaps in the form of extensive printed program notes or a verbal introduction. Yet this particular tour of *Ennosuke's Kabuki* (so the program was billed) was booked into just that sort of hall that has come to be synonymous in the public mind with accessible large-scale entertainment and with the "high" products of our Western culture. My first impulse was therefore to pretend that what we were about to see was exactly like those products of our culture with which we are familiar and thus was something that I could judge directly.

Yet this impulse was stifled by a counter-move of the producers of this event. For the paradoxical novelty of the performances of *Ennoskue's Kabuki* was that the producers acknowledged the existence of this gap by attempting to bridge it in what in fact was an especially interesting way. Next to the candy bars and the opera glasses that were being hawked in the hallway of the Kennedy Center stood enormous signs encouraging audience members to pay $5 rental for a transmitter with an earplug billed as "absolutely essential" to the understanding of the pieces we were about to see. Most of the audience members took the signs to heart, paid their $5, and spent the concert with a wire connected to their ear.

My earplug came with the press tickets, though my inclination was to wing the performance without such a crutch — just as I always pass up the guided tour of a museum exhibit. Better to flounder by yourself, I always feel, than have a great expert Explain It All To You. Ambivalent about the thing in my left ear, I found myself playing games with it, pulling it out and putting it back in — much to the annoyance of the person beside me — trying to answer the following questions: Was it necessary? If not, what remained of the performance for the perceiver without it? If it was necessary in some sense, was the

experience of watching a work for which we need a simultaneous running commentary the same as watching one for which
we don't? How, that is, was the experience of going to the
Kabuki different for the average Western viewer than going to
our fifteenth *Swan Lake*?

To be sure, most of the information provided by the
commentary was unproblematic in theoretical terms, consisting of paraphrased translations of the words spoken by the
actors on the stage. By Western standards, Kabuki is more
drama than dance, and we accept the notion that the words in
a drama are important. The voice in my ear seemed like
another version of the sub-titles in a foreign film, or the opera
supra-titles that troupes like the New York City Opera have
made popular in recent years. And without the synopsis of the
convoluted plot of those scenes from the piece called *Yoshitsune
Senbonzakura* that comprised the evening's pre-intermission
fare, there is no way that an audience member ignorant of
Japanese could have figured out what was going on.

With the aid of the earphone, however, the viewer and
listener slowly picked his or her way through the story of a fox
named Genkuro who had changed himself into the form of a
samurai named Tadanobu in order to be near the drum that
Tadanobu's wife carried with her, which, it turned out, was
made from the skins of Genkuro's parents. By following this
drum wherever it went, Genkuro showed true filial piety,
which the earphone told me was one of Buddhism's cardinal
virtues. I tried understanding this from the props alone in
some scenes and always found myself stuffing the plug back in
my ear, hoping I had not missed too much with my fiddling
around. To its credit, the printed program included lengthy
synopses, though these were so long and complicated that only
someone who had arrived an hour beforehand to study them
could have used them as a guide.

However, plot synopses were not the only kind of information provided by the voice. During lulls in the action it
offered facts considerably more interesting from a theoretical
point of view. It explained the meaning of costumes, gestures,
props, and music, offering a complete semiotic decoding to
what was taking place on the stage. And this kind of explana-

tion will become increasingly necessary as our collective focus shifts to the unfamiliar dance styles of the rest of the world; we are all going to be in the position that I was in with respect to *Ennosuke's Kabuki.*

What was remarkable was that the voice in my ear caused the order of normal experience of this performance to be reversed. For a member of the audience ignorant of the conventions of the form, the performance was turned, through The Voice, into an example of a generic type. For the member of an audience more familiar with the conventions of Kabuki, on the other hand, the generic would be so submerged that all he or she would be conscious of seeing was the particular. And this situation of seeing the particular as an example of the general is fundamentally different one from our experience of any kind of dance performance from our own culture. This includes even avant-garde dance, which strikes us on occasion as similarly hard to understand. With Modern or postmodern, or even postpostmodern dance, we assume the duty of the choreographer is to be comprehensible to the audience. If we don't understand something, we assume the fault lies with the choreographer, for the choreographer has had his or her shot at communicating in the movement. We watch such performances without footnotes. They are, after all, something from our culture; if we don't understand them, who is supposed to?

The explanation through the headset made clear, and so in some fundamental sense actually created, the foreignness of what I saw that evening, just as the explanations of Lucy Snowe in *Villette* create the foreignness of Labassecour in the act of explaining it. The explanation I got through the headsets, through acknowledging the necessity of mediation, made what we saw foreign. It would have been perfectly possible to make sense, in some sort of purely sensory way, of what was happening on the stage—though our conclusions would have been what someone more familiar with the form would have certainly called "wrong" conclusions.

If I had been Japanese, I would have been able to take for granted all of the things about which the voice filled me in, just as I now go to a performance of *Giselle* knowing the plot, accepting a position of turn-out from the dancers, under-standing the mad scene as an essential feature of the work's Romanticism, and not finding inherently foreign the notion that the dead might be conceived as existing in spirit form, flitting through the woods. Without such information I do not understand *Giselle*. Without comparable information for dance from other traditions, partisans of "world dance" would insist, I cannot hope to understand, let us say, the Kabuki. Their conclusion from this is that we members of the audience must educate ourselves as to the givens and the variables in the products of other cultures, just as we learn gradually by osmosis similar things regarding our culture. (That the givens of classical ballet and modern dance are learned is clear to me from teaching dance works from films and performances to midshipmen at the U. S. Naval Academy, who take for granted neither tights, toeshoes, turn-out, nor tutus.)

Learning the givens of the art form is clearly the *sine qua non* of understanding it. But in the circumstances under which I saw this Kabuki performance, the artwork actually changes its boundaries. The work that is perceived becomes the amalgam of what is on the stage and the explanations, much as the bulk of *Villette* consisted of nothing else but the explanations of the narrator to mediate, and so create, the foreignness. This means that our attention is deflected from what is taking place on the stage; we cannot pay attention merely to this. When I didn't understand something, I had to stuff the plug back in my ear, turning as it were to the footnotes. Instead of stopping with the choreographer, that is to say, the buck stopped instead only with the thing in my ear. The result was what I can only call inherently mediated perception of what was taking place on the stage; I could not judge, could only seek to understand.

For example, a few minutes into the first act, some of the Kabuki's female impersonators (the voice gave the correct technical term: *onagata*) playing ladies-in-waiting (information again courtesy of the voice) came onstage holding vaguely Frank Lloyd Wright-ish objects in their hands that the voice told us were lanterns whose purpose was to indicate night. The lights on the stage had not dimmed, but the appearance of these lanterns alone—the voice informed me—sufficed to indicate to the audience the time of day. Would I have had a clue about this without the voice? No. Was the voice necessary? Yes.

My efforts to oppose The Voice were blocked for a second time when Ennosuke, playing both Tadanobu and the fox Genkuro, was about to change from one to the other. His voice (my ear told me) was becoming more high-pitched, as this was the way a fox would talk; we were to notice the paw-like position of his hands and the hair style which suggested ears. When the metamorphosis took place, in one of the three-second costume changes which (the voice in my ear said) are among Ennosuke's innovations in the Kabuki theater, we were supposed to tell that we now had a fox before us because the elaborate samurai pyjamas had been replaced by a kimono of dangling white cords. That curious motion of twirling around on the knee? The voice said this represented grief.

So far so good, I said to myself; as long as I have the voice to explain to me the meaning of these details, I can stay on track, and at this point stopped even thinking of taking it out of my ear. Suddenly the experience of watching the stage with the voice in my ear seemed akin to looking at a black and white photograph on the wall of a museum of a painting that has been removed and having the gallery assistant explain to us what was "really" red and what green and the true size of the piece. And this seemed useful knowledge, given that the viewer could not properly understand what he or she saw without any understanding of the code by which it was to be translated.

As Kealiinohomoku would point out, all art forms rely on codes that we must at some time learn. The Kabuki is no different in this respect than any other highly developed art form. When we Westerners go the opera, for example, we know beforehand that all the words are going to be sung—though a child, or someone from the country, might well find this strange. So too for the postures of our classical ballet, which only a small percentage of our population ever experiences as anything other than artificial. And even these will be quick to admit that the motions of the classical ballet are stylized, which is precisely why so few people can really do them well. To be sure, when animated by an Edward Villella, a Suzanne Farrell, or by a young Gelsey Kirkland, they seem the most natural things in the world. Similarly, the better the choreographer, the more self-evident this expression medium seems: for Balanchine, like breathing, for a Gerald Arpino or a Maurice Béjart, usually an affectation.

No one nowadays would be so xenophobic as to claim that our theater is natural while others' are stylized; it sounds too much like Voltaire's claim that French was the language best suited to the expression of thoughts. The tenor of the times in intellectual circles is a relativistic one. When no absolutes are recognized, what seems stylization to one culture will seem self-evident to another. As for thinking our own traditions less artificial, we have only to remind ourselves that in Shakespeare's time, it sufficed for the actors to announce that it was the forest of Arden for it to be the forest of Arden; surely this is the most artificial way of all of making scenery. And it was only in the nineteenth century that set designers began making paintings with trees painted on them to simulate trees among which the action took place. But are flat images of trees any more "real" than words expressed by actors?

Those who insist that all cultures are nothing but codes would point out that the transformation necessary to understanding a man in pancake makeup as standing for a woman is no greater than that required of Westerners sitting in darkness to look at flat images of moving pictures on a screen. Are the highly stylized Kabuki *onagata* less real than a merciless close-up of Henry Fonda's face? Is the dimming of the lights that, in our theater, would "signify" night any closer to reality than the carrying on of lamps? We might point to the "naturalism" in Western theater that hit its apogee in the works of Ibsen and found its director in Stanislavsky. Yet against Stanislavsky stood Piscator, and through Brecht our stage has become highly "stylized" again. Or should we say, more realistic, in that it acknowledges the stage as a stage? Sweden is announced at the beginning of *Mother Courage* by a piece of cloth painted with the word hanging from the flies; Isamu Noguchi compresses house, church, and frontier into a single set for Martha Graham's *Appalachian Spring*; bare stages and exposed dressing areas are a theatrical commonplace today.

But such an "anthropological" point of view, with all of its implied relativism, was not capable of taking account of what I saw on the stage that night. For even within the enclosed system of the Kabuki we are able to make distinctions between greater and lesser stylizations, between those elements closer or further from what we can only (with apologies for our naivete) call "reality." And such distinctions internal to the system allow us to see how we may ultimately arrive at generalizations regarding it which are not identical to the postulation of Otherness. We may see foreign art forms as foreign, without thereby seeing them as Other.

Late in the play — cut down to three acts from the original five, with omissions — Genkuro's henchmen arrive to foil the evil band of robber priests who have arrived to prey on Tadanobu's master. The voice tells us that they are priests; nothing in their demeanor or costume announced this to me. These henchmen are also, logically enough, foxes, but they were dressed in more "realistic" costumes. They wore one-piece pyjamas with tails and a mask with jaws that covered their faces. Surely this get-up for "fox," which I could understand without The Voice, was, in terms of Peirce's semiotic analysis, more iconic than the other. It looked like the reality it represented in a way the other had not. The objects the samurai carried were more really spears and swords, if only in non-functional stage versions, than the man was a fox. Was it coincidence that I could understand the iconic signs without the voice? Surely we can say that these aspects of the Kabuki are less "stylized" than others.

Yet we may go further. Instances of perceived difference may in fact be generalized to conclusions of difference about the art forms as a whole without turning into the *a priori* assumption of difference that constitutes the postulation of inter-cultural Otherness. In each case it is a conclusion based on specific, perceived differences, a deductive conclusion rather than an inductive postulate. And this, like the conclusion that there are qualities associated with our Westernness, may be the start of a sense of our place in the world that is not based on the essentializing of place in inter-cultural Otherness. Such distinctions within the system of signs that comprises the Kabuki also allow us to make inherent distinctions between this entire system of signs and our own. For example, it may in fact be the case that Kabuki is inherently more stylized than Western theater, all questions of previous familiarity aside.

Certainly we can understand why Sergei Eisenstein thought so when he saw the Kabuki that played St. Petersburg in 1908; he responded with an ecstatic essay claiming that the Kabuki was inherently "cinematographic." It offered "non-differentiated sense 'provocations'" (p. 27), presenting the audience with resolved visual conflict instead of easy harmony. After all, in the Kabuki men play women as well as men; battles are staged as gymnastic displays where the actors remain frontal to the audience; the action is frozen in mid-climax with the actors holding grimaces. Moreover, the actors wear pancake make-up, deliver their lines in a peculiarly "stagey" voice like spoken singing, and enter via a ramp (hanamichi) going through the audience (at the Kennedy Center, along the side of one wall) rather than invisibly, from the wings. Eisenstein called all these "conventionalized." And surely it makes sense to see them as such; at any rate the conclusion that they are so is the result of specific seeing and particular comparisons, not of the wholesale essentializing that constitutes Otherness.

The instantiation of Otherness, as opposed to the perception-without-Otherness which leads us to specific conclusions, prevents us from directly perceiving an art object before us. The alternative to Otherness is point-by-point enumeration of perceived differences, produced without an assumption that there will in fact be any differences. What this means is that we may even end up in the same place by perceiving that we would have ended up in by postulating Otherness. Yet the difference between these two ways of getting to the same place is fundamental.

Futhermore, even if we hold that all culture consists of signs and all signs are arbitrary, so that that my culture is no less arbitrary than anyone else's, this does not change the fact that there remains an absolute distinction *in the fact of perception* between my culture, whatever that is, and the culture of others. This is what we mean when we speak of differences in culture—or at least what, at any rate, we are justified in meaning. For us, the works of our culture are more comprehensible—precisely because we have internalized the underlying assumptions. And this is an advantage that such works possess over others.

In the case of an unfamiliar art form, the process of directly perceiving the artwork cannot take place in a single performance; we simply don't know enough of the presuppositions of the form. Yet despite the novelty of the solution to this difficulty proposed by the producers of *Ennosuke's Kabuki*, we must pronounce it a resounding failure. It alters the nature of the experience so that it is no longer that of a single performance at all. Either see with footnotes, and have the particular become merely an example of the general, or give up the attempt to "understand": these are the mutually exclusive alternatives that face us in the case of art forms from other cultures.

Of course, seeing many performances can lead to understanding a single performance in the future; most Westerners learn the conventions of ballet by being brought up on them, just as all people learn the conventions of a language. But the fact is that within our own culture, we are unlikely to have this kind of repeated exposure to such works. This tends to happen only if (1) we are a foreigner in the land in which they are indigenous, or (2) they are firmly a part of our own culture. In either case we will come to terms with the strange art form. Yet in neither case is the contrast with ourselves that makes them strange worthy of being codified into the postulation of geographical difference at the base of inter-cultural Otherness.

There is one further disadvantage in what I am calling the direct perception of an unfamiliar art object. For whether we achieve this directness by perceiving it outside of its cultural context or learn that context well enough to understand the object the way we understand, say, Brancusi or *Swan Lake*, we lose the sense of the exotic that undoubtedly drove us to seek these unfamiliar things to begin with. The most disappointing fact of life may be that the unfamiliar is only exotic to us insofar as it remains unfamiliar. Without footnotes like the voice in my ear, we fail to understand what we see. With such footnotes, we substitute scholarship for perception; we see the specific as generic. And with familiarity so great that we no longer need footnotes and can again perceive the specific, we are back in the initial position of familiarity with ourselves that probably sparked our hunger for the art forms from other cultures to begin with.

The paradox of the situation is found in the fact that even if, as critics or as audience members, we somehow acquire a minimal fluency in the givens of those few major non-Western art forms that we may expect to see more than once in a life-time, the most we can get from this stumbling acquaintance is a relationship with the works of these other cultures which approaches, perhaps asymptotically, that relationship we already have with those of our own. We can get to know quantitatively more by coming to understand the artworks of other cultures, but we do not hope to know qualitatively more. And it is precisely for this reason, I propose, that we are so prone to the construction of inter-cultural Otherness. For this is what we lose when we see the world in the terms of unitary differences in the manner I am proposing here.

The integration of cultural artifacts from outside our cultural borders is certainly the wave of the future on our performing arts stages. And aside from the problems that became clear in the case of the Kabuki, we should ponder the more fundamental drawback of the attempt to effect such integration. The final, and perhaps saddest drawback of this wholesale rush to bring the outside in is that it can succeed too well and cause us to lose the sense of the exotic altogether. Presenters such as the Los Angeles Festival rely on an initial perception of strangeness; their assertion is however that the strangeness does not exist at all. (In a similar way Paul Bowles relies on the exoticism of the desert only to wave it away.) But what if the audience already takes this lack of exoticism for granted? Will they come? I think not, or at least not more than to works of our own culture. It is precisely the aura of the strange that draws people to unfamiliar art forms to begin with.

We should not delude ourselves that such integration is accomplished in the mere parading of these fragments of other cultures under the rubric of Otherness, even of the positive-valance kind. And we should be aware of what we lose if we take steps to remove this Otherness through education in the generic givens of these forms. Seeing the difficulties and disadvantages may make us aware of what so many Westerners lose sight of—namely that we are not, for all of our openness to the world, identical to the objects of our perception. We are Westerners, people who look outside themselves, people who bring the outside in.

Fueled by our desire for the exotic inherited from the Romantics, the intellectual tenor of our age forces us to deny an interest in the exotic. The problems this produces are the same in the case of world dance as in that of African art which we must either exhibit like Modernist art, or as a subject of anthropology. Do we take out of context and risk incomprehension? Or do we fill in the context, assuming we can find a way to do so without totally destroying the performance as performance, and bring ourselves closer to the same disinterest with this art form that sent us in the first place from the forms we understand? These are the problems of the in-between time in which we find ourselves with respect to world dance.

IV

The World Inside

Chapter Nine

Of Jargon and the Footnote

For better or worse, we are Westerners — limited creatures, doing things the way we do them. The challenge is to see what this way is. Conception in terms of inter-cultural Otherness essentializes the non-us, riveting our gaze on what we are looking at and causing us to lose sight of the fact that it is we who are looking. And this is something of which we can be conscious, in an answer to the Cartesian problem, through the taking account of difference which does not result in the conception of Otherness. We can in fact acknowledge difference, and at the same time have a sense of what we are. Deductive perceptual thinking is what allows us this, however, rather than inductive *a priori* conceptualization in terms of the Other.

Seeing how things are done differently elsewhere allows us to situate ourselves without resorting to Otherness; we can arrive at a formulation of such difference in general terms, but it must be as a result of looking at specific variations. One such Western phenomenon from which much can be learned is the requirement for documentation in the humble footnote, or citation, whose use governs much of our intellectual discourse. For a failure to document properly is fraught with implications, being taken as evidence of the particular moral turpitude we call plagiarism. It is therefore to the footnote that I turn as the first of my attempts, here in this final section, to apply to our own world the lessons we may learn from looking outwards. And ultimately we learn that the attempt to escape from ourselves can in fact only be successful in the confines of our own world, rather than in worlds outside.

At the same time that we learn this, of course, we remark a more general point as well. Namely, that no talk can ever be valid for more than a limited field of reference. This means that the more content we give to the notion of our Westernness, the more quickly we establish the limitation of its field of validity. All words, concepts, and systems are finite in scope, all a part of the world rather than inclusive of it. And we see this by considering the citation.

For if there is anything that those people regulating intellectual discourse in the West feel strongly about, it is plagiarism, which, we are told, can be avoided by the acknowledgement or citation. *The MLA Style Manual*, that Bible of the American humanities establishment, explains to the aspiring writer in its very first chapter that "plagiarism is the use of another person's ideas or expressions in your writing without acknowledging the source" (p. 4). To plagiarize, it continues, "is to give the impression that you have written or thought something that you have in fact borrowed from someone else." Plagiarism can be avoided by acknowledging borrowings through footnotes or, as the current MLA style prefers, citations in the text. The simple footnote or citation saves us from what the *Manual* goes on to call the "moral offense" of plagiarism. In using citations we live up to our "professional responsibility to acknowledge 'academic debts'."

"Moral offense," "professional responsibility," and "academic debts" are weighty words, all of them used with respect to the simple citation. Yet the simple citation is not so simple. It is in fact only the tip of a conceptual structure governing relationships between author and text, between reader and author, and between both of these and the world outside. Once we have articulated this world-view, moreover, we may use it to characterize ourselves with respect to the world outside, and to those elements of our domestic world which remain unacknowledged by it. As it happens, the citation is one expression of the dominant Western world-view all but universally accepted by groups smarting under a position of marginality on the domestic scene. Yet it is based on presuppositions that apply to only a few situations in our own society, and hardly at all outside of it.

For what this consideration of the rules governing talk finally suggests is that the discourse of the intellectual world is quite different from that of the world outside of it. This implies that, just as there is a world outside of us which can be articulated in terms other than those of inter-cultural Otherness, so there is a domestic world which similarly escapes the conceptualization of domestic Otherness. The current discourse of groups is not the expression of such a domestic world outside, for this only ends up affirming the center. I have already intimated, and will claim explicitly in the last chapter of this study, that it is through a perception of art that this discourse can be escaped. But we arrive at this conclusion through continuing my consideration of the world-view implied by an insistence on the footnote or citation.

We may sketch this world-view by reflecting on what we find when we continue on past the first chapter of the *Style Manual*. For what strikes us in subsequent chapters is the extraordinary range of things we can acknowledge and cite in our writing; indeed, if we are to take the book's opening admonitions to heart, the extraordinary range of things we must acknowledge. There is nothing, it seems, which is not amenable to documentation. Our vector arrows of ascription point in all directions. We are obliged to acknowledge our debts not only to books and articles, but also to television shows, recordings, information services, performances, works of art, private letters, unpublished manuscripts, speeches and even private conversations. The world exists, it seems, to end up in a citation.

This list of ways to document suggests further that the world is open to our penetration, and is a world where absolutely particular identification of incidents is possible. We can, and must, identify the sources of our utterances within this world by references to these particulars, which in turn can be identified and individuated through their location on a time-space grid. The main presuppositions of the world-view underlying an insistence on documentation are two: what we may call the subjective and objective presuppositions of the footnote, after the two parts that a citation contains—a reference to the person to whom we are ascribing the idea or particular words, and the time-space co-ordinates in which we place the utterance.

If we are asked to ascribe a thought, an idea, or a phrase to one person, clearly the assumption is that there is a point in doing so. This means that a person fixes words through utterance in whatever medium and makes them his or her own — so that these words forevermore carry that person's name attached to them, like the plaques that go up on the façades of houses where famous people have lived. The second presupposition of the citation, what I am calling the objective presupposition, is that the world is both fixed and accessible enough that we, or more probably our reader, can return to the place where we have pointed with the footnote and find the thing we have indicated.

The world-view of the citation is kin to the empiricist presuppositions that underlie experimental science, central to our way of conceiving the world in the West. Yet the citation adds to these empiricist presuppositions a post-Romantic cult of personality. It implies that ideas are somehow subject to informal intellectual copyright in a way that the facts of science are not, implies that individuals make words and concepts their own. The footnote or citation presupposes the possibility of absolute identification of sources by reference to a time-space matrix, as well as the objective existence of the source so that the reference can, if desired by the reader, be confirmed.

Up to this point, the world-view of the footnote is that of experimental science. Yet experimental science, in contrast to the footnote, subsumes the individual to the material. Though we still speak of Newton's Laws and the Michelson-Morley Experiments, the facts these individuals "discovered" may be quoted and synthesized without citation in textbooks. The world-view of the footnote holds that this never takes place in the humanities, where the individuality of the discoverer takes precedence over the discovery, and where the language of "discovery" is largely replaced by one of "argument" and "assertion." To be sure, the degree of objectification varies from scholar to scholar. An upswing has occurred in the use of quasi-scientific phrases in writing about the humanities: "as X points out," "Y's brilliant insight," and so on. Yet though the language is that of an objective world outside that can be discovered with greater and greater precision, we still demand documentation in the humanities for X's perception and for Y's insight in order to credit the discoverer.

Both of the two pillars of the world-view of the footnote have been subject to attack in recent decades. One of these, the notion that people somehow imprint their identity on words or concepts, has been attacked by Derridean deconstruction, which denies the primacy of the individual author or speaker and emphasizes instead the shared conventions and forms of the material that constitute the text. The strand of contemporary thought that derives from Foucault is even more explicit on the subject, insisting that the "author" is now absent from texts and can best be regarded as a theoretical postulate whose purpose is to unify our perceptions of the words on the page. As it happens, this strand of thought has been especially troubling to theoreticians who are seeking to valorize groups of people hitherto excluded from consideration. Just when excluded groups are poised to demand credit as authors, theorists assert that no one may legitimately receive such credit.

These are attacks on what I am calling the subjective presupposition of the citation. The debate on this subject has been extensive, and we may never arrive at consensus with such philosophical questions. I wish only to indicate the relevance of such questions for my consideration; it is the other kind of presupposition, the objective one, that I am placing in question here. Whatever the theoretical validity of the world-view of the citation, the fact is that the world it rules is terribly small. There is a great deal left when we bracket out that world amenable to its dominion.

The objective presupposition of the world-view of the footnote has been subject to attack too, perhaps most tellingly in W. V. O. Quine's celebrated early article "Two Dogmas of Empiricism." And the later Wittgenstein has spawned an entire school of anti-empiricist thought. Such objections, like the objections to the subjective presupposition noted above, have also been of a theoretical nature. The objections to the empiricist presupposition I make are of another sort entirely, of a practical nature. Nonetheless, these ultimately end up leading to objections that may be more damaging than those spun initially from theory.

When we actually look at the world inside the cultural borders of the West, but most especially outside of them, we discover that there are many types of sources that are not fixed, and many individual sources that are not accessible. Let us consider first the question of fixedness. Footnotes take as their presupposition objects that stay put long enough for someone else to refer to them and see the "same" thing. We would not cite an object that changed daily; we would only refer to it. If footnotes could only refer to this type of source, they would have no purpose whatever, just as, if the results of scientific experiments could never be confirmed or denied, we would no longer require write-ups of the experiments.

In Western culture, it is primarily written works that possess this degree of fixity, with other reproducible media taking on some of their qualities. (I will be arguing here that not all written documents enjoy this quality of fixedness.) Another group of objects enjoys this status as well, namely radically particular objects in museums or other individually identifiable places, such as "the Leonardo in the National Gallery, Washington, D.C.". It is with works like these that footnotes primarily have to do. For though the *Style Manual* gives us a form for documenting more mutable kinds of sources, such as private conversations, these are in a sense limiting cases of citations. We document a private conversation merely to show that we know the necessity of documentation. Such a citation is equivalent to making the unprovable assertion that such and such happened at such and such a time, and at such and such a place, and conceding at the same time that this is unprovable. The author places it on the time-space matrix; the assertion itself, coupled with our belief in the author's probity, functions as a kind of better-than-nothing piece of evidence.

Yet even the private conversation is immutable in theory. It only happened once, and though we cannot confirm the evidence offered us, it might have been open to confirmation if someone else had been there to hear it. But what if the citation refers not even to such a case as this one, but instead to a work of art that cheerfully changes its shape depending on circumstances? In such a case it makes no sense to insist that we give precise coordinates to identify where it can be found on the time-space grid, since its location will alter from one time to the next. Dance, and to a lesser extent film, are just such instances of art forms whose works are radically mutable or subject to alteration in ways inconceivable with written subjects.

Pieces of choreography are constantly being re-made by their choreographers, in the case of twentieth-century, "abstract" works, or, in the case of story ballets, by subsequent producers. The *Nutcracker* we see in one city will not be identical with the one we see in another; it may even vary from performance to performance as steps are interpolated and the staging monkeyed with. Balanchine revised steps, decor, and costumes in *Apollo* countless times for reasons as various as the individual dancers and his changing sensibility. Indeed, I suggest that dance totally lacks any notion of "text," such as is central to the study of literature—even as this study is practiced by those theorists who locate the "text" not in the written pages but in the reader.

Film is another example of a mutable art form. Many "classic" films exist only in subsequent re-editings, such as *Metropolis*; others, such as Erich von Stroheim's epics, were radically cut before release, so that a "complete" print does not exist. Today films are cut for airplane and television showings, and without the disclaimer that should appear on the screen, no one is the wiser. Editing a film leaves none of the wounds that tearing ten pages from a book would, and save through comparison with another version, there is no way to tell that this has happened. Even a printed play script is sometimes "re-shaped" and cut for performance, whether from artistic or political motives. But at least the printed script always exists as something to refer to, at least in the West where a work, if printed at all, will be printed entire.

These are examples of transitory products where the footnote appears theoretically less defensible than it does with written texts. (In the case of dance we get our citation by referring to the particular performance, or to the whole group of variants under their common title.) Yet if the footnote already seems alien to products like these, how much more foreign is it to those sorts of structures that are even more transitory. We do not, for example, attempt to footnote the songs children make up, sing once, and then forget; neither do we cite the chance pattern of trees blowing in the wind or the motions of clouds. It takes a John Cage to put some of these on the stage in controlled circumstances, and such performances we can begin to footnote. If Cage makes a film of these performances, we are on even more secure ground for the purposes of footnoting; when the chance patterns are printed in script form in a book, we are home free. Yet surely Cage's point is that these uncontrolled patterns are far more numerous than the few reproducible patterns we call art. And if the kinds of sources that sit still long enough for our citation of them to make sense are limited in our society, they are almost non-existent in largely oral societies whose art forms are passed down by word of mouth and imitation. In such circumstances, what would we footnote?

These examples suggest that the assumption of fixedness underlying the footnote or citation is valid only for a severely reduced group of cases. A similar conclusion applies to the other assumption of the footnote, that of accessibility. With the presupposition of accessibility, like fixedness, there are paradigmatic cases, limiting cases, and a certain gray area between them. Accessibility or its lack is the result of many factors working together, including geography, politics, and the decisions of individuals. Most of our footnotes in America refer to books published by the same handful of publishing houses in the cultural capitals of wealthy, politically stable Anglophone countries. This means largely London, Toronto, and New York, with a few from selected Continental European capitals or from university presses. A book published, let us say, last year in London by Faber and Faber is a paradigmatic case of the accessibility presupposed of the footnote. It is probably still in print, we can order it with some hope that it will arrive, and our currencies are convertible. Indeed, the local library may already have it.

Let us consider, however, a printed object at the other end of the scale of accessibility, say a handbill produced on a home printing machine somewhere in central America about which we have heard from acquaintances. Like the Faber book, though unlike a work of choreography, this is fixed. But it is almost totally inaccessible, and we would not try to cite a publisher for it. Instead, if we were referring to it in a work of ours, we would reproduce whatever part of the document was relevant to our purposes, if we possess it, or document the conversation in which we heard about it. In other words, we would scan our data until we find something accessible to footnoting, or admit inaccessibility by referring to.a conversation or by explaining that the object itself is now lost. Because books published last year by Faber are accessible we would never refer to a particular copy in our possession, or document our information by referring to a synopsis a friend gave us.

The widely-disseminated London book and the ephemeral handbill of which only one copy is known to exist represent the two ends of the spectrum of accessibility; there is an enormous gray area between them. What, for example, of a political pamphlet published by a tiny, now-defunct printer in Baku in 1873? This may exist in more copies than the handbill, though we would probably still cite from a single copy in referring to it, rather than listing publisher and city. In contrast to the handbill, some library in the world might have a copy. But the chances are that it will be well outside of the Western centers of learning; perhaps the few copies that exist have long ago fallen victim to moisture and rot. It was published, but, we may say, it might as well not have been — for it is not accessible, and the source cannot for practical reasons be verified, or the citation followed up. It may be that the burgeoning sector of desk-top publishing will make this futility even clearer in the contemporary world.

By the same token, we do not footnote a work believed lost; instead we refer to it. This may be brought home most clearly by considering the very real possibility that we may lose many of the works in our libraries to acidic deterioration if some financially feasible means of stopping it is not developed. If this were to happen, who would not say that our insistence on extablishing precise coordinates for citations was misguided and probably silly?

Nor does it make sense to give sources for countries or libraries to which access cannot be gained for political reasons, unless grounds exist for thinking this situation temporary. And many parts of the world are, for all practical purposes, inaccessible in this sense to Westerners – who, after all, are the ones insisting on footnotes and citations. They can be inaccessible because the local regime will not allow Westerners, or perhaps specifically, Americans, to visit their libraries, because the libraries themselves are deteriorating or corrupt, because we have no way of knowing what volumes are in their collections, because the region is embroiled in civil war, and so on. Just as books and articles are not paradigmatic of the world of the other arts, so that portion of the world which enjoys stability and is sufficiently accessible to us that there is a point in citing individual works from it is not paradigmatic of the whole. And of course, accessibility has always meant, accessible to the airplanes of the industrialized West; the necessity to footnote expanded with the reach of our means of transportation.

In fact, an air of maddening provinciality surrounds the way most people live their scholarly lives in America. For there is a world outside; this is the sense of my naive realism. In America we conceive of all printed works entering a central data system that defines the whole world: books to the Library of Congress, articles to one of several bibliographies, dissertations to a central data bank in Ann Arbor, Michigan. And "researching a topic" consists of checking these standard sources. Yet one does not have to go far to step outside of this system to glimpse the vast realms that do not enter into it. Even a society so like the American as Continental Europe remains largely excluded from what constitutes our points of reference.

Anyone who has taken part in the intellectual life of the Continent knows that many highly developed intellectual societies exist other than the Anglo-American one, with completely different benchmark authors. Almost all discussion in the German-speaking world, for example, proceeds from a knowledge of Hegel, who, despite an increase in American interest in matters Continental since the 1960s, is still far from being so generally known in the United States. Until quite recently in Eastern Europe, everything was referred to Marx and Lenin, if only by the most tenuous of strings. Americans, by contrast, are not obliged to refer anything to these sources, even though some similarity of ideas may occur. By the same token, the Germans have never felt the need, so widespread in the United States in the 1970s and early 1980s, to refer everything to Derrida. (I should note too that intention is not the issue here. We must acknowledge the similarity of our ideas to those of the thinkers on our society's short list whether or not we actually took them directly from these sources. Not doing so brands us as naive, or outside of the realm of common discourse.)

The question of obligatory references is central to a consideration of the footnote. In any given intellectual world there is a short list of "individual" sources; the others blur off into the common fund of nameless ideas. If someone is not on the limited current list of our society's benchmark authors, we may borrow this person's ideas without acknowledgement, at least within our own society. And immortality is as limited by geography as it is transitory. Think of all the shrines to Nazi "heroes" whose names were once the very stuff of life in Germany and whose graves disfigured public places; all disappeared without a trace, rightfully too, we would say. Even as I write this, a similar re-writing of history with respect to Marxist-Leninist relics and monuments is going on in Eastern Europe and the Soviet Union.

The precise contents of this short list of people who must be acknowledged is partly determined by the actions of individuals sufficiently powerful to have intellectual epigones spread their ideas. If Althusser is hot this year, then things Althusserian are translated and published. If the thinker of the moment is Adorno, then the character of things that enter our data system will alter because more will be written about him, and because more of his works will be published. The scholarly industry may rest on a theoretical foundation of empiricism, yet its intensely subjective aspect comes to the fore in that it is individuals who decide just what parts of the vast empirical "out there" are currently necessary and acceptable objects of our attention.

What this all means is that nothing at all is absolute about the particular set of givens which constitute the contents of our own list of must-cite data, which is first of all American, secondarily Anglophone, and thirdly Western. England enters imperfectly into the American data system, and Germany only by hearsay. And what of Paraguay or Angola? If we are suddenly freed from the necessity of acknowledging the similarity of our ideas to those of, say, Lenin merely because we have crossed a border, or to those of, say, Adorno because someone influential has decided not to push him this year, then the imperative to footnote of which the *MLA Style Manual* speaks becomes one of practicality, geography, or careerism — which is to say, no moral imperative at all.

Moreover, just as societies exist which contain few of the written works which form the basis of the paradigmatic case of footnoting, some societies utilize not another content of documentation, but no content at all. In these societies there are no information systems to speak of, or those that exist are pale imitations of Western ones. And this means that documentation in these societies has little point.

One such part of the world is Rwanda. Rwanda is rare among the countries that surround it because, at least until recently, it was at peace. It is pro-Western and welcomes Western help with its infant Western institutions such as libraries and universities. The Canadians, building on a teacher's institution that the Belgians had set up in the Rwandan sub-capital of their colonial territory of Rwanda-Urundi, constructed a tiny university in the town in the south now called Butare. In the early 1970s a Rwandan-made spin-off campus for the humanities was built in the middle of potato fields in the north of the country—the home region, not coincidentally, of Rwanda's current president.

The library for the humanities at the National University of Rwanda, therefore, sits at the foot of the central African volcanos. It is stocked largely with the leavings of a single generation of foreign professors, French, Belgian, British, and

American, and with whatever books their respective embassies have been willing to donate. Its collection is only a few thousand in number, including the multiple copies of paperback novels from which I taught. The occasional presence of a literary-critical text on the shelf is the result of chance. A card catalogue for the collection's holdings made under the supervision of a Frenchwoman is based solely on order of acquisition. No indigenous Rwandan indexes exist comparable to our own data systems, and in the entire country there is only one review-type journal, which is Church-run.

The combination of books in this library is therefore completely arbitrary, as well as painfully thin. As a result, scholarly citation of books by Rwandan students takes on the character of references to single copies in the library, not to published works. It is a kind of exercise in documentation "as if," and is thereby, I am suggesting, documentation whose point is lost. Yet this is at least a world in which it makes sense to note that citation makes no sense. In countries with no university or library, with no way for information to flow over the nearest border, or with a history of decades-long political turmoil, not even this is the case. And the countries that fit this description cover far more of the surface of the earth than we citizens of the stable West like to think.

The price we pay for entering into the fiction of a single absolute and non-arbitrary data system is the exclusion of many things from our world-view, such as works of art that don't stay put, like dance, printed materials of more transitory nature, texts from most other languages on the earth, and things that never attain the degree of permanence required of citable objects. Conversely, this means that footnotes only make sense for a limited body of objects, under very precise circumstances, like the laboratory experiments that serve as their theoretical prototype. And the number of cases that fulfill these ideal conditions is severely limited in the world.

Failure to provide a citation may, in fact, break the rules applicable to one particular set of objects in a particular society that possesses the materials and circumstances necessary to set up a specific cluster of written books and articles carefully stored in accessible libraries as a fixed body of reference. But such failure has nothing to do with morality, as the *MLA Style Manual* suggests it does — at least not to the extent that we believe in morality as absolute, a code which transcends the sub-group which invents it. Of course Foucault, drawing on Nietzsche, has rejected precisely this understanding of morality, but neither does Foucault speak of "moral offense" — ethical relativism leads to a quenching of ethical fire.

Partisans of the footnote may find my reasoning so far unconvincing, failing as it does to take account of their sense that the footnote has a purpose not yet addressed. They would be right. I have been considering the footnote as if it were the result of a rationally constructed, if erroneous, world-view. Yet it is just as much the product of purely personal interests. For there is something jealous, almost obsessive about the way we Western scholars insist on the necessity of giving credit to others for their utterances. It is not in fact mere accuracy or the possibility of looking for further information in citations that makes academics so insistent on the necessity of punishing plagiarism.

The emotive force behind our condemnation of plagiarism and our insistence on the necessity of citation comes from footnotes being one of the few ways we have of immortalizing, if only in a brief, admittedly marginal way, the actions of commentators like ourselves, and laying the ground for the possibility that others may someday "immortalize" us. In other words, we become angry at someone who does not acknowledge his or her "intellectual debts" because we fear that we may be similarly passed over some day and hence pass entirely out of scholarly existence. My point is not, therefore, that footnoting and the world it presupposes is illegitimate. On the contrary, footnoting makes sense because part of the world does correspond to the assumption of stability and accessibility that footnoting presupposes. World-views are, after all, views of at least part of the world. The point is that the world of Western talk is very small compared to the world outside. And it is for this reason we are well-advised to admit that this outside world really exists.

We can take another step toward doing so by remaining on the subject of the MLA, taken as a symbol of the American humanities establishment. In doing so, we widen our sights out from the *Style Manual* to a consideration of the Association's annual convention, seen through the eyes of interested outsiders, the journalists who report on it each year. For it may be that these outsiders are better able to situate what they see and hear than those more intimately inside.

Certainly journalists do attempt with great regularity to give us a sense of where scholars and critics of literature fit into the larger scheme of things; every year several handfuls of them attend the annual convention of the MLA in order to produce the articles that their newspapers—*The New York Times, The Washington Post,* or *The Village Voice*—have assigned them to write about the thousands of college professors who make the streets of one major North American city a year run rivers of tweed during the time between Christmas and New Year's.

Someone who regularly scans these articles soon gets a feel for their formulae. The author inevitably begins by commenting on how numerous we are, as if it were more surprising to think that thousands of professors are in the world than, say, lawyers. (Perhaps in fact it is more surprising, given that students tend to think of *the* professor, in the singular.) The author then lists a handful of the more arcane paper titles, with implied sorrow that perfectly good money is being wasted supporting such trivia, and concludes with head-shaking. The pattern of these pieces is so predictable, that is, that we might see them as a literary sub-genre: the MLA article—and at the next MLA meeting have a session on it.

The journalist's point of departure as an observer is frequently the following question: What kinds of words are being used? For this is to say: What kinds of things are being considered? The first thing such outsiders notice about literary critical talk when professors get together is its high level of jargon. Of course, it isn't necessary to go to the MLA to hear jargon. In its more innocent instantiation, jargon takes the form of the patois which societal sub-groups develop for their use, sometimes as much in order to define themselves as to communicate within their boundaries. Such jargon serves what Roman Jakobson would call the "phatic" function in language, those words that mean little intrinsically but re-establish contact with the audience, like "you see," "if you will permit me a digression," and "hear what I'm saying?".

Jargon of this sort plays a role in socializing people, helping them to identify with each other, and placing the group which they thereby constitute in the context of the society as a whole. Indeed, it seems relatively innocent, since the group can usually translate into standard English if forced to; this jargon can be stripped from its utterances without radically affecting the sense. For someone who teaches at the U. S. Naval Academy, the existence of this jargon is taken for granted. The arriving freshmen — or plebes — are systematically taught such jargon. Plebes — itself a jargon word — sleep in a rack rather than a bed, wear a cover rather than a hat, go the head rather than the toilet, and take their English classes on the second deck of the building.

Examples even exist of jargon groups where the jargon words, those that are incomprehensible to other reasonably well-educated native speakers, do refer to things for which we have no perfectly good terms already. The specificity of scientific discovery, for example, demands that many words be used whose sole reference is within this sub-group to delineate entities and distinctions which are no less real for their being invisible to someone on the outside.

Yet there is also a less innocent type of jargon. In defining this, I use the word "jargon" in the sense that Adorno does in his *Jargon of Authenticity*, that searing critique of the Heideg-gerean emphasis in post World-War II German society on a radically subjective notion of "authenticity." Alternately, appealing to Noam Chomsky's widely-appropriated concept, we might call this a "deep-structure" jargon. Such jargon is less innocent because less easily shed or put off. My students can, without much trouble, write a paper in standard English with no Navalacademese; a scientist can, if he or she is forced to do so, explain himself or herself to a grant-giving organization with sufficient clarity to get money for research. But rejecting a jargon that provides the matrix of values and, it may be at its Kantian extreme, thought itself, is a different matter. If the jargon is deeply enough rooted, it may be necessary to act differently before we can begin to talk differently.

Literary criticism clearly abounds in jargon of the more innocent sort. Indeed, much of the work of English teachers consists in the transmission of a large dose of this jargon. We teach students about personae, points of view, omniscient narrators, stream of consciousness, iambic pentameter, and so on, in many cases substituting such terms for those of hero and event to which students are prone, and making distinctions between author and narrator that seem to us real ones. This kind of jargon frequently seems as necessary as it is innocent. How else can we talk about meter in poetry except by using the technical terms invented to refer to it? (The German word for "technical term," *Fachausdruck*, is more clearly separated in German from jargon, or *Jargon*, than its equivalent is in English. And one of the more innocent types of "jargon" is nothing more nor less than what we might call "technical terms.") At any rate, most students are not seared too deeply by the experience. The language we English professors teach is something that our students use during the course, and then by and large later put aside for other things.

Yet literary criticism nowadays is virtually defined by a jargon of the second sort, a matrix of terms and values which cannot be pasted on or peeled off at will. In the last fifty years, in fact, literary criticism has largely shifted from being a jargon of the first sort to a jargon of the second sort, though the paradox is that no particular jargon of the second sort has held the floor for more than a decade. (The more absolute the claims to suzerainty of a jargon, we might say, the shorter period of time it can be allowed to hold the throne.) The self-reflexive jargon of literary criticism today is to a much greater extent part of the very warp and woof of what we say when we talk about literature; it is less easily summarized and characterized than would have been the literary critical jargon of fifty years ago because it expresses a world view.

This is why the reactions of semi-outsiders like journalists can prove so useful. Ten, even five years ago, their ears were catching words like "mise en abîme," "sous rature," and "différance." Now the jargon has changed to one of political relativism, and with it the things critics of literature see. This, at any rate, was the implication of an article that appeared in the *New Republic* after the 1989 Washington MLA meeting. Written by Alex Heard, the title (added, I suppose, by the journal's staff) contains a literary allusion fully as outrageous as any that Heard criticizes in his article: "Jargonauts." This clearly refers to a jargon of the first sort; Heard writes of "fluent lit-theory practitioners [who] play hardball in the conference room, speaking in daisy-chained clauses studded with killer jargon" (p. 12).

Heard is considerably more self-reflexive than many of the practitioners of this sub-genre of the MLA article; he acknowledges the formal constraints to which I have referred above, and seems apologetic about writing an article that conforms, by and large, to these constraints — embodying, we might say, a kind of postmodernist development of the genre.

> Unfortunately the concept I am getting at — that the [participants of the MLA] stumble around . . . speaking in a ademic glossolalia — is an overworked cliché. If you read press accounts of the past 20 years of MLA conventions, you'll see many pieces in which a reporter ventures into this mammoth gathering of literature and language scholars and "discovers" the presence of people whose words he does not understand. Quoting a few dumb-sounding session titles and using phrases like . . . "Tower of Babel," he argues that the MLA has been overtaken by crackpots. (p. 10)

Heard diverges from the paradigm to which he refers by finally talking more about the kind of things scholars said at the MLA rather than the words they used — which seems to indicate that he is more concerned with jargon of the second sort than the first.

A comparable article by Richard Bernstein that appeared in *The New York Times* following this convention was concerned to an even greater extent with jargon of the second sort. The title of this piece provided a useful summary of Bernstein's argument: "Literary Critics Find Politics Everywhere." Bernstein was talking issues, and hence of jargon in the more constitutive sense, a concern which he expressed as follows:

> The most fashionable trend at the association is to see each different group—ethnic minorities, women, and homosexuals in particular—as having its own interests to defend in analyzing works of poetry and literature. Moreover, the former standard "white male" interpretations have, in the view of many at the association today, suppressed what the literary critics like to call these "marginalized subjects." (p. 16)

Yet issues, we know, are expressed in words, and indeed this paragraph ends with a bit of the jargon Bernstein is characterizing. For if we accept "marginalized" (that is, made marginal, not inherently so) we accept an ideology. And at once we are in the thick of the fray. Later in his article Bernstein lists yet more of the terms through which our second-type, deep-structure critical jargon is expressed:

> The words most commonly heard at papers given at the convention reflect the dominating concern with culture's ties to political power. The phrases are these: "empowerment," "patriarchial authority," "the dominant order," "the symbolic order," "discourses of emancipation," "marginalized subjects," "transgressive discourses," "systems of stratification," and "culturally over-determined structures of seeing." (p. 19)

Another article catches the current deep-structure jargon equally well, though this time through a reaction to published works rather than to MLA papers: the article by Renato Rosaldo from which I have quoted in the introduction. Rosaldo turns initially to the last of the books he is reviewing, *The Invention of Ethnicity* by Werner Sollors, producing the reaction from which I have quoted in chapter six, and which I cite in its entirety here.

> Nowadays it's hard to avoid "the-invention-of" books. They're no longer about the light bulb or the wireless; a phrase once applied only to machines now prefaces everything from motherhood and sexuality to ethnicity and Africa. The whole world, it seems, is constructed—socially, culturally, historically. . . . Apparently, few of the inventions-of crowd mourn the passing of age-old essentialisms. Good riddance, they say and hasten to get on with exploring the making of this and that. Humanity has lost its origins. People grow out of the endless accretion of cultural practices, rather than resting, as it once seemed, on solid biological foundations. (p. 27)

Rosaldo then quotes Sollors as—in Rosaldo's words—Sollors "recites the contemporary credo":

> The interpretation of previously "essentialist" categories (childhood, generations, romantic love, mental health, gender, region, history, biography, and so on) as "inventions" has resulted in the recognition of the general cultural constructedness of the modern world. (p. 27)

Rosaldo is hearing the jargon of those on the inside and recognizing it as such: construction, essentialist-in-scare-quotes, system, and so on. What he calls, ironically, a "recognition" is nothing more than a postulate, something on the order of a religious credo—and one, he implies, of passing temporal validity at that. Most critics and professors working today experienced the age of "rature," "différance," and "mise en abîme"; many remember the age of "bad faith," of "Angst," of "thrownness." And who can remember these without a slight blush of shame? The jargon of a bygone era seems as embarrassing—or as endearing—as a taste for fins on Cadillac cars.

This difference in point of view, like last year's hot item in clothing that becomes this year's white elephant, allows us to see the jargon of the past as jargon, as if it had slipped imperceptibly from the "in" column to the "out" column of numerous "What's hot, What's not" columns at New Year's. But why are only journalists able to see contemporary literary criticism and critics from the outside as it is now? Why are literary critics themselves so incapable of seeing what they are at any given moment rather than waiting for history to give them the necessary distance? The most important reason is that we become so intoxicated by our constructions of words that these seem identical with the world as a whole. To someone sitting on the sidelines, they are merely words asserting to be world, not the world itself. Rosaldo puts his finger on this problem with the current jargon: "human beings and their products lose their specific gravity, their weight and their density, and begin to float." Summarizing his position, he speaks of "the postmodern problem of weightlessness."

This is the problem inherent in any jargon. By using terms specific to a small group, the users forget the necessity of taking account of the world that exists outside of their linguistic universe, outside of that world created by their jargon. All jargons tend to create self-contained modules that prevent our seeing outside of them, even if "outside" for their purposes is just as linguistic as the self-contained inside. Yet the contemporary literary-critical jargon is more pernicious than previous ones, because the people who use it can delude themselves that their jargon is different, given that it is a self-reflexive jargon. We can never reach this position of seeing that this is so by talking. A world outside of words does exist, but words cannot ever lead us to it. We should not lose sight of the fact that it *is* a jargon that contemporary critics are talking, and that one day they will wonder why they were ever so taken with it. Like all jargons, it will go the way of Daniel Boone hats, bouffant hair, and shocking pink. For if all flesh is grass, who can doubt that all words are so as well?

Chapter Ten

Proust and the Power of Solitude

What literary critics do is a limited thing, which is not for that reason illegitimate, but only limited. I have considered this collectively; now I turn to something of the same point with respect to the objects of literary criticism and theory, individual texts. My assertion is that art, and its consumption, is something entirely different from a participation in the social world. Thus it is through solitary perception of art that we escape the world of social talk which forces us, nowadays, to conceive in terms of domestic Otherness or its inter-societal relative, Otherness in the world outside. This conclusion is the correlate of my assertion that we can come to terms with the world outside without resorting to the construction of inter-cultural Otherness. Art of our own culture is to the domestic world as travel-without-reporting is to the foreign world.

Indeed, art of our culture is ultimately the more effective way of escaping from ourselves. People who attempt to flee from themselves into the arms of an alien Other world inevitably end up being more conscious than they ever were at home of what keeps them alien. And the alternative to this is the same banalization of the world outside that we can reach with non-Western dance, or that I reached in and with Rwanda. Richard Cronin, in his book on cross-cultural literatures of India, evokes the image of Ruth Jhabvala from her essay "Myself in India" sitting alone in a room with the blinds down, reading Flaubert and Joyce. If we read these authors in a room in the West, we need not put the blinds down—and so may come to be at peace.

The only real escape, in other words, is inwards, toward art. As Emily Dickinson put it:

There is no Frigate like a Book
To take us Lands away.

I argue this point in the present chapter by pointing out that there is an absolute difference between works of literature and works of criticism or theory.   With works of literature we escape the world of others; with works of criticism we enter it. And I arrive at this conclusion through a consideration of a passage from Proust.

In the Preface Proust wrote for his translation of Ruskin's *Sesame and Lilies,* published as "On Reading," he takes issue with the theory of reading developed by Ruskin, which he summarizes as a version of the Cartesian assertion that "the reading of all good books is like a conversation with the most cultivated men of past centuries" (p. 111).   To be sure, Proust can agree with Ruskin that as we read we are "receiving the communication of another thought."   Yet at the same time he holds that reading is not merely a variation on conversation. Like Derrida, who tells us that writing is not a second-order, lesser version of face-to-face speech, Proust insists that reading is not subservient to talk carried out in the presence of the other person. In fact, reading turns out to have a great advantage over face-to-face communication.   For what distinguishes it from conversation is that this reception of communication takes place in solitude.   And this means that we continue "to enjoy the intellectual power we have in solitude, and which conversation dissipates immediately" (p. 112).

As we consider Proust's notion of reading, moreover, it becomes clear that the relation we have to a book read in solitude is nothing like the passive bowing down before the authority of an author that is the nightmare of so many contemporary literary theoreticians.   Like Emerson, who in such essays as the celebrated "Self-Reliance" developed a theory of the use of books for the development of the self, Proust holds that "our wisdom begins where that of the author ends" (p. 114).   He warns us in no uncertain terms about the effects of allowing our solitude to entice us to lazy lotus-eating of other people's thoughts.

Reading becomes dangerous when instead of waking us to the personal life of the spirit, it tends to substitute itself for it, when truth no longer appears to us as an ideal we can realize only through the intimate progress of our thought and the effort of our heart, but as a material thing, deposited between the leaves of books like honey ready-made by others and which we have only to take the trouble of reaching for on the shelves of libraries and then savoring passively in perfect repose of body and mind. (p. 118)

Reading is active; yet it is activity on the individual's terms, rather than on social ones.

The notion of the intellectual power of solitude is central to my consideration here, as is Proust's analogy of written works to honey deposited between the layers of books — what I call the "canned food" paradigm of reading. For we may use Proust's distinction between solitary reading on the one hand and (social) conversation on the other to ground a distinction between texts that much contemporary theory has taken great pains to deny, the distinction between literature and critical-theoretical texts about it. Reading is to conversation as reading literature is to reading criticism; criticism is the talk of the reading world. What differentiates these two sorts of texts is Proust's distinction between solitary and social communication: literature does not involve us in a situation of social communication in the way criticism does. Furthermore, (the reading of) literature has certain advantages over (the reading of) criticism.

Thus, in addition to allowing us to distinguish between literature and criticism, this Proustian vision of the reading situation may serve as a productive goad in these theory-heavy times, a trope to inspire thought and perhaps tease us out of it. For though theory can never be forced to give up its high ground of endless reasoning (since even anti-theories, such as the work of Knapp and Michaels, are only more theories), the vision of reading which takes place in solitude and presents an alternative to face-to-face communication suggests in fact that we can read without theory — and so, in a sense, do without it. This vision of reading in solitude suggests the possibility (or, as some readers will object, the illusion) of an unmediated contact of an individual with a work.

It is virtually an axiom of contemporary theory, which would do everything in its power to avoid being thought "naive," that there is in fact no such thing as acting or reading in solitude, save in the trivial sense of having no one else in the same area at the time. The individual is a mirage, as all of us are socially constructed creatures. Yet this is merely an axiom. I can only suggest that there is another way of seeing things; it would involve accepting the perceptual difference between acting alone and acting among others as basis for a real distinction between reading and talk, and also between literature and criticism. And we must simply ignore the charge of "naivete" which will inevitably follow.

We may therefore ask what, for Proust, constitutes the nature of this "intellectual power we have in solitude" which is the most fundamental quality of reading? And turned around: What is it that conversation dissipates? The best way of answering both questions—and of summing up the difference between reading and talk—is this: we do not have to be polite to a book. We do with a book read in solitude as we choose, and no one is there to say nay. Talk, by contrast, unrolls within the boundaries of the social situation; we are constrained by what we may say, the tones of voice we may or may not use, the givens of who we must refer to in order to establish authority. Criticism does this too, at least to a much greater extent than literature.

Now, it may be that (as theory would be quick to point out) reading unrolls according to equally strict rules. But whatever these are, they are so internalized as to be imperceptible by the individual. What this means is that there is a perceptual difference for the individual between reading (in solitude) and talking (in the social world). In the same way, criticism and theory are in one realm, and literary works are in another. This is so for the same reason that Proust distinguishes reading from talk, namely the real necessity in the case of talk to take account of other people, and the lack of this necessity in the case of literature. Criticism is part of an ongoing written conversation; literature is, to a greater extent, a series of dead-ends. "Criticism," says Northrop Frye in his *Anatomy of Criticism*, "can talk, and all the arts are dumb" (p. 4).

What we call literary works make their contact to the world through a relation of "common-name" reference (which does not coincide with the use or non-use of English words beginning with capital letters), and so belong as much to one reader as to another. Theory and criticism largely employ what I call "proper-name" reference, and so become part of the world of real things around which we must pick our way. Kenneth Burke has pointed out that all works are responses to situations. Yet except for cases like those of the *roman à clef* and satires, the literary work is expressed in terms which intentionally obscure the specificity of the situation to which the situation is a response. It does this through reference to people who did not "really" exist, events which did not "really" take place. This is why biographical critics and New Historicists must dig so deeply to re-create the circumstances under which these responses took place. And even the point of such exceptional cases as these is the extent to which the real-world referents can be half-camouflaged. Criticism and theory as a whole are, much more clearly than literature, a response to objectively extant entities, namely works of literature — though our theory may hold these specifics to be imprecise or composed of to-be-defined qualities. *Hamlet*, whatever its ontic status, is still a more particular reference than the generic "play," and must be distinguishable from *Macbeth*.

By dealing in proper-name objects, criticism institutionalizes an inherent split between the perceiver and the object perceived. The critic must be talking about the "same thing" we are, whatever we hold its ontic nature to be. Criticism, in other words, refers to things which other people than its reader, or for that matter, writer, have every right to judge; it takes place in a social world. And this means that criticism and theory can, by their very nature, go on forever, for the object being referred to is one that is socially identifiable as an absolute particular, or as absolute a particular as we allow to exist. We can therefore have as many perceptions of it as we have people.

Works of literature do not, by contrast, refer to entities of the social world; they use up their objects of reference, because they cause these objects of reference to come to be.

Instead of writing about *Macbeth*, which is a unitary thing in the world outside, they write about Mr. and Mrs. Smith, or Jay Gatsby, or Macbeth, and the work actually consists of the definition of these entities. Of course, some reference is left over to touch the world outside; when works speak of "Julius Caesar" they include some facts, which refer to the world, and fill in the rest. Yet though "Macbeth" is capitalized, it is for the purposes of the work not a proper noun but a common one: the work consists of its definition. It becomes a proper noun only from outside of the work, when we refer to Macbeth as the title character of *Macbeth*.

Criticism involves us necessarily in (written) conversation; works of literature by contrast give us back the "intellectual power we have in solitude." To be sure, literature contains some referents which bring in the social world. The reference to the Brooklyn Bridge in a novel is presumably the same as to the Brooklyn Bridge in a newspaper, though it need not be, as we do not fault Kafka's Oklahoma for seeming to bear little correspondence to other accounts of the place. What distinguishes literature from criticism—or, in this context, from newspaper reporting or history books—is that these bits of the social world are not the most important structures of their works. In novels, the largest structures are traditionally people and strings of events.

When novels talk about cats and trees, we assume that these are the same as the cats and trees we know from our own experience; we do not have to ask about these. Though we may not understand the common-name references, we have no inherent reason to suppose that others will know more. What I am calling proper-name referents, by contrast, are entities in the public world; we are at fault if we do not get information from others about them. Nor does this deny the existence of works in the gray area: so-called historical novels, or works of philosophy so abstract as to become personal expressions of the author rather than structures of the world. Yet the difficulty of classifying these works does not mean that the classifying categories do not exist, simply that we see elements of more than one such category in each of the works in question. Indeed, we can see a proper-name reference turning into a common-name one, as when we start out writing an academic essay on a book and have it end up instead as a personal essay about our state of mind at the time, or when theoretical criticism becomes so abstract as to turn into philosophy, an expression form whose referents are considerably more "common-name" than those of criticism.

One way of characterizing literature, therefore, is by saying that its largest structures are based on referents to which everyone at least in principle has equal access: structures about events and sensations which cannot be proved to have "really" happened or to have not happened. The reader of a work of literature is not alienated from the references the way a reader of a work of criticism or theory is. Thus the possibility for unmediated contact with the common-name referents of literature is a real one.

When we read literature we do not sense ourselves entering a world populated by others; when we read criticism we are in a world much closer to that of talk—though, of course, not yet identical to it. We still have a measure of control over written criticism that we lose when it is presented in conversation; the rigidly controlled situation of formal "presentation" at a scholarly conference falls somewhere between these two.

Such an understanding of the difference beween literature and criticism, which could also be used to found a distinction between literature and history, or indeed literature and some philosophy, requires us to reject as inadequate a number of other discussions of this difference. Among these is John Searle's conclusion, in his attack on the notion that the language of poetry is different from ordinary language, that the assertions of fiction are pseudo-assertions, genial lies. Searle reasons that the statement that "The king is dead" is no different in a novel than in a newspaper. And so what can separate these two statements? Searle locates the difference in his concept of "pseudo" assertion. Yet he sees no way for us to actually perceive this quality of "pseudo," so that it turns out to be a circular concept. And the result is that, looking only at the content of works as he does, Searle is unable to say what separates art from non-art. Of course, there is a difference, though it is not to be found in the sentences on the page but instead in whether or not the reference involves other people in a social situation. And it is this distinction that a consideration of Proust helps us see.

Criticism, therefore—whatever the content of its particular theoretical underpinning—exists as a kind of alternative to direct contact with the work such as Proust's reader enjoys. Indeed, one effect of the institutionalizing of a class of professional critics has been the perfectly understandable tendency to claim that criticism is a necessary mediator between the reader and the work. After all, people who do criticism for a living almost have to believe that their criticism aids reading the work—or, as some of them would go so far as to say, is indispensible for such reading. In many cases, this world of criticism-theory explicitly denies such a possibility of unmediated contact with the work of art; deconstruction has been one of the most egregious offenders in this domain. In other cases, this is simply the all but inescapable implication of the professionalization of criticism. I daresay not even pluralistic critics, to take an example of the less doctrinaire theoreticians, would be willing to say that readings without their help are of the same value as readings with them.

Criticism presupposes a three-sided relation of reading, consisting of the reader, the work, and criticism in the middle. This relation contrasts with Proust's two-sided paradigm of reader and work. The precise contents of the criticism and theories offered to play this role of mediator will vary. But what makes the world of professional criticism and theory possible is the unspoken assumption that there is a slot to be filled between the reader and the work. This is self-evident to many contemporary theoreticians, so all they can emphasize are their differences from one another rather than acknowledging the essential commonality of their undertaking. Yet from the perspective of someone such as Proust who does not assume that there need be anyone between the reader and the work, what is striking is the sameness of all criticism and competing schools of contemporary critical theory.

A passage from a seminal essay by Jerome McGann clarifies the contrast between two-sided and three-sided reading paradigms, and parallels my consideration here in applying it to a difference between texts. Speaking of the predominance of text-centered readings on the contemporary scene, McGann writes:

A text-only approach has been so vigorously promoted during the last thirty-five years that most historical critics have been driven from the field, and have raised the flag of their surrender by yielding the title 'critic' to the victor, and accepting the title 'scholar' for themselves. (p. 18)

McGann shares with his adversaries the belief that the position of the "critic" is the stronger and thus preferable. As a result his theoretical enterprise claims this position for his own New Historicist group, so that it no longer be relegated to the secondary position of "scholar." McGann smarts under the threatened scourge of being a mere scholar, one who does not claim for himself the position of necessary mediator, the person who will tell us how we *must* read the work in question.

I think McGann is correct in his assessment of the contemporary scene. Criticism has in fact tended to assert its own necessity, and hence assert as well the impossibility of any paradigm other than the three-sided one which leaves a spot for it. Scholarship, by contrast, can exist perfectly well in the context of a Proustian two-sided paradigm—which may be why it is thought so undesirable nowadays. Why should McGann not get a share of the same pie that all the other competing schools of contemporary literary theory have demanded and, largely, managed to get? How dreadful to be merely a scholar under those circumstances.

The fundamental difference between "critic" and "scholar," apart from relative importance in the public eye, is that the critic plays the role of *necessary* mediator; he or she tells us how the work must be read. The scholar, by contrast, does not claim necessity for his or her intervention, and does not purport to be part of the initial reading situation at all. Instead, he or she merely adds to a body of what is known; we may pay attention to this person if we so choose, but we are not at all obliged to do so. This is the sense in which criticism tends to claim necessity for its undertaking, even if this claim is expressed in the generous tones of pluralism. Pick any one you want, pluralism tells us, but doing without any is not an option. Yet doing without is precisely what Proust proposes.

McGann's discussion continues to be useful as we apply a Proustian distinction to a difference between types of texts. For McGann acknowledges the very distinction between the work of art and critical literature that I am at pains to re-establish here, and he does so in terms that fit neatly with Proust's—even if he is not willing to let this distinction be the end of the story. In a subsequent passage of his essay, McGann suggests that works of art, in contrast to other works, offer themselves under the "sign of completion." And he explains: "the special character of poetry and art—its universal or eternal aspect so-called—is that it permits its audience to encounter the human experience of the poem as finished" (p. 21).

This, we may extrapolate, is the principle which makes a single work a single work; the principle which unifies it, like the swirls of paint in a Jackson Pollock painting which avoid the edges of the canvas and draw the eye back into the splatters of the center, or the "beginning, middle, and end" aspects of a drama. The principles of unity that McGann concedes to the work of literary art are like the methods used to preserve or can food. They allow the *Stoff* out of which it is made to be separated from the world in which they grew naturally and be consumed by others at a later date, in other climes. And this is what brings us back to Proust.

One critic who has articulated something quite close to Proust's paradigm of reading is George Steiner, with his distinction between "critic" and "reader." In fact, McGann's distinction between "critic" and "scholar" calls this to mind as well, though Steiner's distinction is closer to my dichotomy here of three-sided and two-sided reading paradigms than it is to McGann's pair. For Steiner, the "reader" collapses perceptually into the work, something the "critic" can never allow himself or herself to do. Steiner suggests that precisely because "the critic functions at a certain distance," "there are many and diverse ways in which the critic can assume his stance" (p. 77). In my terms, Steiner is insisting that the plethora of possible critical approaches should not hide from us the fact that all of them are critical, and are all thereby opposed to the more unmediated relation to the text he says is that of the "reader." The differences between critical approaches are built into their common nature as expressions of the "critic."

The longer passage of Proust quoted above suggests that reading (I would say: reading literature), is like consuming preserved food (in his example, honey). He shows both the good news and the bad news implied in this situation. His Emersonian side acknowledges outright the disadvantages of preserves: in comparison with fresh fruit, the strawberries in jam are faded, and taste heavily of the sugar necessary to their preservation. Beans in tins taste of the blanching, and of the tin rather than of sun and warmth. Yet this is not a disadvantage that either Proust or Emerson is trying to forget; remembering it is our protection against thinking that strawberries grow in jars rather than in fields.

Notwithstanding, Proust's emphasis is on the virtues of preserves over fresh food. The first advantage is what, he concedes, Ruskin and Descartes have seen as well: in the unavoidable absence of the fresh (which is to say, the living author to talk to us), the text is certainly better than nothing. Ruskin has gone even further than this, though not far enough for Proust. For Ruskin, the advantage of books is that they allow us contact with the world's best minds in a proportion far higher than that available to us in our own dull lives. Most of us never talk with the most interesting people of even our own age, much less those of earlier ones. We can eat exotic fruits or "thousand year old" eggs only in preserved form.

Proust pushes Ruskin even further. Books have an advantage over conversation that is not only quantitative, but qualitative. Books are better than conversation not merely because they make accessible to us the fruits of worlds that we would otherwise never have tasted; they are better because we can enjoy them on our own time, alone, when and how we will. We enjoy, after all, this "intellectual power of solitude, which conversation would immediately dissipate." We do not have to concern ourselves with either the grower or the pickers to enjoy the strawberry jam on our toast.

Thus it is most fundamentally the fact of preservation, that which makes possible consumption away from the circumstances that produced the fresh food, which separates the work of art from other kinds of works, as it does any written works from any spoken ones. Consumption of art, as opposed to consumption of theory, is like Proust's paradigm of reading as opposed to conversation. It is the only situation where we touch others without their touching us. In Proust's words, "reading . . . is that fruitful miracle of a communication in the midst of solitude" (p. 113). A miracle—which is to say, a strange, almost paradoxical situation unlike any other. Yet the collective force of contemporary literary criticism and theory of all types and all persuasions seems to be aimed at destroying precisely this miracle. According to a three-sided paradigm of necessarily mediated relation to a work of art, we cannot simply read or otherwise consume such a work; we must read it through the filter of theory. The work requires an adaptor, like foreign current. If it did not, after all, theory—and theorists—would be out of a job, or turned into what McGann would characterize as mere scholars. Contemporary literary theory insists with one voice that we should not eat a book alone at all, but must do so in the presence of theory. And this is to say, with the very sort of mediator that Proust was fleeing in the first place.

Interpretation, Susan Sontag said in her famous phrase, is the revenge of the intellectual on art. The enterprise of criticism and theory, similarly, is the revenge of the social on the solitary. It would break down the wall of the garden in which Marcel (or Jean, since this passage was cannibalized from the novel *Jean Santeuil*) reads; it would break the silence that surrounds him. And in this, I would reiterate, returning to McGann's distinction, it contrasts to scholarship. For scholarship plays the role of the guest who knocks on the door at the end of the afternoon, hat in hand; theory plays the role of the uninvited neighbor who breaks in, then looks over the reader's shoulder and comments as the reader turns the pages.

And this is to say that theory violates the conditions on which the perception of art is predicated.

If we accept a two-sided reading paradigm we come to the conclusion that criticism-theory, whatever it says it is doing, is merely scholarship; it is not necessary. Yet if we do find theory unnecessary, we can still reflect on the works we read, and can take account of others' opinions or readings. It simply means that instead of giving others the power to determine the nature of the works read, we hold other people in abeyance to help us when we are in difficulty. And at some point or another all of us are in difficulty. We must run the race ourselves, but we need others to pick us up when we stagger.

Nor, finally, does the acceptance of a two-sided reading paradigm condemn us to being the passive pawns of authors, publishers, or social forces. For as Proust makes clear, the consumption in silence of the art object is only the first step; what comes afterwards is a filling in of the insufficiencies of the text from the store of the self. Yet nothing is in any way effortless or soft about this two-sided reading paradigm. Indeed, for Proust the relation of reader to text is an agon, not an ingestion of "honey ready-made by others" (p. 118). However the agon with the text is a private agon rather than the public one that the literary theoreticians insist we engage in to determine the very nature of what we are about to consume. An insistence on the private nature of artistic experience, or a desire to protect it from violation by the claims of theory does not, therefore, amount to lawless subjectivism. (Of course, in contrast with a truly subjectivist position, even the most reader-oriented of theories seems didactic, judgmental. It too insists that this is the nature of the text, even if we do not think that it is so.) But it does mean that we will accept variations in readings, for the standard with which the reading is compared is not that of other people. Instead it is only that of the development of the self. At the same time, however, we will cease to find these variations theoretically interesting. They will be something which is assumed, not a source of constant Eureka experiences.

Thus reading by a Proustian paradigm, in the absence of theory, is perfectly compatible with the structure of reading in the university—in which much, or perhaps even most, serious reading takes place nowadays. For other people do have a place in the consumption of art, though it is a place both temporally and theoretically posterior to the experience of this consumption, which must take place alone, and in silence. The teacher who meets a class after it has read the assignment conforms to the Proustian paradigm more than he or she does to a literary theoretical one; according to this theoretical paradigm, the students must wait until they get The Word before they may react. Logically speaking, the critical paradigm would require that the class come first, and the reading second. And this is why, in the twentieth century, the writing of theory has diverged so radically from the classroom activities of those who write it.

Reading (or writing) literature escapes the social world in a way that reading (or writing) criticism does not. Talk or talk-writing is part of the social world; literature is not. It is therefore in the world of literature and the other arts that we escape the social world, not in escape to another culture. Those who seek escape in literature are frequently tempted to believe that this escape would be more absolute if it were in real terms. Yet this is not true, given that there are only two ways of encountering the world outside: as Otherness, or in the individual differences which end by banalizing it.

Escape into literature works better, and we can do it at home. Of course, this reeks of the "solution" of the Modernists to the problems of the world, the retreat into Axel's castle which Edmund Wilson took as emblematic of the escape of an entire generation. Yet disappointing as it may be to those who had wished for other kinds of escape—into the world outside, for instance—escape inwards is the most efficacious type of escape. And this implies a distancing from the particular structures of the institutionalized intellectual world, at least in its face-to-face manifestations.

Nonetheless, saying that the somewhat indirect consolation of literature and art is as much as we have in the way of escape from ourselves does not mean that we cannot come to terms more directly with the world of talk, or that we cannot act in the world. Thinking and articulation may create dead ends which must in their turn be escaped; we can nonetheless come to terms with this situation. It may be that our deepest presuppositions are not things we will be able to change in our own lifetimes—even if we do achieve the somewhat limited comfort of articulating them. Perhaps Westernness, as I have been using the term, falls into this category; perhaps it is not so deep. Ultimately, however, the attempt to put off all of our presuppositions may give us the sense of being unable to escape our own skins.

Yet we can achieve a sort of limited triumph over them—and it may be that people have always known this. We taste what limited individuality we can achieve in the world by reflecting and then acting. If we act without reflecting we simply act; if we reflect without acting we end up as Hamlets all. And some hint of how we may function in the world when we are not involved in the private worlds of art and when we are not taken by the will o' the wisps of conception in terms of inter-cultural Otherness may be provided by a consideration of Samuel Butler's now infrequently-read coming-of-age novel and spiritual autobiography, *The Way of All Flesh*, to which I turn in closing.

Chapter Eleven

Mr. Overton's Solution:
On Systems in Thought

The narrator of *The Way of All Flesh* is a certain Mr. Overton, author of light comedies and godfather to Ernest Pontifex, the young man whose life story he is writing. Overton's overt purpose in telling Ernest's story is to lay bare the spirit-crushing aspects of Victorian patriarchy and religious hypocrisy. According to Overton, these two have combined to produce religious dogmatism, which thrives because it is based on systematic belief, a consciously erected system of thought that repels all attackers and is continually shoring up its defenses. For Overton, therefore, the fundamental problem is that of the systematization of thought *per se*. And this is why both his identification of the problem and his proposed solution are relevant to our intellectual situation in the 1990s in America.

To be sure, the orthodoxy regnant in Ernest's Victorian world was one of religions absolutism, a systematization of thought of the first degree: certain things were so, and no questions were to be asked. Today, the tenor of the times is relativistic: nothing is inherently so, and no questions are to be asked. We find ourselves in a period rife with systems of thought, albeit what we may call systems of the second degree; the systems that hold center stage in our intellectual world are skeptical ones, systems-of-no-system of which self-reflexive jargons and culture-relativism are examples. Yet since systems of the second degree are systems as well, they too are amenable to Mr. Overton's criticism and to his solution.

The bulk of Butler's deliciously polemical and shamelessly self-justifying novel — written in the 1870s and 1880s but not published until 1903, a year after the author's death — consists of the description of Ernest's lamentable subservience to his parents and to received religion as taught by his father, a priest in the Church of England. This is also the most satisfying part of the book in purely literary terms, for here the narrator's attack is two-pronged. He convinces us simultaneously of the hero's inherent goodness through the adoption of Ernest's point of view, and of the utter vileness of Ernest's two hypocritical parents by resorting to narratorial omniscience when such point-of-view reporting proves insufficient to make the point. As it happens, Ernest's liberation from his father is effected by fate rather than himself, for it begins only when he is sentenced to prison for propositioning a woman he had taken to be a prostitute, but who turns out to be an "honest woman." Curiously enough, Butler never questions the validity of this sentence, treating it instead as a useful tool in freeing Ernest from his family.

The prison sentence serves the purposes of alienating Ernest from his parents and causing him to abandon his duties as a priest, which he had dutifully taken up in obedience to his father's wishes; he does not yet know that Mr. Overton is holding in trust for him a large sum of money from a deceased aunt that will make him financially independent. In prison he had finally read the Bible with an "open mind," and decided that there was not sufficient justification to accept what it said as truth. Thus, upon his release, he turns for the first time in his life to other writings. Abandoning the religious dogmatism of his father, he searches for truth among what Butler regards as a series of competing secular dogmatisms, systems of organized philosophy. Overton, and through him Butler, look at Ernest's reading program with a jaundiced eye:

> He was continually studying scientific and metaphysical writers, in the hope of either finding or making for himself a philosopher's stone in the shape of a system which should go on all fours under all circumstances, instead of being liable to be upset at every touch and turn, as every system yet promulgated has turned out to be. (p. 319)

Ultimately Ernest, digesting and discarding the Empiricist philosopher Bishop Berkeley, decides that "no system based on absolute certainty was possible," and is "contented." This conclusion pleases Overton a good deal:

> To my relief [Ernest] told me that he had concluded that no system which should go perfectly upon all fours was possible, inasmuch as no one could get behind Bishop Berkeley, and therefore no absolutely incontrovertible first premise could ever be laid. (p. 319)

For Overton, therefore, systems of thought and belief are by definition false, and time-wasters to boot, precisely because they are systems. Every system of thought contains the seeds of its own destruction, regardless of its content. Even a relativistic or self-reflexive system which took as its content the systematic rejection of systems, therefore, would be similarly incapacitated. And it is this last point which links Overton's ruminations with the 1990s.

The urge to erect systems in thought seems universal. We appear impelled to search for a structure of ideas or thoughts that underlie, are taken to be logically prior to, or otherwise substantiate all others. Our quest in thought is to identify a limited set of principles or sentences that, once learned, allow us to treat all others as subsidiary. After all, the world is far too complex and full of data to allow us to take account of all of it. Thus we deal with this plethora of sensations by fore-grounding some and refusing to perceive others, as Gestalt psychology has shown, or by dividing it up into like groups which give structure to what we see and can ingest. And as Foucault has pointed out in *The Order of Things*, writing of the way knowledge is organized by our taxonomies, these structures are themselves contingent.

To take an example of this simultaneous organization and limitation of perception by our own created structures, let us consider the way artistic works "ahead of their time" are rejected as senseless or barbarous according to the understanding of the permissible forms of that time, though subsequently "seen" to be the precursors of other forms. This means that a type has subsequently been established that allows us to re-write our perception of the world in which they first appeared. And this, ultimately, may be T. S. Eliot's perception, in "Tradition and the Individual Talent," that literature of the present actually changes the nature of the literature of the past. As he puts it, we know so much more than our predecessors, and they are what we know.

The value of a system of thought is that it transcends the particularities of time and place, even—or especially—if it includes determinations of time and place within it, such as that of Heidegger for time and that of Hegel for time and place. If a system is true it is true, and is not itself subject to alteration. Of course, the reference to time and place within a system often has the appearance of acknowledging these as external factors. The Marxist system, for example, has attempted to distance itself from other systems of thought using the reason that other such systems, unlike itself, are determined by the "ground" underlying all thought—the social conditions in which such thought develops. Yet insofar as the one set of concepts held to be primary is precisely that of the Marxist system, it becomes no less systematic and dogmatic than any other, no less a part of the "over-structure" of thought from which it wishes to distance itself.

The discourses of inter-cultural and intra-cultural Otherness considered throughout this study as characteristic of the contemporary scene are examples of such second-order dogmatisms, asserting the relativity of each person's own viewpoint save for this assertion itself, the contingency of all perceptions, or the time-boundedness and place-boundedness of all judgment. Indeed, the intellectual history of the late twentieth century in America may be understood as a working-out of Mr. Overton's question of the validity of systems of thought *per se*.

Allan Bloom considered this situation of living in a world of relativisms quickly hardening into absolutisms in his bestseller of the late 1980s, *The Closing of the American Mind*. Much has been made in the critical reactions to this book of Bloom's grousing about such features of modern life as rock music and divorce on demand. Yet the philosophically most powerful discussion in his book is found in the work's Introduction, not the consideration of facets of modern life in the body of the text. The introduction insists that paradoxes inherent in second-degree relativisms of thought are *only* paradoxes of thought, and are not to be taken as identical to the world as a whole. And it is this passage from Bloom which brings us back to some of the primary concerns of my opening chapters.

Bloom is speaking of mandatory university courses in Third World cultures which, he says, have inevitably a "demagogic intention." Their point "is to force students to recognize that there are other ways of thinking and that Western ways are not better." Yet Bloom sees a problem—or, I would say, a paradox—in this situation. For "if the students were really to learn something of the minds of any of these non-Western cultures . . . they would find that each and every one of these cutures is ethnocentric. All of them think their way is the best way." Relativism, or self-doubt, then, is not universal, but particular to the society doing the perceiving, namely the Western one. Bloom makes this point clearly:

> Only in the Western nations, i.e., those influenced by Greek philosophy, is there some willingness to doubt the identification of the good with one's own way. One should conclude from the study of non-Western cultures that not only to prefer one's own way but to believe it best, superior to all others, is primary and even natural—exactly the opposite of what is intended by requiring students to study these cultures. What we are really doing is applying a Western prejudice—which we covertly take to indicate the superiority of our culture—and deforming the evidence of those other cultures to attest to its validity. (p. 36)

The paradox Bloom outlines is that our very attempt to avoid cultural self-centeredness is itself culturally self-centered, our attempt to be value-neutral in our perception evidence of our inability to escape the confines of our particular intellectual system. This development of Western thought from its quite different Enlightenment bases is what Bloom deplores; his deploring this development has acted as a lightening rod for reader ire.

Yet it is through the more generalized lessons of Bloom's argument here that he can be linked to Mr. Overton and to ourselves. If we distance ourselves from the particulars of the argument, we understand Bloom to be insisting on a difference between systematic thought and the world outside of that thought. The most self-coherent system, such as that of institutionalized relativism, can be shown to be limited in application by the introduction of evidence from the world outside; the most intellectually watertight system of thought can be overturned by facts. I would add: the more watertight the system in purely intellectual terms, the more likely it is that facts which are unseen through its very hermetic completeness will overturn it.

This perception of Bloom's may be seen in philosophical terms as simply an example of Gödel's incompleteness theorem. Douglas Hofstedter, in *Gödel Escher, Bach*, perceives Gödel's theorem as a version of the ancient Cretan liar's paradox (wherein Epimenides, a Cretan, made the statement that "All Cretans are liars"), and which Hofstedter paraphrases as saying that "all consistent axiomatic formulations of number theory include undecidable propositions" (p. 17). In technical terms this means that absolute certainty in mathematical systems can never be reached; its practical equivalent is a consciousness of the limitations of human intellect in the world, a kind of humility before the existence of other minds and other things.

This humility, I suggest, amounts to a willingness to accept the fact that though we may polish the creations of the mind to the point where they are perfect and self-enclosed, we can never be sure that the world which exists outside of us may not prove us wrong. If I were to identify one single characteristic of contemporary thought, in fact, it is that it suffers from the sin of *superbia*, pride, an intellectual version of the notion that things must be a certain way because we say they are so.

The attitude of humility I am recommending is an attitude, not a dogma. A dogmatic version of it, to be sure, has always existed, precisely in the organized religion against which Ernest Pontifex was rebelling. Such religion insists that "Der Mensch denkt, Gott lenkt": Man proposes, God disposes. Indeed, the sin of intellectual pride is a sin only within the givens of religion, which stands perennially in danger of making a content out of its the insistence on the ineffability of a power beyond our comprehension. As long as the Church could keep its position of societal primacy, of course, content was the same as that which founded it; in a curious way the Protestant Reformation had already won its points by the realization of its very possibility, based as this was on the notion that there is more than one way of conceiving of these qualities of ineffibility and transcendence.

Thinkers fond of the systematization-of-no-systems approach will be quick to situate Bloom's viewpoint in its proper philosophical and temporal perspective. It presupposes as a given the Cartesian split between mind and matter, so that mind can perfect something which nonetheless fails to take account of the world, as well as the scientific distancing from the world that is the basis for the empirical world view which so many of these systems-of-no-system put into question—most notably Heidegger in *Being and Time*. Indeed Descartes remains the big bogeyman of most contemporary thinkers, as he is of the early Heidegger.

Defenders of systems-of-no-system would assert that no value-free articulation is possible, and hence that there is no way to oppose a world "out there" to a world as perceived by the individual. Even Peirce, who insisted on the capability of the world to bump our foreheads and bruise our limbs and called it "Secondness," as a twin to the mind's "Firstness" that somehow combined with it, in good Hegelian fashion, into a third term that included them both, has been largely read in the modern world—for example by Umberto Eco in *The Absent Structure*—as an idealist pure and simple, rather than the problematic hybrid of idealist and realist that he was.

We are left in a quandry. What are the implications of taking seriously a thorough-going skepticism with regards to systematic thought? On one hand there is the assertion that all systems of thought are relative; yet what if we take this seriously and say that even systems such as these must therefore by definition be so, say that relativism itself must be limited? This is what I see Bloom doing in his discussion of the relativism of Western relativism. Does this land us back in the lap of first-order dogmatisms? Some people perceive this as the only alternative. Indeed, the fight between "creationism" and "evolution" in some high schools today, where they are presented as competing paradigms between which students may "choose," shows the strangeness of a first-order dogmatism (creationism) demanding to re-enter the arena defined by a relativistic system ("secular humanism"): can a first-order system exist within the system of second-order systems, or does the first necessarily overthrow the second?

I have recommended a solution to this paradox of self-reference on the level of inter-cultural Otherness, and now propose the same solution for the world at home: naive realism, which we associate with the name of Samuel Johnson. For every student of philosophy knows the story of Dr. Johnson kicking the stone and saying, "Thus do I refute Bishop Berkeley"; Berkeley insisted that objects were identical with perceptions of them—most immediately, with our perceptions, but ultimately those in the mind of God. Of course kicking a stone to show that objects are "real" both is, and is not a refutation of a position in thought, for it is precisely a refutation by action as opposed to a refutation by thought. From the position of thought, this is no refutation at all. Was this what Ernest Pontifex meant by the impossibility of "getting behind" Bishop Berkeley? In philosophical terms this situation brings us back to the Cretan liar's paradox, or Gödel. In such a situation neither one nor the other of a pair of mutually exclusive opposites will get us out of the bind. As Hofstedter puts it in his gloss on Gödel, there must exist an alternative to either true or false, a cutting of the Gordian knot.

This is the sense of the solution Overton proposes, and the reason why this solution may show us a way out of Ernest's quandry—and ours. Overton considers the difficulty of dealing with first-order dogmatisms through a lengthy reflection on the situation of his hero on the day he exits from prison (pp. 295-296). At this point in his life, Overton says, Ernest is composed of both a changed and an unchanged part; these correspond to changed and unchanged parts of the world outside.

> All our lives long, every day and every hour, we are engaged in the process of accommodating our changed and unchanged selves to changed and unchanged surroundings; living, in fact, is nothing else than this process of accommodation. . . . A life will be successful or not according as the power of accommodation is equal to or unequal to the strain of fusing and adjusting internal and external changes.

This is a combination of Peirce's "Firstness" with his "Secondness" and implies the Cartesian point of departure that seems so inescapable in my reasoning above. Yet this is not the end of Overton's reasoning:

> The trouble is that in the end we shall be driven to admit the unity of the universe so completely as to be compelled to deny that there is either an external or an internal, but must see everything both as external and internal at one and the same time, subject and object—external and internal—being unified as much as everything else.

Here Butler anticipates the anti-Cartesian, post-Hegelian strain of thought. Yet he does not leave this strain of thought holding the palm of victory more firmly than what it has overthrown. Instead, he continues cheerfully as follows: "This will knock our whole system over, but then every system has got to be knocked over by something."

We are back at the question of systematization of thought *per se*; the question being raised here concerns the validity of any system of thought, even of skepticism as a system. The solution Overton proposes goes Dr. Johnson one better; he is a Dr. Johnson who neither subscribed to Berkeleyen idealism as a system, nor felt that kicking a stone proved anything at all.

> Much the best way out of this difficulty is to go in for separation between internal and external—subject and object—when we find this convenient [that is, Cartesianism as a point of departure], and unity between the same when we find unity convenient. This is illogical, but extremes are alone logical, and they are always absurd, the mean is alone practicabale and it is always illogical. It is faith and not logic which is the supreme arbiter.

This position, by no coincidence, is what Ernest has already adopted with respect to the received religion in which he was brought up. Religion cannot be proven logically and must be accepted, if it is to be accepted at all, on faith. This at once robs religion of its imperative and of its dogmatism. We may well accept the tenets of religion, but this must be an individual decision, and cannot be either arbitrated or legislated.

It is at this point that Butler-Overton produces his summing-up, his denial of system that at the same time wishes to resist the impulse to be made into a system in its turn. And it is this solution that offers a way for us today out of the systems of internally so horribly coherent thought in which we find ourselves imprisoned.

> They say all roads lead to Rome, and all philosophies that I have ever seen lead ultimately either to some gross absurdity, or else to the conclusion already more than once insisted on in these pages, that the just shall live by faith, that is to say that sensible people will get through life by rule of thumb as they may interpret it most conveniently without asking too many questions for conscience's sake. Take any fact, and reason upon it to the bitter end, and it will ere long lead to this as the only refuge from some palpable folly. (p. 296)

Systems of thought should be regarded as objects of use, things to be gone through and disposed of as circumstances determine. Yet, it will be objected, this is what most people do who have never been instructed in philosophy, even if they do so without knowing it. Philosophy, after all, is the art of developing out of precise actions the bases on which these implicitly rest. Yet Butler has anticipated this objection, even if his response appears wanting to us. And even poor Ernest, who learns so dreadfully slowly, knows that this is so, apologizing to Overton for having taken so long to come to the conclusion that most people reach long before their twenty-sixth year. Indeed, Ernest's hero throughout his life remains a certain Townsley, a "golden boy" of his time at Cambridge who is well-bred, rich, good-looking, and rather stupid, so that Townsley has never gone through the rigors of thought that have plagued Ernest and been for that reason further along from the beginning. (One thinks of the dumb blondes of both sexes idolized by Thomas Mann's quintessentially Romantic-Modernist gentleman artist, Tonio Kröger.)

It may be that this conclusion of Ernest and Overton will seem no less dogmatic than the received religion from which it is ostensibly a diversion, being intuitionistic and anti-intellectual, while at the same time a glorification of the financially self-sufficient bachelor "gentleman" of early capitalism. After all, Overton talks unembarrassedly of "the just," thereby ending up himself in a system akin to G. E. Moore's intuitionistic understanding of "the good" whose effect was to valorize the cliquishness of the Bloomsbury circles that received it so eagerly.

The response to this objection may be found in Bloom: we must accept that our matrix of thought, whether it talks a language of first-order or second-order dogmatism, will by definition be limited by factors that may be totally invisible to us. We must therefore acknowledge our way of talking as ours, and accept the definite qualities associated with our discourse, rather than pretending that we alone have no such qualities, or re-writing the world so that all others seem to share ours. We need not as a result cease to talk of "the just," or to talk in any terms whatever, simply because we come to understand that others hold different notions of these. Instead, our realization is that all absolutist terms are absolute only for a limited time and place, a particular set of circumstances — which nonetheless are ours. When these circumstances change, we may hope for the grace and wit to change our absolutes in response. As for the question of whether others must share these absolutes, well, this will be decided by our perception of whether they are like us so far as these determinative factors are concerned, or unlike us.

The realization of the contingency of human thoughts — the frailty, to use a religious term, of people in the face of the universe — is a realization that lies too deep for tears. It may undergird a way of life, but it cannot provide the justification for a system of thought. It gives us an orientation in life, but not a content to it. In this sense, Mr. Overton's solution may be a viable one for us today, as a way out of the paradoxes with which our urge to systematic thought has plagued us in the final years of the twentieth century.

Works Cited

Achebe, Chinua. "An Image of Africa." *Massachusetts Review* 18 (1977): 782-94.

___. *Things Fall Apart.* London: Heinemann, 1958.

Achtert, Walter S. and Joseph Gibaldi. *MLA Style Manual.* New York: Modern Language Association, 1985.

Adorno, Theodor W. *Jargon der Eigentlichkeit: Zur deutschen Ideologie.* Stuttgart: Suhrkamp, 1964.

Ashcroft, Bill, Gareth Griffiths, and Helen Tiffin. *The Empire Writes Back: Theory and Practice in Post-Colonial Literatures.* London: Routledge, 1989.

Bernstein, Richard. "Literary Critics Find Politics Everywhere." *New York Times* 1 Jan. 1990: 16, 19.

Blake, Michael. *Dances With Wolves.* New York: Bantam, 1988.

Bloom, Allan. *The Closing of the American Mind: How Higher Education Has Failed Democracy and Impoverished the Souls of Today's Students.* Foreword by Saul Bellow. New York: Random House, 1987.

Bohannan, Laura. "Prince Hamlet in Africa." *The Norton Reader: An Anthology of Expository Prose.* 3rd ed. Ed. Arthur M. Eastman, *et al.* New York: Norton, 1973. 498-507.

Bowles, Paul. *The Sheltering Sky.* New York: Vintage 1990.

Brantlinger, Patrick. "*Heart of Darkness*: Anti-Imperialism, Racism, or Impressionism?" *Criticism* 27 (1985): 363-385.

"Breakthrough Books." *Lingua Franca* June 1990: 6.

Brontë, Charlotte. *Villette*. Intro. by Tony Tanner. Baltimore: Penguin, 1979.

Butler, Samuel. *The Way of All Flesh*. Intro. by Carl Van Doren (1945). New York: Books, n.d.

Claridge, Laura and Elizabeth Langland. *Out of Bounds: Male Writers and Gender(ed) Criticism*. Amherst, Mass.: University of Massachusetts Press, 1990.

Clifford, James. *The Predicament of Culture: Twentieth-Century Ethongraphy, Literature, and Art*. Cambridge, Mass.: Harvard University Press, 1988.

Cronin, Richard. *Imagining India*. New York: St. Martin's, 1990.

Dances With Wolves (Film). Director Kevin Costner. With Kevin Costner. Orion, 1990.

Diamond, Stanley. *In Search of the Primitive: A Critique of Civilization*. New Brunswick, NJ: Touchstone, 1974.

D'Souza, Dinesh. "Illiberal Education." *The Atlantic Monthly* 267/3 (March 1991): 51-79.

Duras, Marguerite. *The Lover*. Trans. by Barbara Bray. New York: Harper, 1986.

Eagleton, Terry. *The Ideology of the Aesthetic*. Oxford: Blackwell, 1990.

Eco, Umberto. *La struttura assente*. Milan: Bompiani, 1968.

Eisenstein, Sergei. "The Unexpected." *Film Form*. Ed. and trans. by Jay Leyda. New York: Harcourt, Brace, 1949. 13-27.

Frye, Northrop. *Anatomy of Criticism: Four Essays*. Princeton: Princeton University Press, 1957.

Gilbert, Sandra, and Susan Gubar. *The Madwoman in the Attic: The Woman Writer and the Nineteenth-Century Literary Imagination*. New Haven: Yale University Press, 1979.

Goodman, Nelson. *Languages of Art: An Approach to a Theory of Symbols*. Indianapolis: Bobbs-Merrill, 1968.

___. *Ways of Worldmaking*. Indianapolis: Hackett, 1978.

Hammond, Dorothy and Alta Jablow. *The Myth of Africa*. New York: Library of Social Sciences, 1977.

Heard, Alex. "Jargonaut." *The New Republic* 29 Jan. 1990: 10, 12.

Hemingway, Ernest. *For Whom the Bell Tolls*. New York: Scribner's, 1940.

Hofstadter, Douglas. *Gödel, Escher, Bach: An Eternal Golden Band*. New York: Vintage, 1980.

Kealiinohomoku, Joann. "An Anthropologist Looks at Ballet as a Form of Ethnic Dance." *What Is Dance?*. Ed. Roger Copeland and Marshall Cohen. New York: Oxford University Press, 1983. 533-549.

Kermode, Frank. *The Sense of an Ending: Studies in the theory of fiction*. New York: Oxford University Press, 1968.

Kinkead-Weeks, Mark. "'Heart of Darkness' and the Third-World Writer." *Sewanee Review* 98/1 (1990): 31-49.

Knapp, Steven and Walter Benn Michaels. "Against Theory." *Against Theory: Literary Studies and the New Pragmatism*. Ed. W. J. T. Mitchell. Chicago: University of Chicago Press, 1985. 11-30.

Lentricchia, Frank. *Ariel and the Police: Michel Foucault, William James, Wallace Stevens.* Madison: University of Wisconsin Press, 1987.

Lévi-Strauss, Claude. *Tristes Tropiques.* Trans. by John and Doreen Weightman. New York: Atheneum, 1977.

Los Angeles Festival, September 1 thru 16, 1990; Program and Ticket Information. Los Angeles, 1990.

McGann, Jerome J. "Keats and the Historical Method in Literary Criticism." *The Beauty of Inflections: Literary Investigations in Historical Method and Theory.* Oxford: Oxford University Press, 1985. 15-66.

___. *The Romantic Ideology: A Critical Investigation.* Chicago: University of Chicago Press, 1983.

Mbiti, John S. "The Concept of Time." *Contemporary African Literature.* Ed. Edris Mackward and Leslie Lacy. New York: Random House, 1972. 392-402.

Meyers, Jeffrey, ed. *Ernest Hemingway: The Critical Heritage.* London: Routledge and Kegan Paul, 1982.

Miller, Christopher L. *Blank Darkness: Africanist Discourse in French.* Chicago: University of Chicago Press, 1985.

___. *Theories of Africans: Francophone Literature and Anthropology in Africa.* Chicago: University of Chicago Press, 1991.

Naipual, V. S. "Our Universal Civilization." *New York Review of Books* 38/3 (31 Jan. 1991): 22-25.

Norris, Christopher. *What's Wrong With Postmodernism: Critical Theory and the Ends of Philosophy.* Baltimore: Johns Hopkins University Press, 1990.

Porter, Dennis. *Haunted Journeys: Desire and Transgression in European Travel Writing*. Princeton: Princeton University Press, 1991.

Proust, Marcel. "On Reading." *On Reading Ruskin*. Ed. and trans. by Jean Autret, William Burford, and Phillip J. Wolfe. New Haven: Yale University Press, 1987. 99-129.

Rabubm Steve. "Kenya: AIDS as if it Mattered." *The Washington Post* Nov. 17, 1991. C-5.

Rosaldo, Renato. *Culture and Truth: The Remaking of Social Analysis*. Boston: Beacon, 1989.

___. "Others of Invention: Ethnicity and Its Discontents." *Voice Literary Supplement* Feb. 1990: 27-29.

Said, Edward. *Orientalism*. New York: Basic Books, 1978.

Schneider, Peter. *The Wall Jumper*. Tr. Leigh Hafrey. New York: Pantheon, 1985.

Searle, John. "The Logical Status of Fictional Discourse." *New Literary History* 6/2 (Winter 1975): 312-332.

Sontag, Susan. *On Photography*. New York: Farrar, Straus, and Giroux, 1977.

Steiner, George. "'Critic'/'Reader'." *George Steiner: A Reader*. Oxford University Press, 1984. 67-98.

Steiner, Wendy. "The Critic as Saviour." Review of Patrick Brantlinger, *Crusoe's Footprints: Cultural Studies in Europe and America*. *Times Literary Supplement* 25 Jan. 91: 7.

Stocking, George W., Jr. *Victorian Anthropology*. New York: Free Press, 1987.

Tanner, Tony. Introduction. Charlotte Brontë. *Villette*. 7-51.

Thompson, Robert Farris. *African Art in Motion: Icon and Act in the Collection of Katherine Coryton White*. Berkeley: University of California Press, 1974.

Torgovnick, Marianne. *Gone Primitive: Savage Intellects, Modern Lives*. Chicago: University of Chicago Press, 1990.

Watts, Cedric. "'A Bloody Racist': About Achebe's View of Conrad." *Yearbook of English Studies* 13 (1983): 196-209.

Waugh, Evelyn. *Brideshead Revisited: The Sacred and Profane Memoires of Captain Charles Ryder, a novel*. Boston: Little, Brown, 1945.

Webb, James. *A Sense of Honor*. Englewood Cliffs, N.J.: Prentice-Hall, 1981.